CLASSICS IN EDUCATION
Lawrence A. Cremin, General Editor

☆   ☆   ☆

THE REPUBLIC AND THE SCHOOL
Horace Mann on the Education of Free Men
Edited by Lawrence A. Cremin

AMERICAN IDEAS ABOUT ADULT EDUCATION
1710–1951
Edited by C. Hartley Grattan

DEWEY ON EDUCATION
Introduction and Notes by Martin S. Dworkin

THE SUPREME COURT AND EDUCATION
Edited by David Fellman

INTERNATIONAL EDUCATION
A Documentary History
Edited by David G. Scanlon

CRUSADE AGAINST IGNORANCE
Thomas Jefferson on Education
Edited by Gordon C. Lee

CHINESE EDUCATION UNDER COMMUNISM
Edited by Chang-Tu Hu

CHARLES W. ELIOT AND POPULAR EDUCATION
Edited by Edward A. Krug

WILLIAM T. HARRIS ON EDUCATION
(in preparation)
Edited by Martin S. Dworkin

THE *EMILE* OF JEAN JACQUES ROUSSEAU
Selections
Translated and Edited by William Boyd

THE MINOR EDUCATIONAL WRITINGS OF
JEAN JACQUES ROUSSEAU
Selected and Translated by William Boyd

PSYCHOLOGY AND THE SCIENCE OF EDUCATION
Selected Writings of Edward L. Thorndike
Edited by Geraldine M. Joncich

THE NEW-ENGLAND PRIMER
Introduction by Paul Leicester Ford

BENJAMIN FRANKLIN ON EDUCATION
Edited by John Hardin Best

THE COLLEGES AND THE PUBLIC
1787–1862
Edited by Theodore Rawson Crane

TRADITIONS OF AFRICAN EDUCATION
Edited by David G. Scanlon

NOAH WEBSTER'S AMERICAN SPELLING BOOK
Introductory Essay by Henry Steele Commager

VITTORINO DA FELTRE
AND OTHER HUMANIST EDUCATORS
By William Harrison Woodward
Foreword by Eugene F. Rice, Jr.

Vittorino da Feltre and Other Humanist Educators

By WILLIAM HARRISON WOODWARD

With a Foreword by
EUGENE F. RICE, JR.

CLASSICS IN

No. 18

EDUCATION

BUREAU OF PUBLICATIONS
TEACHERS COLLEGE, COLUMBIA UNIVERSITY
NEW YORK

Library of Congress Catalog Card
Number 63–22510

First published 1897
Reprinted by permission
of the Cambridge University Press
Second Printing, 1970

Manufactured in the United States of America
By Edwards Brothers, Inc.
Ann Arbor, Michigan

Contents

Foreword

By EUGENE F. RICE, JR.

The humanist idea of education is among the permanently influential legacies of the Italian Renaissance. Four short Latin treatises published between 1400 and 1460 define it admirably: Pier Paolo Vergerio's *De ingenuis moribus et liberalibus adolescentiae studiis;* Leonardo Bruni's *De studiis et literis;* the *De liberorum educatione* of Aeneas Sylvius, who later became Pope Pius II; and Battista Guarino's *De ordine docendi et studendi.* Translated into English by William Harrison Woodward and framed, on the one hand, by his description of the famous school founded by Vittorino da Feltre in 1424 at the court of Gianfrancesco Gonzaga, marquis of Mantua, and, on the other, by a judiciously balanced analysis of the aims and methods of the humanist educators, these important texts form the heart of a book that has remained for almost seventy years the fundamental study of early Renaissance educational theory and practice.

When Renaissance humanists wrote about education, they

wrote as professionals. To be sure, not every humanist was
a pedagogue. A very few, like Petrarch, managed to support
themselves as independent men of letters; a few—the great
Venetian printer Aldus Manutius is an example—were
scholarly editors and publishers; others were civil servants,
who combined research and writing with jobs as secretaries
in the chancelleries of Rome, Naples and the cities and
principalities of central and northern Italy. But more
humanists earned their living by teaching than in any other
way. Their very name confirms this. For the word *humanista*,
or humanist, was coined toward the end of the fifteenth
century to designate members of a particular professional
group: teachers of subjects variously described in Renaissance texts as literature (*studia litterarum*); the good, human
or liberal arts (*bonae artes, humanae artes, artes liberales*); or,
most frequently and expressively, the humanities (*studia
humanitatis*).

Humanitas is a classical word and a classical idea. From
it have come, not only *humanista*, but also "humanism"
(a term first used by German scholars in the early nineteenth century to denote an educational theory based on
the Greek and Latin classics) and, by way of the meaning
Renaissance teachers attached to the phrase *studia humanitatis*, our present conception of the "humanities." Cicero
used it to translate the Greek *paideia*, education or culture.
The second-century grammarian Aulus Gellius defined it
as "knowledge and instruction in the good arts" (*eruditio
institutioque in bonas artes*). Fourteenth- and fifteenth-century
humanists revived the word. "To each species of creatures,"
wrote Battista Guarino, "has been allotted a peculiar and
instinctive gift. To horses galloping, to birds flying, comes
naturally. To man only is given the desire to learn. Hence
what the Greeks called παιδεία we call 'studia humanitatis.'
For learning and training in Virtue are peculiar to man;

therefore our forefathers called them *Humanitas*, the pursuits, the activities proper to mankind."

So comprehensive a purpose—to perfect the individual in wisdom (*sapientia*), learning (*doctrina*) and virtue (*scientia moralis*)—would seem, theoretically, to demand an encyclopedic curriculum. Cicero, after all, had defined wisdom as "knowledge of all things divine and human and their causes"; and Vittorino da Feltre himself, reports his fifteenth-century biographer Bartolomeo Platina, "used to praise that universal learning that the Greeks call ἐγκυκλοπαιδεία [from *kyklos*, circle or orbe, and *paideia*, and so an all-embracing education], saying that to benefit his fellows the perfect man should be able to discuss natural philosophy, ethics, the motion of the stars, geometry, harmony, arithmetic and surveying." In practice, however, the subject matter of the *studia humanitatis* was more limited. Humanistic writing shows a fairly consistent pattern of intellectual interests: grammars, poems, orations and histories; letters, plays and biographies; learned editions of literary and historical texts; dialogues and essays on moral philosophy. Humanist teaching shows the same pattern. A humanist did not teach everything; he was a specialist. When teaching his subject professionally, whether publicly or privately, he taught the Latin and Greek languages and literatures, history and moral philosophy. These were the "good and liberal arts," which were counted on to make men learned and virtuous. The same arts define the content of the *studia humanitatis* and the basic curriculum of a humanist school.

The very limitations of this curriculum reflect a new educational purpose: to produce free and civilized men, men of virtue and taste, with a sense of beauty, rather than professionally trained doctors, lawyers, merchants, philosophers or theologians. In the Middle Ages education had been at once professional and clerical. Formal education

—in the sense of the transmission of knowledge through the systematic study of literary, philosophical, legal and scientific texts—was largely a clerical monopoly. The medieval university had neglected the layman; his training, at home or in town or guild schools, was narrowly functional. Since, for example, it was the social function of nobles to fight, they were taught the rudiments of religion, the aristocratic ideals of their class—those notions of courage, honor and *noblesse oblige* which we call chivalry—and, above all, how to fight on horseback in heavy armor, none of which necessarily involved learning how to read and write. Merchants and a growing number of craftsmen were literate, but the purpose of literacy was trade, not sweetness and light. The aim of a humanist education, on the other hand, was to embellish the leisure and fortify the virtue of that approximately 2 per cent of the population of the Italian city-states who controlled the levers of political and economic power. It was more civic and more secular than in the past: civic because the aim was to train citizens rather than monks or scholars, secular because the aim was to train laymen rather than priests and to train them in literary and philosophical disciplines that had been formerly a clerical preserve. Inevitably, it was also classical. For by using the term *humanitas* to name their highest intellectual and moral ideal, Renaissance humanists consciously identified Cicero's admiration for the cultural achievements of the Greeks with their own renewed delight in the arts and letters of antiquity, condemned their own more recent past as a "dark age," and polemically announced a reform of education based on the critical and historical study of ancient literature renascent after centuries of alleged barbarism and decay.

Humanist theorists of the first half of the fifteenth century constantly emphasize the civic end of education. "Respecting the general place of liberal studies," says Vergerio, after reviewing the principal subjects taught in a proper school, "we remember that Aristotle would not have them absorb the entire interests of life: for he kept steadily in view the nature of man as a citizen, an active member of the State. For the man who has surrendered himself absolutely to the attractions of Letters or of speculative thought follows, perhaps, a self-regarding end and is useless as a citizen or as a prince." Human beings are capable of action and contemplation. They must pursue both in order to bring distinction to their family and city and to earn for themselves "fame and honor in the world." A man whose interests are purely scholarly or professional is a tree without fruit. Action in the world should be the end of contemplative scholarship, as art and letters should be the recreation of civilized leisure. Vittorino quoted Cicero to prove the point: "*virtutis laus omnis in actione consistat*"; and Aeneas Sylvius reminded his readers that Cicero had reproached Sextus Pompey for spending too much time on geometry: "His reason was that the true praise of men lies in *doing*, and that consequently all ingenious trifling, however harmless in itself, which withdraws our energies from fruitful activity, is unworthy of the true Citizen."

This is why humanist educators stressed eloquence, that is, grammar and rhetoric, rather than logic; moral philosophy rather than science and metaphysics; and gave to history so novel an importance. For rhetoric, ethics and history are disciplines of doing uniquely appropriate for training scholar-citizens. Moral philosophy teaches us "the secret of true freedom." It teaches us that man is free, like Hercules at the crossroads, to choose the path of virtue or that of vice; it teaches us self-knowledge, practical wisdom, and our duties to God, family, friends, country and ourselves; and it draws us from the abstract preoccupations of natural philosophy and metaphysics into the world of human action. History gives us concrete examples of the precepts inculcated by philosophy. The one shows what men should do, the other what men have said and done in the past and what practical lessons we may draw for the present day. Finally, eloquence is indispensable, not only because formal and stylistic beauty is pleasurable in itself, but also because it persuades our fellow citizens to follow the lessons of history and the precepts of philosophy in their private and public lives.

Humanist emphasis on physical training reflects a similar civic and human purpose: specifically, to train the citizen in arms so that he "may be found ready to defend [his city's] rights or to strike a blow for honor or power"; more generally, to develop fully all an individual's capacities, strength and grace of body as well as intellectual and moral vigor. An age which redefined happiness, with Aristotle, to include money, beauty and health as well as virtue; which redefined wisdom, with the Stoics, to include knowledge of human as well as divine things; which, for the first time since antiquity, used the nude to express its image of perfect beauty—such an age was inevitably concerned to educate body as well as mind, to prize as peculiarly liberal and humane the harmonious cultivation of every admirable human potentiality. The training of aristocratic boys in riding and fighting, which in the Middle Ages had had a strictly professional purpose, acquired a new and more general significance when fifteenth-century schoolmasters made gymnastics and organized sports an integral part of a liberal education. Until the sixteenth century this sporting emphasis could be found only in Italy. In England, where sport was ultimately to bulk so large in the ideal of the gentleman, football was considered base and mean. In Florence, it was played by the sons of the patriciate, and it was said "to make the body sound, dexterous and robust and to make the mind

awake, sharp and desirous of virtuous victory." Therefore, said Vergerio, as soon as a boy is able to use his limbs,
"let him be trained in arms; so soon as he can rightly
speak, let him be trained in letters." Men, to be sure, have
different aptitudes. Some will excel in arms, others in
letters. But the perfect man, just as he cultivates both
intellectual and moral virtues and combines the contemplative and active lives, excels in both. A favorite subject
of Renaissance painting was the loves of Mars and Venus.
The pictorial message was also the ideal of humanist
education: the necessary and desirable coexistence of
speculation and war, contemplation and service to the
state, *humanitas* and physical excellence.

Such a conception of man, the humanist believed, found
its highest expression in ancient literature. A humanist
education, therefore—aside from the fact that Latin was
the indispensable language of the church, diplomacy, scholarship and the professions of law and medicine—was necessarily classical and literary. Study of letters meant study
of Latin letters. Latin, and later Greek, literature was the
core of education because, as Erasmus bluntly put it in the
sixteenth century, "within these two literatures is contained
all the knowledge which we recognize as of vital importance
to mankind." Ancient literature was the voice itself of
humanitas, the civilizing force which made man free and
whole, refined his sensibility and molded his moral attitudes.
A man was liberally educated who had achieved self-
knowledge through an accurate understanding of ancient
literature, whose imagination was stirred by the ideal pattern of classical humanity, who modeled his life after the
image of man in the Greek and Latin classics in the same
way that Scipio and Caesar had kept before their eyes the
image of Alexander. Indeed, the idea of *humanitas* itself
suggested the claims that a classical education was peculiarly

human, that it, pre-eminently, civilized the rude and uncultured, that it made a human being more fully and more
perfectly a man. "We call those studies liberal," wrote
Vergerio in a seminal passage, "which are worthy of a free
man; those studies by which we attain and practice virtue
and wisdom; that education which calls forth, trains and
develops those highest gifts of body and of mind [honor and
glory] which ennoble men, and which are rightly judged to
rank next in dignity to virtue only." Classical studies free,
civilize and perfect.

Such a commitment implied no necessary blunting of
Christian zeal. It did pose acutely the problem of reconciling Christian values with the humanist's enthusiasm
for heathen literatures, whose fundamentally secular assumptions were increasingly revealed as knowledge of
antiquity became more accurate, critical and historically
sophisticated. Humanist educators offered an initial solution by coupling their enthusiasm for pagan antiquity
with a parallel emphasis on Christian antiquity, by em-
bracing the whole of ancient letters, pagan literature and
the writings of the Church Fathers in a comprehensive
admiration.

Leonardo Bruni underlined the significance of the Church
Fathers for education in a key passage: "True learning has
almost died away amongst us. True learning, I say: not a
mere acquaintance with that vulgar, threadbare jargon
which satisfies those who devote themselves to Theology, but
sound learning in its proper and legitimate sense, viz., the
knowledge of realities—Facts and Principles—united to a
perfect familiarity with Letters and the art of expression.
Now this combination we find in Lactantius, in Augustine,
or in Jerome; each of them at once a great theologian and
profoundly versed in literature." These sentences are a
manifesto: an attack on medieval learning and scholastic

theology, a justification of the *studia humanitatis*, an assertion that true learning has a double source, classical literature and patristic theology.

For the Fathers, in the humanist view, were themselves classical men of letters. By reading and quoting Homer and Virgil, Plato and Cicero, they sanctioned the study of pagan literature and philosophy by the moderns. Several had written poetry; several more ranked in style and eloquence with the greatest of their pagan contemporaries and predecessors. By contrast, the religious writings of the scholastics, wrote Bruni, "are utterly destitute of sound and melodious style, and seem to me to have no attraction whatever." Nor was it simply a question of style. Humanist educators considered patristic theology more appropriate for the religious training of the young than the arrogant subtleties, in their view, of scholastic theological science. By combining the purity and simplicity of the early church with a sophisticated literary culture, the Fathers had created an "eloquent wisdom" and a "learned piety." Therefore, they were the most appropriate models for Christian eloquence and Christian philosophy, for a holy rhetoric simpler and more moving than the crabbed and Gothic "questions" of the schoolmen, for a piety stripped of the factitious complexity of dialectic and closer to the scriptural text. In patristic literature humanists found a Christian vision of antiquity. The Fathers had reconciled the tension between Christianity and the ideals of classical culture. Their example convinced humanist educators that they could do the same.

The principles of the fifteenth-century Italian humanist educators were restated with only minor shifts of emphasis by Erasmus and Juan Luis Vives, the greatest educational theorists of the sixteenth century, and took firm institutional form in the secondary schools, both Catholic and

Protestant, of the early modern period. They remained the dominant ideal of education until the end of the nineteenth century. When Woodward, writing in England in the 1890's, subtitled his book "An Introduction to the History of Classical Education," he clearly assumed that he was describing the origins of modern education, or, as he put it himself, the "educational practice of a period whose originating impulse is still, within that sphere, powerfully operative among us." And he was right. The educational treatises of Vergerio, Bruni, Aeneas Sylvius and Battista Guarino, and related humanist works, are the sources of the modern notions of the humanities, of belles-lettres and of a liberal education. Renaissance humanists created the modern idea of the gentleman, whose nobility is conferred by virtue and learning, in short, by education in the *studia humanitatis*, rather than by birth; of training the whole man, both in sport and in the Greek and Roman classics; of an education at once civic and nonprofessional with its inevitable function of civilizing and perpetuating a leisured ruling class. Our difficulty today (and this is why we read Woodward's book with a perspective very different from his) is that these ideas are modern no longer. Like the men of the Renaissance, we live in a period of profound and rapid transition, a period in which most Renaissance values are in a state of disintegration or transformation. This is as true of education as it is of the sovereign state, of capitalism, of Newtonian science and of an art based on perspective. Specifically, the conviction that much, to say nothing of Erasmus' "all," of what is best and vitally important to mankind can be found in the texts of classical antiquity is shared by a diminishing band. The undermining of this fundamental assumption has drained the idea of liberal education of its traditional meaning. But by understanding what humanistic education meant in its historical origins and what cultural and social needs it was designed to meet, we can perhaps decide on more adequate evidence whether it has become a historical curiosity or whether, and to what extent, its traditional principles and ambitions can be given new meanings appropriate to our own society and to our own sense of what a civilized man should be. For this purpose no book is better than Woodward's scholarly and therapeutic study.

BIBLIOGRAPHICAL NOTE

Woodward's versions are in many passages paraphrases rather than translations. The original texts are best read in critical editions published since he wrote: Vergerio's, edited by A. Gnesotto, in *Atti e Memorie della R. Acc. di Scienze, Lettere ed Arti in Padova*, N.S. XXXIV (1918), 96–146; Bruni's, edited by H. Baron, in *Leonardo Bruni Aretino humanistisch, philosophische Schriften* (Leipzig-Berlin, 1928), pp. 5–19; Aeneas Sylvius', in R. Wolkan's edition of the letters of Pius II, *Fontes Rerum Austriacarum. Diplomataria et Acta*, LXVII (Vienna, 1912), 103–158 or, in the text and translation of Brother J. S. Nelson (Washington, D.C., 1940). There is as yet no modern edition of Battista Guarino's *De ordine docendi et studendi*. A fifth important educational treatise by an Italian humanist of the first half of the fifteenth century is the *De educatione liberorum et eorum claris moribus* of Maffeo Vegio (1407–1458). It is conveniently available in a modern edition by Sisters M. W. Fanning and A. S. Sullivan, in The Catholic University of America, *Studies in Medieval and Renaissance Latin*, I, fasc. 1 and 2 (Washington, D.C., 1933–1936). E. Garin, *L'educazione umanistica in Italia* (Bari, Italy, 1949) is a valuable collection of texts, with commentary, which usefully supplements Woodward with documents on the life and educational methods of Vittorino and with selections from Salutati, St. Bernardino of Siena, Matteo Palmieri, Leon Battista Alberti, Guarino Veronese and Antonio de Ferrariis. More valuable still is *Il pensiero pedagogico dello Umanesimo*, edited by Garin (Florence, 1958), a second collection of texts that includes the Latin originals as well as Italian translations. Bartolomeo Platina's life of Vittorino da Feltre has been translated and republished by G. Biasuz (Padua, 1948). Two other major sources for the early history of the new education are the letters of Guarino Veronese, edited by R. Sabbadini, in *Miscellanea di Storia Veneta*, Vols. VIII, XI, XIV (Venice, 1915–1919) and those of Vergerio, edited by L. Smith (Rome, 1934).

Since the publication of Woodward's *Vittorino da Feltre* (Cambridge, England, 1897) and his *Studies in Education during the Age of the Renaissance, 1400–1600* (Cambridge, England, 1906), the best general works on the educational theory and practice of the Italian humanists have been G. Saitta, *L'educazione dell' Umanesimo in Italia* (Venice, 1928) and Garin, *L'educazione in Europa (1400–1600)* (Bari, Italy, 1957), a stimulating synthesis by a master of the sources. Readers who care to explore further will find useful the following more specialized studies: G. Bertoni, *Guarino da Verona fra letterati e cortigiani a Ferrara (1429–1460)* (Geneva, 1921); A. Gambara, *Vittorino da Feltre* (Turin, Italy, 1946); V. J. Horkan, *Educational Theories and Principles of Maffeo Vegio* (Washington, D.C., 1953); and R. Kelso, *Doctrine for the Lady of the Renaissance* (Urbana, Ill., 1956).

Our understanding of the humanist idea of education is, of course, influenced by our interpretation of Renaissance humanism as a whole. Several recent interpretative and bibliographical studies are helpful guides through the maze of controversial literature: P. O. Kristeller and J. H. Randall, Jr., "The Study of the Philosophies of the

Renaissance," *Journal of the History of Ideas*, II (1941), 449–496; C. Angeleri, *Il problema religioso del Rinascimento* (Florence, 1952), A. Buck, "Italienischer Humanismus," *Archiv für Kulturgeschichte*, XXXVII (1955), 105–122; XLI (1959), 107–132; W. K. Ferguson, "The Revival of Classical Antiquity or the First Century of Humanism: A Reappraisal," The Canadian Historical Association, *Report of the Annual Meeting held at Ottawa, June 12–15, 1957*, pp. 13–30; W. Bouwsma, *The Interpretation of Renaissance Humanism* (Washington, D.C., 1959); Kristeller, "Changing Views of the Intellectual History of the Renaissance since Jacob Burckhardt," in *The Renaissance: A Reconsideration of the Theories and Interpretations of the Age*, edited by T. Hilton (Madison, Wis., 1961), pp. 27–52 and "Studies on Renaissance Humanism during the Last Twenty Years," *Studies in the Renaissance*, IX (1962), 7–30.

The decisive works that have formed the contemporary image of Italian Renaissance humanism are less numerous than bibliographical articles might suggest. The following are indispensable: Ferguson, *The Renaissance in Historical Thought* (Boston, 1948); Garin, *L'Umanesimo italiano: filosofia e vita civile nel Rinascimento* (Bari, Italy, 1952); Baron, *The Crisis of the Early Italian Renaissance* (2 vols.; Princeton, N.J., 1955); Kristeller, *The Classics and Renaissance Thought* (Cambridge, Mass., 1955) and *Studies in Renaissance Thought and Letters* (Rome, 1956); and E. Panofsky, *Renaissance and Renascences in Western Europe* (Uppsala, Sweden, 1960).

VITTORINO DA FELTRE

AND OTHER

HUMANIST EDUCATORS:

ESSAYS AND VERSIONS.

AN INTRODUCTION TO
THE HISTORY OF CLASSICAL EDUCATION

BY

WILLIAM HARRISON WOODWARD,
CHRIST CHURCH, OXFORD;
LECTURER IN EDUCATION IN VICTORIA UNIVERSITY.

CAMBRIDGE:
AT THE UNIVERSITY PRESS.

INTRODUCTION.

THE present volume is offered as an introduction to the study of the education of the first period of Renaissance, the century which followed the death of Petrarch. The work falls into three divisions. The first treats of the career of the characteristic Humanist School-master, Vittorino da Feltre. The second consists of four noteworthy treatises on education produced during this period, not now readily accessible to students. These are here presented in English versions. In the third section I have aimed at setting forth a general review of education as conceived by humanist scholars.

The subject is of interest in more than one direction. It bears immediately upon the broader conceptions which we form of the civilisation and ideals of the Renaissance in its earlier and less self-conscious stage; inasmuch as the educational aim of any age, if scientifically thought out, must express, with some precision, the moral and intellectual temper of the time. In the next place, though less directly, light is thrown by such enquiry as the present upon the development of classical scholarship. Its relation to the history of educational ideals and methods needs no insistence. In limiting the present Study to the period of the early Renaissance I have not been guided by considerations of space alone. Recent critics of Humanism, both in England and Germany, appear to me to have overlooked the distinctive character of this period of 'Origins.' Whether as regards spirit or practice, the Mantuan school of Vittorino can by no possibility be classed under one head with the school of Sturm at Strassburg.

In this difference is implied a constant process in which the ideal of the greater Humanists was slowly narrowed and hardened till it reaches the pedantry which rouses the scorn of Montaigne. It is not merely that the Latinity of Vergerius or Guarino was freer and less artificial, nor that with them literature was something more than a sequence of model passages: the scholars of the first half of the Quattrocento had a far broader grasp of the true content of education, and with it a more sincere conception of the relation between the antique and the modern world.

To bring out, even at the cost of some repetition, this decisive feature of early Humanism has been an object which I have throughout kept steadily in view. In Italy the distinction is sharply drawn by such ardent and clear-sighted students of Humanist literature as the late Prof. Combi, and that most industrious enquirer and powerful critic, Dr Sabbadini of Catania. It is one worthy of attention, not only from professed students of the Revival of Learning, but from all who are concerned in the status and the methods of classical teaching. Humanist education, alike of the Elizabethan schools, and of those of to-day, is, no doubt, open to criticism, either in respect of its aims, or of the methods of attaining them. It will serve good purpose if, in weighing what is alleged, we can fall back upon the experiences and the avowed ideals of a period in which our classical education of to-day received its first and in some respects its noblest impress. We shall then not refuse our recognition to the wonderful gifts, scholarly and educational, which mark the little band of students and school-masters, who within the space of hardly more than one generation, could establish a concept of education wholly new to the modern world and could devise, from material in large part unfamiliar, a working method which has for five centuries remained, with but slight modification, adequate to the highest needs of intellectual culture.

I desire to record my obligation for help received in the compilation of the present work from Dr Sabbadini, Professor of Latin in the University of Catania; from Principal Rendall, of University College, Liverpool; from Dr Garnett, and the officials of the Reading Room, and of the Manuscript Room of the British Museum, whose courtesy is never failing; from Dr Copinger; and from Mr John Sampson, the Librarian of University College, Liverpool, who has kindly read the proofs, and whose bibliographical knowledge has been of great assist-ance, notably in the preparation of the *List* which concludes the volume.

VITTORINO DA FELTRE: AUTHORITIES.

The AUTHORITIES for the life and work of VITTORINO DA FELTRE are the following:

1. The Dialogue of Francesco Prendilacqua. Born at Mantua about 1422 he was a pupil of Vittorino in 1440; some years later he served as Secretary to Alessandro Gonzaga. At school he was contemporary with Federigo di Urbino, with whom he maintained friendly relations in after years. Prendilacqua had special opportunities of information in all that concerned the personal character of Vittorino and of his methods of instruction and discipline. The date of the Dialogue is uncertain, but in any case it was composed some years after the death of Vittorino (1446).

2. The Letter of Sassuolo da Prato *De Victorini Feltrensis vita ac disciplina*. Sassuolo is found at the Mantuan school in 1437, and is still there in 1443. He acted as assistant in Mathematics and Music during part of this time. His Letter is referred to by contemporaries as a valuable authority upon the work of Vittorino.

3. Francesco di Castiglione prefixed a short account of Vittorino, whose pupil he was for eight years, to his life of Antonino, Archbishop of Florence.

4. Bartolomeo Sacchi, known as Platina, is in some respects the most important of all contemporary authorities. He was not a pupil of Vittorino himself, but of his beloved scholar and successor Ognibene da Lonigo. Platina in his turn followed Ognibene, as head of the Mantuan School, in 1453, remaining there for three years. His position enabled him to gather minute and accurate information upon all details of subject and method adopted by Vittorino. Platina is best known by his *Vitae Pontificum* and

Historia Urbis Mantuanae. He was the first 'Praefectus Bibliothecae' of the Vatican (1475).

5. Giovanni Andrea, afterwards Bishop of Aleria, was, like Sassuolo, one of the free pupils of Vittorino. He is referred to on p. 88, below. He devotes a portion of his Preface to the *Editio Princeps* of Livy to a recognition of his debt to his old master, from whose emended copy of Livy he was said to have printed the Text.

6. The memoir by Vespasiano da Bisticci, the famous Florentine bookseller, though inaccurate and not very definite, is interesting on the personal side. Vittorino made his acquaintance during his visit to Florence in 1443.

7. Certain letters of Vittorino to the Marchioness Paola Gonzaga, brought to light within the past ten years from the remains of the Mantuan archives, throw an interesting light upon the relations between the Gonzaga family and the master of the Palatine school. The Correspondence and *Hodoeporicon* of Ambrogio Traversari are valuable upon the literary side.

The work of Cavaliere Rosmini, *Idea dell' ottimo Precettors, nella vita e disciplina di Vittorino da Feltre*, published in 1801, is a most appreciative and stimulating memoir of the Teacher, written, as the title implies, mainly from the educational standpoint. It is based chiefly upon Prendilacqua, though Rosmini showed extreme diligence in collecting all the scattered notices of Vittorino available from printed sources. But the wider and more precise knowledge of Humanism which we owe to the research of the past half century enables us to define much more exactly the place of Vittorino in the Revival of Letters, and in the general history of Education.

The bibliographical list which is placed at the end of the volume, p. 251, will facilitate reference to the editions of works actually quoted in the text or notes. Although it is by no means a complete list of authorities consulted it will serve to indicate the active research now in progress in Italy and Germany in connection with the literary aspects of the Renaissance. It is only right to acknowledge the special debt due from all students of the subject to Dr Sabbadini.

VITTORINO DA FELTRE.

Vittorino da Feltre was born at Feltre, one of those
picturesque little towns which nestle under the southern
slope of the Eastern Alps with their faces turned toward the
great Venetian plain. It is near enough to the southern edge
of the Dolomite region to be called Titian's country; its natural
centre is Venice, though at the end of the fourteenth century
its dependence was either upon the Visconti or the Carrara,
the famous condottieri and lords of Padua. Vittorino was the
son of one Ser Bruto di Rambaldoni and Monda his wife; the
family was held in high respect[1], but latterly it had fallen upon
evil days, and only the tradition of place and fortune survived
at the time of Vittorino's birth in 1378. Bruto Rambaldoni
was a writer or notary, and in later years his son recounted
how from time to time the household lacked even the bare
necessaries of life. Vittorino, however, in spite of a slight and
unimpressive figure seems to have been possessed of a sound
constitution, which certainly the bracing air of his native hill
country could not fail to strengthen. Of his boyhood we
know practically nothing. Feltre could offer little in the way
of masters or books. It lay remote from any large town and
no highway of importance passed through it. Vittorino, who
manifested as he grew up an intellectual keenness which Feltre

---

[1] Castiglione writes of Vittorino (whose pupil he was for eight years)
"Non ex ignobili genere in Feltrensi civitate natus est." Mehus, *Ambr.
Trav.* ccccviii.

could not satisfy, left his native town at the age of 18 and in 1396 entered the university of Padua, where, as his pupil records, 'all the Arts had their home.'

The position of Padua, still part of the Lordship of the Carrara, was at this moment one of some peculiar interest amongst the universities of Italy. The year 1396 is at the same time one of the great dates in the history of learning. For in the spring of this year the Studium of Florence addressed an invitation to Manuel Chrysoloras, at Constantinople, to accept the chair of Greek letters as the first Professor of the Greek tongue in the West. From this invitation, couched in terms of grave dignity worthy of the men who sent it, date the beginnings of Greek learning in Italy. We are naturally accustomed to associate the revival of the study of antiquity primarily with Florence, with Boccaccio, Salutati and Niccoli, and to regard the municipality[1] or the court rather than the established universities as the more potent influence in the rise of Humanism. This is no doubt in the main true of all cities of Northern Italy. But there is strong evidence that Padua, the second great Italian university of the time, stood in more friendly relation to the new studies than any other 'Studio Pubblico' of the peninsula except perhaps Pavia. The spirit of Petrarch—in the study of the Renaissance we find ourselves inevitably harking back to Petrarch—was still a living force in Padua. He had lived for many years in its immediate neighbourhood. He had been equally intimate with the ruling family[2] and with the learned circles of the University. Francesco Carrara was his admirer, correspondent

---

[1] The Florentine Studium was revived in 1348; it had never been reckoned amongst the older universities, which had their origin from Bologna. The terms of the invitation shew that it was with the citizens rather than the students or regents of the Studium that it originated. The Studio of Florence was curiously lacking in vitality. See Voigt, i. 340.

[2] See Zardo, *Il Petr. ed i Carraresi*, Milan, 1887. The letter on the character of a prince in *Ep. Senil.* ed. Fracassetti, xiv. 1.

and close personal friend. One of Petrarch's most important letters was addressed to him, bearing directly upon the state of the university city itself. His correspondence reveals how deeply interested Petrarch was in all that concerned education, and his anxiety for its reform. Petrarch's library[1], the most remarkable collection of ancient books formed since classical times, was for some years after his death preserved at Padua, where his many friends kept alive his keen enthusiasm for Latin learning in the University and throughout Venetia.

But Petrarch's connexion with Paduan scholarship is even more directly marked by the presence there of Giovanni Conversino da Ravenna. This great figure in the history of Humanism was the man upon whom in a special sense the mantle of Petrarch may be said to have fallen. He had passed the critical years of early manhood as 'famulus' and pupil in the house of Petrarch. In 1379, shortly after the poet's death, we find him at Padua; three years later he is 'Artis Rhetoricae Professor.' A period of wandering follows; he is Chancellor to the municipality of Ragusa, or school-master at Udine, until, some time after 1392, he is found in the capacity of 'Protonotarius' to the Carrara at Padua, combining with that office the lectureship on Rhetoric and Latin literature in the University. Conversino was thus, by his position, a man of no little influence. He was a man of great ability, far above the level of the ordinary Master of Grammar. He had the confidence and high esteem of the reigning Carrara prince, whose sympathies were, as we know from other sources, heartily on the side of the revival of Latin letters. The Carrarese had indeed been for two or three generations men of serious tastes, and had chosen as administrators officers of a congenial type: in which course they were followed, after the extinction of their power in 1405, by the Venetian Council. Scholars rather than soldiers or ecclesiastics were sought for as

[1] Nolhac, *Pétrarque*, ch. ii. p. 77 seqq.

tutors to their children; and their influence in the University, direct and indirect, was favourable to the new studies[1].

Even in such subjects as Theology and Dialectic Padua had already, by the end of the fourteenth century, given evidence of a new, a more objective, method of treatment. In the hands of Paulus Venetus and of P. P. Vergerius, both men of warm sympathies with Latin letters, the purely scholastic method in Logic or Theology had no place. It would seem as though Padua were, consciously or not, affected by its neigh-

---

[1] The identity of Giovanni Conversino with Giovanni Malpaghini, a confusion which dates from Cortesius in the fifteenth century, has been maintained by Voigt, by Rački and by Gloria. But the question may be regarded as definitely settled in the opposite sense by the research of Sabbadini (*Giornale Storico* &c. v. 156), of Klette (*Beit.* i. 44), of Novati (*Epist. Salutati*, ii. 404) and of Lehnerdt (Voigt, *Wiederbelebung*, i. 213, 3rd ed.). The identity of Conversino with the Giovanni da Ravenna who was in 1364 living under Petrarch's roof has been most ably proved by Lehnerdt : but Klette and Sabbadini (*opp. cit.*) identify Malpaghini with Petrarch's pupil. Malpaghini was professor of Latin at the Studium of Florence and afterwards lecturer on Dante. Gloria (*Mon. Univ. Padov.*) maintains that both Florentine and Paduan records prove the identity of the two scholars (ii. 534) but from Gherardi's collection (*Statuti dello Studio Fior.*) we derive, as Klette shews, the opposite conclusion.

The discussion is hardly yet closed; and Rački's important body of facts drawn from a MS. collection of the letters of Giovanni Conversino in the library of Agram has not yet been fully weighed (*Rad. Jugo-Slavenske Akad.* 1885, p. 135 seqq.). Lehnerdt's new section in his edition of Voigt's *Wiederbelebung*, i. p. 213, is the latest and most conclusive reconstruction of this much disputed chapter in the history of Humanism. Gaspary and Novati are right in stating that there were *three* contemporary scholars known as Giovanni da Ravenna. Cf. Gaspary, *Letterat. Italiana*, ii. 335.

Conversino was an able teacher: Sicco Polentone, Guarino and Benvenuto da Imola, besides many able scholars of less name, were his pupils. Cf. the anon. letter addressed to him in Voigt, *Briefs. Petrarca's*, p. 92. His writings, however, were tasteless and hardly survived him : but he definitely made Padua the leading university centre in the Latin revival, and for our purpose this is his chief importance. As a scholar Vittorino, of course, far outstripped him.

bourhood with Venice. There, interest in Greek lands was a habit of daily life ; and scholastic learning or ascetic morals had no attraction for a people whose ideals were above all things practical, external, social. Not only did Venice contribute perhaps the largest share of the students of the University, but in turn she drew from it her schoolmasters, jurists and doctors. Thus when Vittorino came to Padua in 1396 he found an atmosphere as favourable to the revived taste for ancient learning as existed in any Italian city, Florence alone excepted. Certainly in no other of the universities would a student be so likely to find that love of erudition, that critical spirit, that clearness of intuition, that objective intellectual habit, which were to become the characteristic marks of Italian scholarship.

The repute of Padua at this period was very high, not in Italy only but beyond the Alps. We find both English and Scottish names amongst its students ; and others came from the Low Countries, France, Germany, Hungary and the East. Medicine, Canon Law and Mathematics attracted the larger proportion of students ; but the Arts subjects, Grammar, Dialectic, Rhetoric and Philosophy, occupied a more important place than at Bologna, the only other university of the same standing and popularity.

It is uncertain to which of the higher Faculties Vittorino proposed to devote himself. But at the outset he enrolled himself under the faculty of Arts, attending the courses of Giovanni da Ravenna in Grammar and Latin letters[1]. He had as fellow-pupils many men afterwards distinguished, and amongst them one destined to become not less famous than himself as a teacher, Guarino da Verona. Vittorino soon became known as himself an able teacher of Grammar. For

[1] Conversino came to Padua in the second half of 1392 ; and he seems to have remained there as Chancellor of the Carrara (a non-academic office) and Professor of Rhetoric until 1405. See Novati, *Epistol. Salutati*, ii. 405 ; Klette, *Beit.* i. 44.

his poverty compelled him to undertake the thankless post of
'magister puerorum' or master of the rudiments of Grammar.
This was an altogether private venture, carrying with it neither
university status nor stipend. It was probably ill-paid work,
monotonous and laborious, but only in this way could Vittorino
find the means to enable him to attend the courses on Dialectic, Philosophy and Rhetoric. Dialectic was taught by
Paulus Venetus, a man of some distinction, who combined
with his chair the teaching of Theology. Nicolas di Cusa,
some twenty years later, came from Trèves to Padua to learn
from Paulus Philosophy and Mathematics. He was, apparently, as Rossi describes him, 'originale pensatore in
molteplici discipline[1].' Vergerius was at this time at Florence
(1397—1400). As we hear of Vittorino attending also a
course on Canon Law it is possible that he contemplated
ecclesiastical service: later on, as we shall see, his bent lay
decidedly towards the religious life. We have no allusion to
the teaching of Greek at Padua at this time: the first public
chair there in this language was not founded until after
Vittorino's death. Florence alone in 1400 possessed a master
of the forgotten tongue. For we must remember that in spite
of Boccaccio and of Petrarch Greek was absolutely an unknown language in Italy when Chrysoloras came to Florence
early in 1397[2].

Vittorino remained at Padua for nearly twenty years.
Like most of the Humanist scholars of the time he was at
once a teacher and a learner; attending the lectures of public
professors even after he had received his Laurea (the Degree

---

[1] G. Rossi, *Niccolo di Cusa*, p. 11.

[2] This no longer admits of dispute. Nolhac, *Pétrarque*, describes the
true position of Greek in relation to Petrarch and L. Pilatus. Nolhac, *Pét.*
p. 339. There were of course trade relations between Venice and
Southern Italy and Greek lands. But it is agreed that no one was to be
found in Italy who could teach the grammar of ancient Greek or
explain an ordinary passage from a Greek author. See the complaint
made by Vergerius, infra, p. 106.

of Doctor.) So Vergerius, a man of fifty, with the *Laurea* of Arts and Medicine, did not hesitate to sit side by side with boys for three years in the lecture room of Chrysoloras[1]. The subjects in which the *Laurea* of Arts was gained at Padua were the Grammar and Literature of Latin, Rhetoric or Composition, Dialectic, and Moral Philosophy[2]. The date of his degree we do not know. It was in any case some time before 1411[3]: probably much earlier. But it was characteristic of the man that he refused to wear either the ring or the gown which marked his academic rank.

After receiving his degree Vittorino turned to the study of Mathematics, at that time regarded as a subject outside the usual university courses. There was no public Professor of Mathematics at Padua: indeed there is no evidence that a chair with public stipend existed in any Italian university at the beginning of the fifteenth century. Natural Philosophy was combined sometimes with the chair of Moral Philosophy (as in the case of Paulus Venetus) or with that of Astrology (as with Pelacani). But in any case Mathematical teaching was dependent, in any Studium, on the accidental presence of a capable master who could attract private pupils.

Biagio Pelacani da Parma was the ablest of these private masters in Mathematics. He was apparently a man of real capacity. His connexion with Padua dates from 1387[4], perhaps earlier; and he died there in 1416. Early in the century

---

[1] Vergerius himself refers to his own 'cupiditas discendi,' which led him to attend courses in the universities even when well advanced in years. Vid. *Ep.* 104 (*Epist. Verg.* p. 159).

[2] Gloria, *Mon. Pad.* ii. p. 84.

[3] Vittorino after receiving his Laurea learnt Mathematics from Pelacani, who left Padua in this year. Gloria, *Mon. Pad.* ii. p. 416.

[4] He is then referred to as 'Doctor Artium profundissimus.' In 1386 he had successfully predicted a defeat of the Veronese. He has left many treatises in MS., including several on Aristotle. Some on astronomy and geometry are decidedly in advance of the popular teaching of the day. Gloria, *Mon. Pad.* l.c.

Pelacani was teaching Geometry privately at high fees. It is recorded that Vittorino though now holding the degree of Doctor (Artium) was still so poor that, unable to pay the charges of the class conducted by Pelacani[1], he offered himself as 'famulus' in the Professor's household. In that capacity he acted for six months, winning a grudging respect from his master, who had the reputation of a hard man even amongst private teachers. Vittorino made rapid progress with Euclid, and when his course was completed acquired great popularity as a mathematical teacher. This probably implies some knowledge of Algebra as well as of Euclid, though Astrology was never a favourite subject with him. Vittorino's name indeed was associated especially with Mathematics all his life, as is shewn by the medal of Pisanello reproduced on the frontispiece. Possibly this may be due to the unfamiliar nature of mathematical studies at the time and the paucity of masters. For we have but the slightest reference to the extent of Vittorino's use of Geometry in his school courses.

Vittorino seems to have maintained himself at Padua as master of Grammar and private teacher of Mathematics until 1415 when he left the university city. His repute grew steadily, and both in mathematical and in literary subjects his teaching was much in request. During these years the fortunes of the University[2] underwent some variations. The final absorption of Padua into the Venetian State in 1405 led to the departure of many personal adherents of the Carrara family,

---

[1] Castiglione in Mehus, *Vita Ambros.* ccccviii. Gloria, ii. 416, says that Pelacani had to quit Padua for a time by reason of discredit due to his grasping nature. As Mathematics did not form part of the usual courses in any faculty the private teaching by regents was arranged on a strictly commercial basis. Pelacani seems to have been able to drive good bargains because of his special ability, though on the part of one who was in another subject a 'Professor publicus' this was probably regarded as unworthy.

[2] Interesting light is thrown by Rossi, *Niccolo di Cusa*, Pisa, 1894, on the temper of intellectual life at Padua about this period.

and deprived the University of a sympathetic patron. But Venice, proud of her new acquisition, took care to appoint as her representative a scholar, Sicco Polentone, and shortly afterwards we find Padua not only the most popular of all Italian universities but marked perhaps by the greatest breadth of intellectual aim. The discipline, however, of the students was less satisfactory. Writing in February 1414 Guarino has occasion to pass a severe judgement upon the student life as he saw it. The tutelary deity of the Paduan students is Bacchus : they celebrate his feast, not annually, but daily, and indeed more than once a day. How different from the School of Socrates or the Academy of Plato ! ' In illis namque disputari solitum aiunt, in his vero nostris dispotari, immo trispotari quaterque potari frequens patriae mos est. Academici de uno, de vero, de motu disserunt, hi nostri de vino, de mero, de potu dispotant[1].'

A sudden influx of foreign students, especially from countries north of the Alps, the influence of Venice, the freedom accorded to students, often not more than fourteen years of age, serve to account for that laxity of discipline and morals which Guarino portrays. We shall see Vittorino at a later date driven to resign his university chair by reason of similar disorders. It is probably true that in other universities the same disorders prevailed. But we must remember how intense was the devotion to the New Learning in Italy at this time, especially in Padua, Florence and Pavia : how absorbed in the work of deciphering or interpreting the classical authors were the few scholars upon whose shoulders lay the burden of the ancient literature. It was bad enough in their eyes that young men with so great a harvest of honour and virtue before them could be frivolous or debauched. But that a scholar whose years were all too short for the great task awaiting him should waste precious hours upon such auditors was an impossible thing.

---

[1] Inedited letter, dated Flor. iiii. Kal. Mart. 1414, quoted by Sabbad. *Epistol. Guar.* p. 61.

So perhaps Padua was in reality no worse than Montpellier or Paris. But Vittorino derived from his experience there his lifelong conviction that the critical years of youth demand first of all close and watchful care: and that this can hardly be secured amid the distractions or temptations of a university city.

It is necessary now to consider more closely the influences which at Padua tended to mould Vittorino's intellectual nature, and definitely imbued him with the finer Humanist spirit.

In 1407 Padua was so fortunate as to secure for the new chair of Rhetoric[1] the greatest Latin scholar of the time, Gasparino Barzizza, who had gained a considerable reputation at Pavia, where he had formed an acquaintance with Chrysoloras. It was by Barzizza, we may safely affirm, that the Ciceronian tradition was definitely established in the revival of classical learning. Guarino Veronese, and there could be no better authority, wrote of him at a somewhat later date "cuius ductu et auspiciis Cicero amatur, legitur, et per Italorum gymnasia summa cum gloria volitat[2]." He was indeed the first to approach Cicero in a thoroughly scholarly spirit, bringing to bear upon the text an analytic and comparative method to which no ancient author had hitherto been subjected. At the same time we must be careful to distinguish the Latin scholarship of the first decades of the 15th century from the stricter Ciceronianism represented by Bembo. The purely imitative treatment of Cicero was not the aim of Barzizza and of the scholars whom he typifies, such as Zabarella, Vergerio and Vittorino. In the widest sense, these men set before themselves the reconciliation of the ancient learning with the Christian life, thought and polity of their own day; they had no dream of a dead reproduction of the past. So in language. Latin was to them a living tongue, to be adapted as

---

[1] The stipend was fixed at 120 ducats, increased to 160 ducats in 1412, owing to Barzizza's poverty.

[2] In 1422, Letter of Guarino, Bodleian Libr., Laud. MS. Lat. 64. 3.

such to the needs of learned intercourse and literary treatment. Thus Barzizza—and it is equally true of the other scholars I have just mentioned—definitely set himself to enter into the spirit of Cicero's style; partly because in Cicero, orator, correspondent, popular philosopher, they found a model peculiarly useful in the various needs of literary or public life. But they did not refrain from adding to his vocabulary for the purposes of the actual life of their own day; and, especially in the epistolary style, they practised as much elasticity and freedom as was compatible with the general form and construction of the Ciceronian sentence. And indeed we may claim for the Latinity[1] of this particular stage of the Revival a spontaneity and Italian colour which we look for in vain when the middle of the century has been turned. It is necessary to bear this in mind in judging the literary methods of the period under review. The Italian scholars, the successors of the Romans, aimed at restoring their literary inheritance by utilising Latin for all grave and serious purposes. In reality they were already too late; and by the end of the century it had become evident to their successors that in the vernacular a not unworthy instrument was ready to hand even for the higher purposes of Literature. Poliziano[2] and Bembo used both Latin and Italian indifferently. Thereupon, as an inevitable consequence, Latin became once for all an artificial language, and therefore merely imitative. In Bembo and Dolet the most rigid type of Ciceronianism, quite logically,

---

[1] Vid. Combi, *Ep. Verg.* p. xxvii.; Sabbad. *Ciceron.* p. 14, contrasting Barzizza's freedom with Valla's formal and pretentious style; and the same writer's tract upon Ognibene da Lonigo, 1880. The school of Barzizza is essentially different from that of Perotti in its simplicity, and its readiness to adapt Latin to current needs.

[2] The definitive revival of Italian, modified and strengthened by the classical influence, is due to Poliziano and dates from the last quarter of the fifteenth century. Reumont's remarks upon the effects of Humanism on the developement of Italian are of much weight : *Loren. dei Med.* ii. 8 seqq. (English edition).

appears. Henceforward structure, metaphor, vocabulary, usage—all the elements of style—must be supported by strict Ciceronian precedent. Where the subject-matter is alien from classical modes of thought, as in Christian doctrine, the greatest ingenuity must be exercised to bring its expression within Augustan terms. But this was a hundred years after Barzizza[1].

Barzizza began by a careful exposition of the *Letters*; the treatises *De Senectute* and *De Amicitia* followed; afterwards he dealt with the *De Oratore* and other rhetorical works of Cicero. Upon the *De Oratore*[2] Barzizza had from 1407 bestowed an extraordinary amount of labour. He had to deal with a text mutilated and corrupt. In order to connect the isolated passages Barzizza provided sundry marginal glosses, not in any way foisting them into the text, but solely for the purpose of giving a certain continuity to the fragmentary work. Correspondents forwarded to him MSS. of this and other classical texts for revision; and most interesting notices are preserved as to his practice in this most delicate function of scholarship[3]. His own letters were deservedly prized as models of composition[4]; so too his Academic addresses. His reputation for taste is shewn by the fact that the oration on the death of Manuel Chrysoloras by Andreas Giuliani[5] was submitted to him before publication. Barzizza represented indeed the Humanist spirit on its best side, and from his

---

[1] It is interesting to notice the close association of Ciceronianism and Padua, from Barzizza and Vittorino to Bembo and Dolet.

[2] See Sabbadini, *Studi di Barz. su Quint. e Cicerone.* Barzizza devoted much time to the *Rhetoric* of Aristotle, which, however, he never edited. His labours on the *De Oratore* did not cease till his death.

[3] Sabbad. *op. cit.* pp. 10, 11.

[4] Bodl. Library, Codd. Canonic. Misc. 360. 1. "Gasp. Barzizzae Bergomatis Epistolae centum triginta tres ad exercitationem accommodatae." See B. Mus., Add. MS. 14,786. There are works by him *De Orthographia, De Etimologia* and a *Vocabularium.*

[5] Sabbad. *op. cit.* p. 28.

appointment at Padua we must date the introduction of sound critical scholarship into the University.

Now Barzizza was a man of slender means. His stipend was a poor one. To supplement it he received into his house both fellow scholars, men of established reputation, and also young students. Amongst them were such men as George of Trebizond, who had come to Italy to learn Latin and to seek his fortune ; Francesco Filelfo, who acted as Barzizza's deputy ; and Vittorino[1]. We do not know in what year Vittorino began residence with Barzizza; but he was thirty years old when the latter first came to Padua in 1407 ; and he left Padua for Venice seven years later. Thus Vittorino came under the direct influence of Barzizza, the first Latin scholar[2] of the age, and in a most important sense imbibed his spirit and continued his work. Indeed it is not too much to affirm that after the death of this great scholar Vittorino was the foremost representative of the best type of Latin learning—the rational Ciceronian. His own pupils, especially Gaza and George of Trebizond, a brilliant scholar whose Latinity he definitely formed[3], and others like the Bishop of Aleria and Ognibene da Lonigo, were all free from the pedantry of purism and upheld the flexible elastic treatment of the Latin tongue.

But apart from his place in scholarship Barzizza was a notable force in Padua in other ways. His relations with

---

[1] Sabbad. *Giorn. Ligust.* xviii. p. 25. Vittorino was probably still with Barzizza until he left Padua to join Guarino.

[2] " La maggior autorità letteraria di quel tempo," says Sabbadini of him. *Op. cit.* p. 28. Aeneas Sylvius declares that the 'Praecepta' of Barzizza were in his day the best guide to sound prose composition, vid. *Rhet. Praecepta,* Prologus : Aen. Syl. *Opera,* p. 992.

[3] Any doubt on this point is definitely set at rest by the extracts from inedited letters of G. of Trebizond himself (Vatic. MSS. 2926) lately published by Sabbadini (*Giorn. Storico d. Lett. Ital.* xviii. p. 230) " ...cum ego Graeca a meis, Latina a Victorino Feltrensi acceperim"; "a quo (Victorino) cuncta quae ad Latinitatem pertinent hausimus"; "si quid Latinae linguae in me est, te doctore, o Victorine, post deum est."

Guarino[1], a professional rival, who took from him more than one of his most creditable pupils, reveal a frank and generous disposition, not too common amongst scholars of the time. An observer peculiarly competent records that his pupils are so taught that not merely "probe ex arte dicere valeant," but also "vivendo morum praecepta sequantur[2]"; "ut ornatissime quis dicit ita et recte vivat" was a well-known motto of Barzizza. Further, with the same master in his mind, Vergerius adds, "eo vero demum praeclara consonantia mihi videtur, cum in homine diserto mens cum lingua concordet et sermo cum opere[3]." These words are taken from a letter of P. P. Vergerius, who, notwithstanding his resignation of the chair of Logic in 1405, still kept up close relations with Padua and was a regular correspondent of Barzizza.

Vergerius himself was a powerful force upon the side of literary study in Padua during this period. He was a teacher in Arts[4] ('Doctor Artium,' May 1391) at the time when Vittorino arrived at the University (1396). But his fame may probably have reached the young student a year or two before that date. For in 1392[5] he had published a work "De Ingenuis Moribus," addressed to Ubertinus, a prince of the house of Carrara, in which the claims of Latin letters are, for the first time in a systematic treatise, upheld as an integral part of higher training. Vergerius indeed lays down tentatively, but with clear conviction, the bases upon which Humanist education was presently to be built up. The book was regarded throughout the following century[6] as of profound importance and undoubtedly

---

[1] He was ever ready with advice and encouragement in the establishment of Guarino's school at Venice, and was both in public and in private a generous advocate of his claims as a scholar and a teacher. Sabbad. *Giorn. Ligust.* xviii. p. 24.

[2] Combi, *Epist. Verger.* p. xlix.

[3] *Op. cit. Ep.* xliii. p. 62.

[4] Gloria, *Univ. Pad.* ii. p. 491.

[5] The date fixed by Combi, *Ep. Verger.* p. xix. Infra, p. 93.

[6] In MSS. in nearly every learned library: at least 40 editions printed

exercised much influence upon the growth of classical study. The scholarship[1] of Vergerius was recognised on all sides. A crucial proof of his distinction is given by the fact that to him the sorrowing friends of Manuel Chrysoloras turned in 1415 as to the one man worthy to compose the epitaph upon the great scholar which exists to-day in the old monastery at Constance[2]. To him also we owe the first translation made by an Italian scholar from the Greek, the History of Arrian; and the first introduction to Quintilian[3]. Vergerius would have the further attraction for Vittorino that, although nearing his fiftieth year, he threw up his career at Padua to attend the course of Greek Grammar lectures which Chrysoloras was (1397) then giving at Florence. His treatise (which is to be found in full upon page 96 below) and his Letters reveal to us a man whose strong religious temper was ample security against the perversities of Humanists of the type of Valla. For we find in all that he wrote that endeavour to combine in his ideal the 'virtus' of the ancient world with obedience to Christian duty[4] which has already been noted as the characteristic of the nobler scholars of that age. It was of prime importance that the first, and perhaps the most widely read, of the many tractates on Education called forth by the Revival of Learning, should have distinctly upheld

before 1600. Paulus Jovius says that it was a recognised school text-book in the sixteenth century. Infra, p. 94.

[1] A volume of his letters in form of Epistles from and to Cicero exists in Bod. Libr., MSS. Canon. 166. 17 and 18. See also Combi, *Epist. Verg.* p. xlviii: "Ben si può dire che quanti erano allora conosciuti latini o greci che fossero tutti ei li avesse letti e meditati."

[2] Guarino, who would naturally be critical in the matter, recognised the fitness of the choice.

The Inscription, still perfectly legible (in the kitchen of the Hôtel Insel!), is printed in Legrand, *Bibl. Hellén.*

[3] This 'compendiolum' is referred to by Combi, *Epist. Verg.* p. xxi.

[4] "Nel Vergerio l' umanista ed il credente mai si contradicono, ma vivono quasi a dire l' uno per l' altro." Prof. Combi's judgment is borne out by every page of Vergerius' correspondence. *Epist. Verg.* p. xix.

the Christian standard of faith and life. His influence upon Vittorino we can well understand; as a scholar, as a thinker, and as an educationalist, he was fitted to leave the impress of his personality upon so sympathetic and earnest a nature as that of the young scholar from Feltre. There is little doubt that, next to his intercourse with Barzizza, the treatise of Vergerius, enforced by its writer's life and example, served mainly to determine Vittorino in the great decision of his life. One defect, of which Vittorino was keenly aware, remained to be satisfied. Padua offered no regular opportunity of learning Greek[1].

But the wave of excitement produced by the presence of Chrysoloras at Florence (1397—1400) and subsequently at Pavia (1400—1403)[2] undoubtedly reached Padua. The great scholar would naturally pass through the city on his way to Venice and Constantinople. It is however incorrect to say that Chrysoloras taught Greek at Padua[3], or that Vittorino learnt the rudiments of the language from him. Vergerius and Guarino however were both links between the University and the pioneer work of Chrysoloras. Guarino, who had lived for some years (1403—1408) in the house of Chrysoloras, and in intimate relations with members of his family, at Constantinople, left Florence in 1414[4] and definitely settled in Venice. There

---

[1] Neither Giovanni Conversino nor Barzizza taught Greek: the former probably knew none; the latter very little.

[2] The chronology of Chrysoloras is not yet finally determined. He left Florence in 1400, partly on account of the Plague. He was teaching at Pavia between 1400 and 1403 when P. C. Decembri saw him in his father's house. In 1403 he returned to Constantinople accompanied by Guarino. In 1404 he was at Venice, again in 1408, 9, and 1410. Klette, *Beit.* i. 50–52. Sabbad. *Giorn. Stor. d. Letter. Ital.* 1885, p. 156. Legrand (*Bibliogr. Hellénique,* Paris, 1885) must be read subject to the corrections of these two scholars.

[3] Mullinger, *Cambridge,* i. 393.

[4] He was still at Florence in February, but at Venice in August. Sabbad. in *Vierteljahrsschr. Cult. Ren.* i. 103 seqq.

he opened the first humanist school established in Venice, and probably in the beginning of 1415 Vittorino joined him. Guarino had been for some years in close correspondence with Chrysoloras during the sojourn of the latter in the West, he had maintained very friendly relations with Barzizza, whom he visited at Padua, and he had acquaintance with all leading scholars. Vittorino thus felt it a valuable privilege to come under the instruction of so distinguished a scholar[1]. Guarino was undoubtedly the best Greek scholar of whom Italy could boast. He had spent five years in Constantinople, at first as 'famulus,' in the house of Chrysoloras. He had seen Manuel Chrysoloras only at intervals, owing to his long absence in Western Europe in the service of the Emperor. Guarino speaks of him always in terms of deepest reverence and affection[2]. Guarino could speak and write Greek; the only other scholars of the first quarter of the century who could do the same were Filelfo (who married a niece of Chrysoloras) and Aurispa. Guarino edited, with a Latin version, the little manual of Greek accidence which Chrysoloras dictated to his pupils in lecture, and for many years this remained the only introduction to Greek available to Western students[3].

[1] The chronology of Guarino has been entirely reconstructed by Sabbadini in his *Epistolario di Guarino* (1885) and in his short biography of the scholar (Genova, 1891).

[2] There seems to have been something very impressive about Manuel Chrysoloras. P. C. Decembri's recollection of him in the days of his work at Pavia is interesting: "Memini me puerulum adhuc Emmanuelem Chrysoloram saepius admiratum esse, cum in hac urbe" (Pavia or Milan) "litteras Graecas edoceret. Fuit illi cum patre meo summa familiaritas; tanta itaque illi virtutis emulatio, bonorum caritas, litterarum studium inerat, ut non hominem videre, sed angelum quempiam intueri saepenumero existimarem." Letter of P. C. Decembri (Riccard. Codd. 827), printed *Arch. Stor. Lomb.* Marzo, 1893, p. 9.

[3] *Erotemata Chrysolorae*, the accidence of Greek *in* Greek, accompanied by Guarino's Latin version, in question and answer. It is to be found in MS. in nearly every old library in Europe, and in numerous printed edd. of the fifteenth and sixteenth centuries. Theodore Gaza's Grammar dates perhaps from 1445 and that of C. Lascaris from 1460.

The relations between Vittorino and Guarino at Venice were of the most friendly character. We are told that Guarino taught Vittorino Greek in return for instruction in Latin. This may imply a joint conduct of the school which Guarino had opened at Venice; but it most probably means merely that the latter recognised the finer Latin scholarship of Vittorino and gladly availed himself of the chance of improving his own. It is clear that Vittorino worked unremittingly at Greek under Guarino, and during the eighteen months which they passed together (1415—1416) at Venice laid the foundations of a mutual affection and respect which lasted until death. We are expressly told that Guarino bestowed special pains upon the method of teaching the language to beginners—no light matter where neither grammar, dictionary nor text was easily available.

In 1416 the Plague drove Guarino from Venice for a time and broke up his school. He returned, however, a little later, finally quitting Venice on his marriage[1] in 1418. Vittorino had followed Guarino to Padua late in the autumn of 1416, and although Guarino returned to Venice in 1417 and re-opened his school it is uncertain whether Vittorino accompanied him. The scanty information which we have of his movements at this period shews him, next, settled in 1420 at his old University. He enjoys now a high reputation as a scholar and as a teacher. Following the custom of Barzizza and Guarino he receives into his own house a number of students (*contubernales*) who board with him, presiding thus over a student family (*contubernium*). This privilege, which seems to have been common to the regents of most universities of the time, was ordinarily regarded merely as a profitable means of livelihood. But to Vittorino, as to Barzizza and Guarino, the 'contubernium' presented itself as a most important responsibility. Padua was, as we have seen, beset with dangers for the mixed body of young men—many of them not more than

---

[1] The date of his marriage, 27 Dec. 1418, according to Sabbadini (*Giorn. Ligust.* xviii. 39).

fourteen years of age—who attended the public and private courses of the University, and who provided their own maintenance independent of official supervision in matters of living and morals. Vittorino thus took into his house a limited number of students whose homes were at a distance from Padua. For some of these, who were personally recommended to him, he provided everything at his own charge; to others, the sons of Venetian merchants and wealthy proprietors, he charged high fees, intending, as the Bishop of Aleria records, to equalise the treatment of the whole household, repressing indulgence on the one hand, and lifting the burden of poverty on the other, and thus to all alike "libris, domo, victu, vestitu-que optime consulebat." He firmly refused, now and always, to increase the number of his pupils beyond a limit which made it possible for him to exercise direct personal supervision, and to gain an intimate knowledge of the character and capacity of each student. He had no hesitation in dismissing any who proved unsatisfactory in morals or, though with more reluctance, who were of slow intellect or disappointed their early promise. He cultivated friendly relations with parents of his pupils, giving them careful advice on the future careers of their sons. The instruction which he gave would no doubt include all the Arts subjects, with the addition of Mathematics; and he made provision for the teaching of subjects outside his own courses.

Vittorino was, we are told, a most welcome member of all University reunions. Apart from the attractiveness of his personality he was one of the most conspicuous scholars now in Padua. As a Latinist he was probably unequalled by any one there except Barzizza himself: few had enjoyed so good opportunities of acquiring Greek; whilst in Mathematics he had the reputation of the ablest master of the day. We are told that he always held himself at the disposal of the students of the University; and he was not less esteemed by the citizens of Padua, who prized the high tone of life and aim which he imparted to their sons.

In 1418 Barzizza had received an invitation to Milan which
led in 1422[1] to his definite resignation of the chair of Rhetoric
at Padua which he had held with slight interruption since 1407.
This chair was now offered to Vittorino[2], the students urging
its acceptance upon him as the one man worthy of the succession to the great scholar and teacher who had held it with such
distinction. But Vittorino yielded only after much hesitation
and more than one refusal. He was conscious of a call to the
monastic life, and it wás only after he had convinced himself
that he could, as a teacher, do much to further true religion
and to strengthen character, that he consented to waive his objections and to accept the office. He was now forty-four years
of age ; and from the fact that Padua was gradually becoming
recognised as a University in which humanist sympathies were
in favour[3], he assumed a position at once of considerable
importance in the world of scholars.

The picture which we are enabled to form of Vittorino at
this juncture is both clear and attractive. In person he was
slight and in appearance frail. But by dint of rigorous self-
discipline and of active habits he had built up a constitution
capable of sustaining the gravest exertions. For the greater
part of his life he never admitted a day's illness. The careful
practice of gymnastic had given him a peculiar suppleness and
grace of movement. His expression was grave though not
austere. Sympathy and affection, we are told, readily beamed
from his face, though his eye had a penetrative quality before

[1] This date is fixed in correction of that (1418) given by Mazuchelli,
s. v. Barzizza, ii. p. 499. See *Arch. Stor. Lomb.* Marzo, 1893, pp. 28, 29.

[2] Prendilacqua, p. 32, says that the chair was expressly established
for Vittorino by the Municipality. There is no reason to think that this
was a new creation ; the corrected date of the removal of Barzizza to Milan
simplifies the matter. Philosophy was added to Rhetoric to increase its
emoluments, which since 1412 had been 160 ducats.

[3] Contrast Vittorino's position of influence with that of Aurispa at
Bologna shortly after this date: he could gain neither sympathy nor
audience as Professor of Greek at 'stately, scholastic Bologna' in 1424–5.

which conscious wrong-doing stood confessed and ashamed. Strong passionate instincts were by constant watchfulness reduced to obedience and a temper prone to anger became softened and restrained. The simplicity of his nature shewed itself in his dress; the long cloak of rough cloth for the summer, with a fur lining for the winter, contrasting with the richness of dress customary in Venetia. He was careless of cold, believing artificial heat to be a source of many humours. We trace something of the rigour of the old Roman discipline in Vittorino's temper, in his notion of authority, of reverence to elders, of manliness and endurance. But we shall be wrong if we ascribe to the Pagan ideal any other place than this in his view of life. Vittorino was before all else a Christian imbued with the spirit and the doctrine of his faith. This indeed is the dominating note of his personality. It was this which preserved him from exaggerations and moral perversities which disfigured some of his contemporaries and gave an evil name to a certain type of Humanist. It was Vittorino's aim to graft ancient learning upon the stock of Christian training; and we shall see that within the next five-and-twenty years this had become his achievement.

Vittorino was however destined to sad disappointment in the hopes he had formed for his new career at Padua. Allusion has been made to the state of discipline amongst the students of the University. Whether the prevalent disorders affected those whom he lodged under his own roof and for whom he felt himself directly responsible, we do not know[1]. But Vittorino was in any case unwilling to subject those for whom he was answerable to temptations against which he could very imperfectly guard them; so feeling himself powerless to remedy the vicious tendencies around him he decided to leave Padua[2].

[1] Ticozzi says that it was so. *Storia dei Letterati*, p. 15.

[2] No Humanist stayed so long at Padua as Barzizza: and he was so very poor that with his family he found it difficult to consult his own choice. Still Padua was more congenial to the Humanist than any other

He resigned his chair and once more betook himself to Venice. This occurred probably in the course of 1422. In 1423 we find him conducting a school for the sons of Venetian patricians and others, who were attracted by his high repute from various parts of Italy. At Venice he continued the custom of receiving boarders into his house, and as before this privilege was much in request, parents offering large fees to secure the admission of their sons.

The work in which Vittorino was now engaged was thoroughly congenial to him. He was rapidly becoming recognised as the most trustworthy and most capable teacher of the New Learning in Italy. He had in Venice excellent opportunities of acquiring Greek texts from Eastern sources; he had left privation once for all behind him. Padua was close at hand; Barzizza indeed had gone to Pavia (1422), but Guarino was at Verona, and Venice itself was favourably placed for intercourse with scholars. Vittorino had barely time to settle in his new home, and to gather his pupils around him when in 1423[1] an invitation reached him, the acceptance of which profoundly modified his prospects.

Gianfrancesco Gonzaga, the head of the family which held the Lordship of Mantua, was on the whole a favourable representative of the type of Condottiere prince. He was respected by his subjects as a 'benevolent' despot, was on good terms with the neighbouring states of Venice (in whose pay he was), of Milan, and of Ferrara, and was a fairly satisfactory son of the Church. His assassinations were not obtrusive, and though, as was only too often the case, he remained

university except Pavia and Florence. The Courts however competed for scholars and paid them far better. Gonzaga for instance offered 300 ducats, whilst Padua paid 160, and that under pressure.

[1] Probably towards the close of this year. Sabbad. *Epist. Guar.* p. 65: Paglia, in *Arch. Stor. Lombardo*, 1884, p. 150: Luzio, *Arch. Venet.* vol. 35, p. 330. Rosmini's date, 1425, must be definitely surrendered, though accepted by Voigt.

for some years in mortal quarrel with his eldest son, he was induced ultimately to pardon him and to restore him to place and favour.

Now the condottiere prince, as the 'new man' amongst the dynasties, with an illegitimate title, was compelled to rely upon personal qualities for due recognition of his status. 'Virtus' and 'Gloria'—personal consequence and repute— were the qualifications for distinction which alone were open to him. "With his thirst for fame it was talent not birth which the despot needed. In the company of the poet and the scholar he felt himself in a new position, almost indeed in the possession of a new legitimacy[1]." This 'fama' could be secured by employing great architects or painters to create or embellish a cathedral or palace. But the characteristics of this particular period led naturally to a preference for a dis-tinguished humanist. It was in this way that the Carrara had engaged Giovanni Conversino da Ravenna, and Vergerio; or the Visconti, Chrysoloras or Barzizza; or the D'Estes, a little later, Guarino and Gaza. Gonzaga, therefore, wishing to ac-quire for himself a new dignity, which would be at once recognised and be a source of envy, turned to search for a scholar whose presence would add lustre to his Court. He had a young family for whose education it was now necessary to make provision. What better step could he take, to his own glory and to their future consequence, than to engage the services of a renowned humanist? Two men were now foremost as educators in northern Italy—Guarino da Verona, and Vittorino da Feltre. To Guarino, now married, and settled at Verona as master of Rhetoric in the service of the Municipio, the invitation was first sent, probably in 1421[2]. It was declined. The Marquis Gonzaga then approached °

---

[1] Burckhardt, *Renaissance*, p. 9 (Eng. trs.).

[2] In 1421 or "al più tardi il 1422," Sabbadini, *Giorn. Ligust.* xviii. p. 113. But Guarino was settled at his native Verona amidst relatives and friends, with a small property, and his fellow-citizens appear to have made much of him.

Vittorino through a Venetian patrician who was intimate with both. Vittorino was busily occupied as we have seen with the school which he had lately opened in Venice. He disliked the unsettled habit which had been forced upon him by circumstances since 1415, and at first was inclined to give the same answer as Guarino—that he was happily employed and had no desire to move. But the invitation was pressed: Vittorino then declared his aversion for court life, his anxiety for peace and useful work, his indifference to all external show, and his dread of a position certain to arouse jealousy and ill will. He acknowledged the liberal purpose of the Gonzaga, who had left Vittorino free to fix his own stipend, in attaching so great importance to the education of his children. Finally he agreed to go to Mantua, thinking, we are told, that in training the future head of a state in the right way he would be benefitting his subjects, and that such a career was not less a life of service than the monastic life which he would now be called upon definitely to abandon. His friend Prendilacqua records that on reaching Mantua Vittorino laid down one condition: "I accept the post, on this understanding only, that you (i.e. the Marquis Gonzaga) require from me nothing which shall be in any way unworthy of either of us: and I will continue to serve you so long as your own life shall command respect."

The reply to this somewhat outspoken declaration satisfied Vittorino, who, as the event proved, never had occasion to regret his decision, finding in the Gonzaga and his wife Paola di Malatesta faithful friends and firm supporters of his authority. Vittorino was at work at Mantua at the end of 1423. He was now forty-six years of age. He stayed there in the service of the Gonzaga family until he died in 1446. During these two-and-twenty years he established and perfected the first great school of the Renaissance—a school whose spirit, curriculum and method justify us in regarding it as a landmark of critical importance in the history of classical education. It was indeed the great typical school of the Humanities.

Let us here recall the influences which had aided in shaping Vittorino's educational ideals up to this time. The impulse given originally by the intercourse with Giovanni Conversino, Vergerius, and Barzizza had been strengthened, and directed to a specially educational bent, by the Treatise of Vergerius and his friendship with Guarino.

During the twenty years of his first residence at Padua (1396–1415) Vittorino had thus become imbued with the purest spirit of the Humanist revival. At Padua the study of Grammar, Scholarship, Dialectic and Philosophy had already far more affinity with modern than with mediæval conceptions of these great subjects. But more than this we can point to certain specific incidents which gave a most important impulse not only to humanist enthusiasm but to its educational method; these all fell during the ten or twelve years immediately preceding Vittorino's call to Mantua.

The first is the publication of Guarino's translation of Plutarch's treatise Περὶ παίδων ἀγωγῆς, the date of which may now be regarded as fixed at 1411. The importance of this translation in the development of the humanist ideal of education can hardly be over-estimated. The number of MS. copies scattered through the ancient libraries of Western Europe and the long series of printed editions prove the depth of the interest which it excited. The new sense of the dignity of the educated man, of the status of the teacher, of the breadth of the educational aim, which mark Vittorino, Aeneas Sylvius and M. Vegius, were found there for the first time. Its effect on the notion of punishments, and of the function of games, or on the age of beginning the study of Letters, was due less, perhaps, to the novelty of Plutarch's suggestions than to the authority which his name gave to more or less inchoate ideas. The second event referred to was the discovery by Poggio at St Gallen of the complete text of Quintilian[1]. This

---

[1] The well-known letter of Poggio in Shepherd, *Poggio*, p. 108. Vergerius wrote a 'compendium' some years before, which was un-

discovery, whilst it aroused excitement throughout the entire
world of scholars, specially affected Padua through Barzizza.
For this scholar had for many years made a close study of the
Institutio, hitherto available only in an imperfect state, and
beyond doubt the work formed an important subject in his
courses on Rhetoric at Padua. Vittorino, living under Barzizza's roof, could not fail to become thoroughly familiar with
his master's work on this author, which was of an elaborate
character. It was natural, therefore, that one of the earliest
transcripts made from the St Gallen archetype should be sent in
all speed to Barzizza. In June 1418 we find him utterly
absorbed in its study. Copies were in the hands of Bruni and
Niccoli at Florence, and another reached Guarino a little later.
The insight into Roman oratory, and not less the fuller conception of Roman education, now available for the first time,
were henceforward most important factors in determining the
course of humanist thought upon the aim and method of
teaching Letters. This impulse was reinforced by the discovery, five years later, of the entire text of the *De Oratore*
at Lodi in 1422[1]. This again had been known to scholars for
at least a century[2]; but only in a mutilated state. Barzizza's
interest in this work has been already referred to. He had
now left Padua for Pavia, whither the newly discovered Codex
was at once sent to him. Vittorino, as an enthusiastic
Ciceronian, lectured constantly on the *De Oratore*, the study
of which he may very probably have begun under Barzizza; in
any case the extreme importance attached by him and other
scholars to the eloquence of Cicero was confirmed by the
enthusiasm created by this discovery of the complete text

doubtedly familiar to Vittorino as a hand-book to the *Institutio*. On
Barzizza's work upon Quintilian, see Sabbadini, *Studi* etc., p. 3 seqq.

[1] This famous Codex (belonging perhaps to the ninth century) was
again lost to view in or after 1428 (not 1425 as usually stated). Sabbadini,
Guarino e le Opere Rettoriche di Cicero, p. 433.

[2] Petrarch possessed a copy, Nolhac, *Pétrarque*, p. 210 (note), (as
against Koerting).

of the rhetorical treatises. It may seem hardly possible that
the so-called discovery of the bones of Livy at Padua in 1413
should have affected Latin scholarship. But in the temper of
the time such an incident appealed to more than sentiment
and imagination. Vittorino, and indeed every scholar of his
day, was susceptible to such associations in a degree which we
can hardly realise[1]. It is not in the least unreasonable to
trace his enthusiasm for Livy and his devotion to the textual
criticism of the great Paduan, in part at least, to a discovery
which sent a thrill from one end of Italy to the other.

But permeating and controlling this humanist enthusiasm
the Christian spirit retained its supreme place. With Vittorino
this was the result both of rational conviction and of devout-
ness of temper. Amidst the temptations of life at Padua or
Venice, amidst the distractions of Pagan ideals, to which so
many scholars succumbed, he had always lived up to a high
standard of Christian faith and conduct. So that he brought
with him to Mantua a desire to combine the spirit of the
Christian life with the educational apparatus of classical
literature, whilst uniting with both something of the Greek
passion for bodily culture and for dignity of the outer life.

It has been said that Vittorino was the first to conceive
and to carry out a system of education framed on this ideal.
It is worth while at this point to distinguish between this—the
humanist conception of education on its noblest side—and
such of the mediæval attempts as at first sight seem not unlike
it. The best of the pre-Renaissance schools, as the Cathedral
schools of Chartres[2] or that of the Brethren of the Common

[1] We may recall the incident of the discovery of the body of a Roman
lady in one of the tombs of the Via Appia, Symonds, *Ren.* i. 23, and the
fierce outburst of indignation against the Malatesta who destroyed the
statue of Vergil at Mantua, and called forth the denunciation of Vergerius.
See Combi, *Ep. Verg.* 113.

[2] At Chartres Livy was specially studied. But nowhere north of the
Alps could such an incident as that of Niccoli and young Pazzi have been
possible. See Symonds, *Revival of Learning*, p. 41.

Life at Deventer, were acquainted with ancient authors, such as Livy or Ovid. But the characteristic note of the Humanist is wanting. In none of these schools was Latin studied with a single eye to the understanding of Roman literature, history or civilisation. There was no consciousness of a re-entering upon a forgotten and long-lost possession. Individual instances of scholars of a real humanist enthusiasm may be quoted, such as Bernard[1] and Landulph[2] at Chartres, or John of Salisbury[3]; and probably in Westphalia or the Low Countries there were occasional scholars who in happier days might have developed the powers of Agricola or Reuchlin. But these cases are so to say sporadic: except perhaps at Chartres we can detect no tradition of scholarship. On the contrary, as L'Abbé Clerval justly sums up the evidence, speaking of John of Salisbury: "Lui seul a cultivé la littérature pour elle-même à l'exemple de Bernard de Chartres: les autres ont été amenés à la mettre exclusivement au service de la philosophie et de la théologie[4]." The ancient books when they were read at all were studied in dependence upon scholasticism and theology. This attitude remains even in the fifteenth century. The case of Paris is significant[5]. In that century Chairs were decreed—they were never filled—in Classics and Oriental languages: but with what object? To facilitate the conversion of Mahommedans. At Paris, indeed, all classical studies were despised as purely 'grammarian,' i.e., as subjects fit only to be dealt with by the 'magistri puerorum.' At Chartres an interest in ancient writers was in a certain degree traditional; and Livy, especially (rather than Cicero, whose writings were scarce), was read as history and literature, and not as a mere collection of grammatical examples. Composition also was encouraged in prose and verse. But even there—and Chartres (1200–1400) is the most favourable case that can be offered—this interest was absolutely insignificant com-

---

[1] Clerval, p. 225. [2] Ib. p. 409. [3] Ib. p. 228 sqq.
[4] Ib. p. 230. [5] Thurot, *Enseign.* p. 83.

pared with that taken in Law and Theology, as we can easily
see from the records of the Chapter library. The idea of
Literature, or of an ancient author as a complete subject, was
unknown outside Italy in the fourteenth century. Now in
Italy, especially in Florence, and the Lombard cities, many
Latin schools (municipal or private, not ecclesiastical) sprang
up, partly at least as a consequence of the influence of
Petrarch. These were not intended to provide preparatory
courses for higher classical study, though they did, as it proved,
serve that purpose. Their chief aim was to teach Latin as
a subject of practical use in life. But when the wave of
enthusiasm for the literature and the arts of the ancient world
swept through the centres of cultivated life in Northern Italy
and brought with it a new measure of the knowledge best
worth having, by an inevitable process the ideal of Education
was modified in the same direction. The humanist school-
master was the natural product of the humanist tastes of
the rulers or citizens of Milan, or Florence, or Ferrara. For
in every period the educational aim obeys the dominant intellectual or religious ideals; at best it personifies them; it
can never create them.

The children of the Gonzaga constituted Vittorino's immediate charge. There were at that time three boys, Ludovico the eldest, born in 1414, Carlo, and Gianlucido. Their
ages ranged from nine years to three. Cecilia, the second
daughter[1], was born in 1425 and another brother, Alessandro,
two years later. With them Vittorino was empowered to
associate at his discretion, as fellow pupils, a certain number
of the sons of the leading Mantuan families. Further, after a
year's experience, he accepted the sons of personal friends of
his own[2], from Venice and elsewhere in Northern Italy, at

---

[1] Margherita, the eldest girl, married Leonello d'Este, but I can trace
no allusion to her education. She was several years older than Cecilia. Cf.
Sabbadini, *Vita di Guarino*, p. 100.

[2] Francesco Barbaro recommended (in 1443) the son of an intimate

fees varying according to the position of the parents.   By
degrees the neighbouring reigning families[1] sought to place
their sons under so able and so trustworthy a master.   Thus
Frederic of Urbino, 'ancor fanciullo,' was sent to Vittorino,
who held him in much affection, and we are told[2] how deep a
love of letters marked the after years of this characteristic
figure of the Renaissance.   Vittorino, moreover, mindful of
his own early struggles, and true to the scholar's instinct of the
equality of genius, continued to receive free of all charges
promising boys, commended to him by trusted friends.   These
he treated absolutely on the same footing with the rest of the
boys, and in some cases he undertook the entire cost of their
maintenance, clothing, and books, for ten years or more.   One,
Ludovico da Feltre, probably had some home associations with
the master; another was taken at the instance of Sassuolo da
Prato[3], a favourite scholar.   The greatest scholars of the time,
Guarino[4], Poggio[5] and Filelfo[6] sent their sons to Mantua.
They were well aware of the temptations that beset youth in
most university cities; with Vittorino they knew that their

friend, Fr. Clarici, as a pupil.   And this practice was probably very common
with past pupils of Vittorino.

[1] Ambrogio mentions "two sons of other princes each about ten years
old" (Mart. et Dur. iii. 553).   One of these may well have been Frederic of
Urbino, who was born in 1422, and went to Mantua when about eleven
years of age.   Dennistoun, i. 64.   He was knighted by the Emperor
Sigismund as he passed through Mantua in 1433.

[2] Castiglione, *Il Cortigiano*, p. 5.   For many years a bust of Vittorino,
with an inscription, stood in a place of honour in the great palace of
Urbino.   Ottaviano Ubaldini, brought up as his brother, was a fellow
pupil of Frederigo, and may have been the second of the two princes
referred to by Ambrogio.   Holtzinger, *Frederigo* &c. p. 210: and the
verses devoted to Vittorino by G. Santi, the father of Raphael, in his
Cronaca di Federigo, i. ii. 28 seqq.

[3] *Saxolus Prat.* ed. C. Guasti, pp. 18, 19.

[4] Gregorio, born 1432; Sabbadini, *Epistol. Guar.* p. 81.

[5] Probably Bartolomeo, born 1425.   Poggio sent his eldest legitimate
son to Guarino in 1456; Vittorino had then been dead ten years.

[6] Platina, p. 23.

boys were certain of most careful guardianship. The Marquis of Mantua, perhaps under the influence of his wife Paola, who always regarded Vittorino with the deepest respect, allowed him the fullest responsibility in this matter of the choice of scholars. The Mantuan School rapidly became the recognised 'Ginnasio' for the aristocratic youth of Northern Italy, a dignity of which its patron was thoroughly conscious, and its repute gradually extended to France, Germany and even to Greek-speaking lands.

The ages of the scholars varied considerably. L. Valla left in 1430, when he was 23; he probably acted as assistant for part of his stay. Sassuolo was 21 when he entered, and remained till he was at least 27; Corraro and Perotti came at the age of 14; Beccaria was younger than this; Ognibene was probably eleven; others were as young as 6 or 7. The number of scholars seems to have steadily increased with the fame of the School. Mention has been made of the practice of Vittorino at Padua and Venice of receiving children of poor parents[1]; at Mantua he extended this principle by a type of scholarship which we are told, and it is not difficult to believe it, was much appreciated. In addition to the free maintenance of the scholar he provided an income for the parents secured upon the State treasury[2].

The Marquis of Mantua had set apart for the use of Vittorino and his pupils a favourite palace, in close neighbourhood of the Curia or family residence of the prince and his household. This detached villa or Casino, had been built in 1388 and the following years by Francesco Gonzaga IV., and it had borne the name of La Gioiosa, or, in Venetian dialect, 'Zoyosa': the Pleasure House. It lay upon the ridge of slightly rising ground which commands the valley of the Mincio upon the north-eastern corner of the city. The

---

[1] Sassuolo says that at one time (about 1440) as many as 40 scholars were received as free scholars. Guasti, p. 51.

[2] Platina, p. 26.

present Piazza di Sordello and the Piazza della Fiera occupy
in all probability the site of the Casa Zoyosa, and of part of its
gardens[1]. The name of the future school-house did not however commend itself to Vittorino. But his ingenuity quickly
surmounted the difficulty. La Gioiosa became easily La
Giocosa[2]. The associations of La Giocosa were not less
bright and cheerful than those of the older name of doubtful
intention : it was still 'the Pleasant House' : and there was
besides a suggestion of the Roman name for a school which
accorded with the ingenious taste of the time. The house was
probably at Vittorino's suggestion decorated anew, with frescoes
of children at play, and this also, together with the pleasant-
ness of its situation, gave further point to the name by which
Vittorino's school was universally known.

The house was of stately proportions. The interior was
spacious and dignified. Broad corridors, rooms lofty and well
lighted, gave to it an air of distinction which suited well
Vittorino's idea of what a school-house should be. For, as
its name implied, it was to be regarded as a 'house of delight.'
He believed that a certain brightness of surroundings conduced
to sound intellectual work. The notion so widely held that
the needs of study demanded that a school should be placed
in a gloomy, unhealthy situation[3], was foreign to the true
humanist. La Giocosa was, on the contrary, surrounded on
three sides by a large enclosed meadow, bordered by the river;
this was laid out with broad walks, lined with well-grown
trees. The open grass-covered space was highly prized by
Vittorino, who made much use of it as playing fields.

---

[1] The local surroundings of La Giocosa have been cleared up by
Paglia, after much research in the Mantuan archives. *Arch. Stor.
Lombard.* 1884, p 150 seqq.

[2] Gioiosa, from gioia (gaudia): giocosa is jocosa (jocus). Jocus is again
a synonym for ludus (sport) while the latter is the usual name for school.
As Paglia says, La Casa Zoyosa became "la casa di ludi letterarie e
di delizie spirituali dopo essere stata la casa delle gioie lussuriose." p. 153.

[3] Mullinger, *Cambridge*, i. 339.

La Giocosa was from the first ordered as the school house, and there Vittorino himself and the princes had their home. Part of the scholars were lodged in a house close at hand, not unlike the palace itself in character, where they were under the close supervision of the Master and his assistants. All met for school work in La Giocosa. It would seem that all alike were boarders; and indeed the special discipline of Vittorino would hardly have been possible on any other system.

But whilst he rejoiced in the dignity of proportion which the school house offered, he ruthlessly stripped it of all its luxurious furnishings, its ornaments and plate[1]. The princes received no peculiar consideration in this respect or in any other. Their father trusted entirely in the judgment of the Master and firmly upheld his authority in such wholesome changes as these. For Vittorino had made it clear that, unless temptations to luxury, idleness or arrogance were once for all removed, and all scholars of whatever rank put upon the same footing of plain and sober living, he could not attempt his task with hope of success.

He found it necessary at the outset to discard certain companions whose influence upon the Gonzaga children he distrusted. It was a delicate task, for the children dismissed belonged to important houses, but the Marquis supported his action without hesitation. A scarcely less difficult matter was the choice of suitable officers and servants ready to adapt themselves to the new regimen. The Gonzaga family life was, we know[2], of a creditable type, but the new discipline was unusual in a palace. Strict watch was kept over the egress of the scholars, who found ordinarily ample room for games and exercise in the grounds surrounding the school.

---

[1] An inventory of the contents dated 1406 is preserved, enumerating seventy beds and a very large array of hangings, furniture and appointments, as belonging to the palace.

[2] Mart. et Durand, iii. 830. The reference is to 1425 or 1426 This letter is quoted infra p. 77.

Vittorino definitely held himself the father of his scholars. It was with him no formal claim [1]. His school entirely absorbed him. He watched the youngest with affection and hope, the elders with pride and confidence. Himself moving always amid the larger things of life, the power that went forth from him insensibly raised the tone of thought and motive in those around him. His singleness of purpose was quickly felt, and a word or even a glance of disapproval was, with the keenly sensitive Italian youth, often sufficient to bring tears of shame and repentance to the eyes of a culprit. Living a common life with his scholars in meals, in games, in excursions, always sharing their interests and pleasures, his control over the sixty or seventy boys under his charge was such that harsh punishments were not needed. Naturally quick-tempered, he had schooled himself to a self-control which never gave way except in face of irreverence or looseness. Corporal punishment was very seldom resorted to, and then only after deliberation, and as the alternative to expulsion. For ill-prepared work the penalty imposed was the compulsory re-learning of the task after school hours. But it was part of Vittorino's purpose to attract rather than to drive, and to respect the dignity and the freedom of his boys. So he refused, after fair trial made, to force learning upon an unwilling scholar, holding that nature had not endowed all with taste or capacity for study. It is characteristic of the time that Vittorino could appeal with confidence to the personal and family distinction conferred by excellence in the study of Letters. It was a motive to which most youths of spirit eagerly responded.

[1] It was no doubt this characteristic of Vittorino's method that attracted Pestalozzi, who is not usually supposed to have shewn much knowledge of, or interest in, Renaissance education. Guasti, in his edition of Sassuolo, has this note: 'E qui pure dirò che l' avvocato Giovacchino Benini di cara memoria senti dalla bocca del Pestalozzi, che la vita di Vittorino scritta dal Sassuolo era stimabile sopra tutte l' altre, e meritava d' essere fatta meglio conoscere con una traduzione.' p. 31.

We are told that Vittorino watched carefully habits of self-indulgence in eating and drinking[1], and by discipline in these matters eradicated even gross faults : whilst he was equally attentive to those whose appetite seemed deficient. Like other educators of the time, he discouraged resort to artificial heat[2], even during the severe cold of the Mantuan winter. He never stood near a fire, though his hands and feet were often numbed with cold. Clapping the hands, stamping the feet, or, better still, discussion and reading aloud were the proper remedies for anyone in health : for cold was generally the result of idleness of mind or body. The healthy activity of childhood was always encouraged, and skill in games was cultivated in all his pupils. Two little boys were overheard by him talking earnestly apart ; hearing that they were discussing their lessons, he exclaimed, 'That is not a good sign in a young boy,' and sent them off to join the games. Regular exercise in all conditions of weather he regarded as the foundation of health, and health as the first necessity of mental progress. The health of the boys under his charge was a matter to which Vittorino paid much attention ; in this respect again we feel how remote he was from the mediaeval standards. In the excessive heats he made provision for sending or accompanying parties of his scholars to the villas owned by the Marquis at Goito, or at Borgoforte, or to the Lake of Garda, or the lower Alps of the Veronese. If any fell ill his care was unremitting. Indeed the tie of personal affection which united him with his pupils was manifest in all relations. His keen desire for their progress, and his pride in it ; his peculiar insight into individual character ; the absence of all considerations of self, so affected

---

[1] The use of wine, though discouraged, was not actually forbidden. It was always diluted. He himself drank very sparingly a light and sweet wine.

[2] There was nothing peculiar to Vittorino in this opinion. The cold of the Monastery or university Hostel must have been severely felt. Rashdall, *Universities,* ii. 665. Vegius, *De Lib. Educ.* i. § 4.

the methods of discipline that in the truest sense La Giocosa was an ideal school, and, so far as a school ever may be, an ideal home.

What is here written may seem a fancy sketch based on the adulatory method of criticism common to the fifteenth century. But we have the correspondence, fragmentary but most significant, of Vittorino himself, the unvarying testimony of scholars[1] who spent their youth and early manhood under Vittorino ; the indirect evidence afforded by those of his pupils who became famous schoolmasters in their turn ; and the respect of men of so wide experience and such ample opportunity of information as Guarino, Ambrogio, Filelfo and Poggio, —a respect due not only to his attainments but to the noble temper by which Vittorino gained and kept his unique authority. We may trace the characteristics of this new discipline, if we will, to the study of Plutarch's Treatise, and of Quintilian. Something no doubt was due to the revolt of the Humanist against the doctrine that the body is the enemy of the mind and of the spirit. But most of all do we feel that Vittorino could dispense with harshness just because he was intensely sympathetic with the young, was master of his task in all its detail, and pursued it with an undivided mind. Moreover, we know that he was aided by able colleagues, men of like mind with their Master ; for most of them had been trained by Vittorino himself. But the last word that can be said is after all just this : the secret of his authority lay in the genius of the man himself.

The aim of Vittorino, the aim of the true humanist educator, was to secure the harmonious development of mind, body, and character[2]. As compared with the other great schoolmaster of the time, Guarino da Verona, we may say

---

[1] Esp. Sassuolo, who wrote during Vittorino's life-time (1443) ; Prendilacqua, the Bp of Aleria, Castiglione.

[2] He aimed at creating ' the complete citizen,' says Ticozzi. The real Humanist had a very practical end in view. Ticozzi, p. 18 : infra, p. 182.

that whilst Guarino, the better Greek scholar and more laborious reader, bent his efforts rather to turning out clever and eloquent scholars[1], Vittorino aimed at sending forth young men who should 'serve God in church and state,' in whatever position they might be called upon to occupy[2]. But both agreed in this, that the subject matter, the educational apparatus, to be employed, must in the main consist of the literature of Greece and Rome. If we contrast the Humanist curriculum with its mediaeval predecessor, we shall find that it is scarcely accurate to say that the ancient Trivium and Quadrivium have disappeared and have been replaced by something absolutely new. But it is still less accurate to say, as M. Benoist says of Erasmus, 'Trivium Erasmus intactum reliquit, neque in quadrivio quidquam aliud mutavit nisi quod geometriae in locum cognatam doctrinam, geographiam substituit.' On a superficial view it is possible to recognise in the Humanist school course the 'Seven Liberal Arts,' Grammar, Dialectic, Rhetoric, Arithmetic, Geometry, Astronomy and Music. But the identification loses all serious meaning when we realise, first, the immense difference in the relative importance of the subjects as understood by the new Teachers, and secondly, the revolutionary interpretation they placed upon their contents[3]. Undoubtedly, in Italy, as every student of the Renaissance soon learns, the classical tradition had never been wholly lost,

---

[1] Cortesius, *De hom. doct.* p. 226. Voigt, i. 551, and Burckhardt, *Ren. in Italy,* p. 215, both concur in this judgment. Cf. Schmidt, *Gesch. der Pädag.* ii. 403 for a concise review of the educational aim of Vittorino.

[2] Prendilacqua, p. 86. Vittorino's practice was that advocated by Vergerius and by M. Vegio in their works on Education. This broad view of education may be contrasted with that set forth by Bapt. Guarino (son of the elder Guarino), whose tract *De Ordine Docendi et Studendi* represents a narrower idea. See below, p. 160. Vittorino's ideal, worked out at Mantua, was seldom so fully realised in later times.

[3] Benoist, *Quid de Puerorum &c.,* p. 44 : in many respects a valuable study of Erasmus and the later Renaissance.

and Latin was at no period a dead language, hardly even a 'learned' language. The consciousness of race and of imperial position was kept alive by the ruins of Rome, by the *Aeneid* or by the tales of Livy: it was expressed in the Papal power and in the Roman Law. But the Humanists, as has been already said, quickened this consciousness by bringing to bear upon the whole field of ancient culture a strict method of study, and an enthusiastic adaptation of the past to the needs of the present. So that the spirit in which they handled the constituent subjects of the Trivium was wholly different, even in Italy, from that of educators of the previous centuries. For example, the figment of the four senses of a passage—the literal, the metaphorical, the allegorical, the anagogical—which grammar and dialectic jointly endeavoured to exhibit, gave way to a desire to find out what the author's words meant to a plain intelligence. To Vittorino Grammar and Rhetoric, combined, implied the critical scholarship of Greek and Latin, a facility in composition in either language, and a power of entering into, and absorbing, the spirit of the literature, history, and thought of the ancient world. Dialectic, instead of dominating all other subjects, especially Grammar[1], sank into a comparatively insignificant place. All was rational, objective, in method; the aim was erudition and not speculation, as a means of adorning and moralising life. The essential foundation of education was Letters; the rest was subsidiary. As Aeneas Sylvius and Erasmus said of mathematics or dialectic, 'degustasse sat erit.'

Vittorino found himself entrusted with pupils of varying ages. He preferred that they should come to him before they had much to unlearn. He devised for the youngest letter-

[1] The terminology of grammar, and the spirit in which the subject was studied, were much affected by current Dialectic: the practice of Disputation as applied to Art-subjects led to unreality in their study. The subject is treated of in the Dialogue of L. Bruni d' Arezzo (1401). Klette, *Beit.* ii. 53 seqq.

games by which children of four or five years of age might be
insensibly taught to read and to spell: and with this he combined simple exercises in speech.   Much importance was from
the first attached to right enunciation.   He insisted upon the
necessity of opening the mouth properly, of drawing the breath
at right intervals; of the clear enunciation of each syllable, of
avoiding sibilation, or thick guttural utterance.   He repressed
loudness in reading or speaking, and insisted on great attention to proper emphasis and intonation, accent and quantity[1].
Grace of address, he taught, must accompany dignity of carriage
and refinement of manners.

Reading aloud was one of the regular exercises of each day,
and was generally taken in presence of Vittorino himself.   In
the scarcity of books this practice found wide scope.   At meals
rigid silence was enjoined whilst the prescribed author was
read.   In later stages of classical teaching he held that reading
aloud was both an aid to and test of the intelligent understanding of historian or poet.   This practice was derived from
Chrysoloras and was much valued by his pupil Guarino[2], from
whom possibly Vittorino in turn acquired it.   Declamation
was also carefully taught as a needful training in eloquence.
Both reading and recitation were considered to be very health-
ful exercises, fortifying the body against cold, and aiding
digestion.   Of what did the subject matter of Reading and
Declamation consist?   Young scholars were early taught to
recite with reverence and intelligence the chief religious exercises.   They were then practised in repeating short and easy
passages of Ovid and Vergil; and we know that some of
Vittorino's pupils could, by the age of ten, recite Latin compositions of their own.   Recitation, of prose and verse, was,
in an age when books were scarce, a favourite exercise: and
the length and difficulty of the works thus learnt by heart

[1] Sadoleto, in the following century, used the device of reading back-
wards as an aid to fluency.

[2] Rosmini, *Guarino*, i. 113 (nota 76).

is evidence that the memory was much stronger and a far more ready instrument of education than it is to-day. With Perotti, the famous scholar of Vittorino, as with Quintilian, memory is 'primum ingenii signum[1].' Its cultivation led to remarkable results in young children. Whole orations of Cicero or Demosthenes, books of Livy and Sallust, besides large portions of Vergil and Homer, were recited with accuracy and taste by boys or girls of less than fourteen years of age. And this art of Recitation[2] was regarded as of the greatest importance by Vittorino, as evidence of intelligent appreciation of the matter and form of classical reading.

We have no allusion to the reading or recitation of Italian. Dante, for instance, is never mentioned in any references to the school of Vittorino or to that of his friend Guarino at Ferrara.

This brings us to the interesting but difficult enquiry—Was any place allotted to the language and literature of the vernacular in the education of the time? It seems indeed most unlikely that the Italian language was used at all except in rudimentary instruction, and in conversation. It is improbable that it was thought worthy of a place in a scheme of serious education[3]. Translations into Italian there were, in much larger numbers than we, perhaps, imagine; one, a history of

---

[1] *Rud. Gramm.* f. 4 (Romae 1473), cf. Vegius p. 238. Ficino said that memory was amongst the chief requisites of a philosopher. See interesting quotations from Vespasiano in Fioretti, p. 113.

[2] One of the Gonzaga boys recited a book of the *Aeneid* a day. Prendilacqua.

[3] See however the expression (very rare in a scholar) of a different feeling in the title of a little manual by Filelfo 'Exercitatiunculae Latinae et Italicae' (first ed. Milan 1483) '...genus exercitiorum quo duce non solum Latinae linguae flosculos decerpent verum etiam ipsius linguae vernaculae (quod non ab re fuerit) elegantiam sibi comparabunt....' Filelfo's own literary Italian was chiefly a string of Latin words with Italianised terminations—pedantic and artificial. L. B. Alberti represents the reaction in favour of Italian on its strongest side.

St Clement of Rome, was dedicated to Cecilia Gonzaga[1], herself a pupil of Vittorino, to whom the original Latin would have offered no difficulty. Dante was honoured with a Chair at the Studio of Florence, though rather in spite of, than because of, the language in which he wrote. Salutati[2] regretted the poet's choice of Italian, which Bruni curtly said was due to his gross ignorance of Latin. But in truth there was at this time little doubt felt that Latin was destined to be henceforth the common tongue of the educated world, and that all delay in acquiring it by speech and writing was so much wasted opportunity. 'La lingua volgare' might indeed be convenient for common life. But it was rather a series of dialects than an authoritative literary instrument[3]: hence it could in no way be regarded as equal to the task of expressing and interpreting the vast range of ideas now being revealed in the monuments of ancient civilisation. The eternity of Rome attached also to the Roman speech; anything worthy of survival must therefore be expressed through that medium[4].

---

[1] I only know of one copy, MSS. Ital. Canon. in the Bodleian Library (Catalog. ed. Mortara, 1864, No. 5).

[2] Salutati (in the *Dialogue* of L. Aretinus) is represented no doubt accurately as saying, 'si alio genere scribendi usus esset,' he would have placed Dante amongst the great figures of literature. See Klette, *Beit.* ii. 59. The chair of Dante was held by Giovanni Malpaghini and by Filelfo, both, of course, Latinists.

[3] Cf. the criticism of Gebhardt, *Les Origines de la Renaiss.* p. 171-2, and of Reumont, *Lorenzo dei Medici* (Eng. ed.), i. 486 (upon the absence of grammatical apparatus). The same feeling marks Erasmus' attitude towards modern speech nearly a century later: and Vives attached the greatest importance to the practice of talking in Latin (*De trad. Disc.* iii. 298).

[4] The extreme Humanist contention is best stated in the *Dialogue* of L. Aretinus already quoted. Niccoli is speaking: 'Quos tu mihi Dantes, inquit, quos Petrarcas, quos Boccatios?... Nam quid est in illis quod aut admirandum, aut laudandum, cuiquam videri debeat?' p. 60. 'Ego, mehercule, unam Ciceronis epistolam atque unum Virgilii carmen omnibus

Italian was unfixed, crude; it had no definite grammatical method; no sanction from great names of the past. The truly historic language of Italy could only be Latin. Vittorino's practice coincided with this prevailing opinion. As early as possible, so we may safely conclude, ordinary conversation, just as all teaching, at the Giocosa, was carried on in Latin, and the use of Italian discouraged.

Although Vittorino thus regarded Latin as the natural medium of instruction, he by no means limited his curriculum, whether for younger or elder scholars, to language alone. No mistake is more common amongst superficial students of the history of education than this misconception of the place accorded to Grammar by the teachers of the Renaissance. We are expressly told that the school hours were divided amongst a varied range of subjects. 'Laudabat illam quam Graeci ἐγκυκλοπαιδείαν vocant, quod ex multis et variis disciplinis fieri doctrinam et eruditionem dicebat' says Platina[1]. Indeed, Prendilacqua tells us that no subjects of instruction were wanting, and that special masters were provided to secure effective teaching. Arithmetic, which he valued highly for its training in accuracy and businesslike habits of mind, was in the rudimentary stage taught by games, 'following the practice of the ancient Egyptians, whose method in the subject Vittorino highly commended[2].' Geometry, in which Vittorino had gained a high reputation at Padua, and with which we may believe that he associated the elements of Algebra, he taught in conjunction with drawing, mensuration and surveying. We hear much less than we should expect of Vit-

vestris opusculis (those of Dante, Petrarch or Boccaccio !) longissime antepono.' p. 65.

Manetti, though holding Italian in genuine esteem, is compelled to write in Latin : 'Cuncta, quemadmodum gesta erant, conscribere atque perpetuis et aeternis Latinarum literarum monumentis mandare statuimus.' *Chron. Pistoriense, Praefatio, s.f.,* in Muratori, xix. p. 992.

[1] p. 21.   [2] Sassuolo, p. 70.

torino's teaching of mathematics, when we consider his interest in the subject and his credit as a master in earlier years[1]. The medal by Pisanello expressly records his fame in this department of knowledge. We are told that he engaged masters to teach the elements of Natural Philosophy and Euclid. At Padua Mathematics and Astrology had been closely associated[2]. Vittorino discarded Astrology for Astronomy, and lessons on the heavenly bodies were included in the course. Natural history was not neglected, though we may suppose it to have been of an uncritical sort, like our own sixteenth century 'bestiaries.' Music was admitted, although under careful supervision[3]. There was much anxiety amongst educators at this time respecting the moral influence of music and musicians. Indulgence in the art tended, it was feared, to sensuous excitement, or to mere indolence. To listen to music was an excuse for doing nothing; to practise it might lead to loss of complete self-control. Music masters, carefully chosen, paid special attention to those likely to excel. But Vittorino held fast to the Attic distinction between base and elevating harmonies. With these precautions he admitted instrumental music, choral singing, and dancing.

Vittorino held the opinion that not only was the alternation of study with games and exercise needful to real intellectual quickness, but that the teacher must provide ample variation in the subjects of instruction themselves. It was an illustration common with the Humanist writers on Education that the mind needs variety of food no less than the body[4]. The range of

[1] Ambrogio however writes from Goito in 1435, of Gianlucido, the third son : 'ostendit propositiones duas in Geometria Euclidis a se additas cum figuris suis, ut aestimare plane iam nunc licet quam sit valiturus ingenio.' Mehus, *Vita Ambros.* Epist. vii. 3 (p. 332).

[2] Astrology had affinity on one side with Mathematics and on the other with Medicine. See Rashdall, *Univ.* i. 243.

[3] 'modo educata sit in philosophiae gremio' says Sassuolo speaking of Vittorino's views.

[4] 'Animus alternatis studiorum generibus refici solet,' says Platina,

school subjects was undoubtedly narrow, as a consequence of the meagre field of knowledge available at the period; and their adaptation to school purposes was certainly most imperfect. But it still remains true that in the best Italian schools of the fifteenth century the restriction of school work to a mechanical study of Latin and Greek Grammar and Delectus was unknown.

Indeed, from the nature of the case, in its early stages the teaching of the classical languages was in such a school as that of Vittorino of necessity freer and more attractive than it was when school tradition had become formally settled. In the scarcity of books an oral method and clear intelligent exposition were indispensable. For it was necessary for each scholar to accumulate, by gradual induction from the usage of authors, both vocabulary and syntax. A small manual of Accidence, in the case both of Latin and of Greek, might be placed in the hands of every pupil, possibly the Elementarium of Papias, and the Erotemata of Chrysoloras[1]. But idiomatic usages, synonyms, irregularities of inflexion, were learnt by observation and practice. Grammar thus provided in the hands of a good teacher a valuable mental discipline: it deserved the title claimed for it by Vergerius 'scientia primordialis pedagoga,' which 'dirigit et administrat singulas facultates,' and so forms 'fundamentum solidum cuiuslibet alterius disciplinae[2].' It was a study calling into play many other and higher mental processes than verbal memory. The habitual use of Latin as a spoken language enabled the grammar of it to be employed with much freedom, and rapid

explaining the practice of Vittorino, p. 20. Compare Aen. Sylvius, p. 156, below.

[1] The manual compiled for the use of his classes at Florence and Pavia by Manuel Chrysoloras. It was abridged, with Latin version, by Guarino, and remained in that form (often under the title of *Erotemata Guarini*) the most popular elementary Grammar of the century. It is written in form of question and answer, as the name implies.

[2] Vergerius, *Epistol.* p. 5.

progress both in Greek and Latin was common amongst pupils of average intelligence.

Vittorino treated Grammar under four heads[1], which he required to be thoroughly mastered before definite reading of authors, or continuous composition was entered upon. The master first provided sufficient vocabulary by dictation, and with the words themselves their chief inflexions. Then easy passages from poetical authors were delivered, explained, no doubt translated, and then treated as exercises in accidence. Parallel with this ran a similar course in historical narrative or moral anecdote, in which more stress was laid upon the matter, in view of subjects for elementary composition or disputation[2]. Accent, especially with northern strangers, quantity, and enunciation were taken in hand as an integral part of every lesson. These, the 'quattuor officia grammaticorum,' were in the eyes of Vittorino the foundation of good teaching. It is evident that so elastic a method of handling grammar gave scope to a high order of teaching ability. Guarino in his schools at Venice and Ferrara followed a somewhat similar method, which was applied by Vittorino both to Greek and Latin.

Upon the foundations of Grammar thus understood Vittorino proceeded at once to raise the edifice of Letters. Cicero and Virgil, to speak first of Latin writers, were naturally the corner-stones. Passages from both authors were from the first committed to memory[3] as the basis of style, and as aids to vocabulary, and to prosody. With them Vittorino coupled

---

[1] This is derived from Sassuolo da Prato, a very good authority on points of this kind. He was pupil at Mantua between 1437 and 1443; and for some time was assistant to Vittorino.

[2] Sassuolo compiled a little book, which contained a selection of such passages in Latin and Greek; it is unfortunately not now to be traced. Compiled at Mantua, no doubt it represented the method pursued by Vittorino himself.

[3] It is said that not a few of his pupils could before leaving school repeat the whole of Vergil, entire speeches, treatises and letters of Cicero, large parts of Livy, and the whole of Sallust. Bernardi, p. 114.

Lucan and Ovid. But before prescribing a piece for recitation he took the greatest care in the explanation and rendering
of the selected passage. His method in 'reading' an author
is described as follows. He dealt, first of all, with 'verba,'
i.e. the exact meaning of each individual word and its construction in the sentence: that led up to the second part of
the lesson, the exposition of 'genus dicendi' or style; and
this includes 'ordo,' 'nexus,' and 'rhythmus verborum,' as
characteristic of the individual writer. Then the passage was
further explained under 'descriptio locorum,' or allusions, and
under 'affectus personarum,' or characters. All these points
were illustrated from other passages of the same, or of another,
author. We have here undoubtedly a direct reminiscence of
Quintilian and Plutarch[1] applied to elementary teaching.
Vittorino used always the simplest and most direct language
in class, avoiding all display and redundancy. He had great
power of illustration, and of putting his meaning in different
ways. His expressions were clear and carefully adapted to the
intelligence of individual scholars. His voice was musical and
penetrating, reaching every-one present in the room. The
matter thus given out was taken down by each member of
the class, who formed, each for himself, his own written
vocabulary, and collected examples of syntax and of prosody.
The reverence of Vittorino for Vergil was characteristic of his
age, and of his city. The art of the Augustan Age appealed
strongly to the Humanists. 'Cura et diligentia Homerum
superasse' he said of Vergil. Lucan he admired 'propter

---

[1] Quintilian, i. 8; Plutarch, *De aud. Poetis*, §§ 5, 6, 12. Erasmus'
advice to a master on this subject (*De Ratione Studii*, Opera I. 527) is
interesting : 'Ad haec si qua insignis elegantia, si quid prisce dictum......si
durior aut perturbatior ordo, si qua etymologia, si qua figura...diligenter
admoneat. Tum loca similia ex auctoribus conferat, si quid diversum, si
quid affine, si quid imitatum, si quid allusum, si quid aliunde translatum,
aut mutuo sumptum, ut sunt pleraque Latinorum a Graecis profecta, ne id
quid taceat.'

ardorem et concitationem.' Ovid he distrusted on moral
grounds; but his helpfulness in forming sound poetical taste
was so clearly recognised that a volume of extracts from this
poet was never out of Vittorino's hands. Other elegiac poets
he used sparingly: there was nothing morally bracing in them.
Terence, whose 'proprietas' he rated highly, and Plautus, he
would read only with pupils of whose strength of character he
was assured. So, too, the satirists, Horace and Juvenal, needed
excisions, and even then were better postponed to the last
year of school. The Odes, on the other hand, were models
of grace and elegance of diction. The tragedies of Seneca
attracted him by their loftiness of sentiment, their grave
diction, and the seriousness of their situations. None, however,
amongst the poets equalled Vergil in refinement of thought
and in perfection of technique[1].

Amongst historians Valerius Maximus[2], though unduly
prone to flattery, presents great variety of character and incident. Elegance, acumen, and verve are alike characteristic of
Caesar. In spite of accusations of provincialism in style and
inaccuracy in matter (which Vittorino indignantly rejects)
Vittorino is a warm admirer of Livy, as a master of a flowing
narrative style. Upon Livy Vittorino lectured frequently. He
indeed laid the foundations of the critical study of the text.
The famous editor of the *Editio Princeps*, the Bishop of Aleria,
was a pupil of Vittorino. He has left a touching record of his
debt to his old master in the Preface to that splendid book.
He tells us that Vittorino lectured upon a large part of the
history of Livy, and goes on to affirm 'si quid in recognitione
profeci, auctori acceptum Vittorino referatur.' This points to a

---

[1] Platina, p. 22.

[2] Salutati valued Valerius Maximus, 'non tam excerptorem historiae
quam moralium praeceptorem uberem.' *Epistol.* ed. Novati, i. 10. This
represents the usual attitude of the earlier Humanists towards historians. It
is probably even true of Erasmus. Cf. Benoist p. 137 '...forte hanc ei (i.e.
historiae) praecipuam utilitatem tribuit, ut praeclara apophthegmata pulchrasque sententias philosophis suppeditaret.'

systematic correction of the text of Livy, a task for which the scholarship of Vittorino aided by his rich collection of MSS was peculiarly qualified. Sallust and Quintus Curtius were used in younger classes. The *Natural History* of Pliny[1], though little read hitherto, was valued for its matter at least as much as for its style. Quintilian took a high place in Vittorino's estimation. We find him discussing this author at much length with Ambrogio, and we do not doubt that in conjunction with the *De Oratore* of Cicero, upon which he lectured almost continuously[2], it formed the basis of his teaching of Latin Oratory. We have a reference to the reading of Seneca the philosopher. The philosophical writings of Cicero are alluded to later on.

There is occasional notice of the Christian Latinists. A work of St Augustine, *De Musica*, and another, *De Cataegoriis*, are spoken of by Ambrogio as amongst Vittorino's books; but we have no reference to Lactantius, who was usually regarded as the Christian Cicero by Humanist teachers[3]. Vittorino undoubtedly had learnt from Barzizza to regard Cicero as the best material for the foundations of scholarship; nor was he tempted to make use of such collections of model epistles, orations or academic exercises, as served for substitutes for Cicero in many schools[4]. Vittorino, again, does not seem to

---

[1] Pliny was little known at this period, and MS. copies of his works were rare. Lud. Gonzaga had a copy at Mantua in 1376; there was none at Florence in 1378; and apparently none in the Milan library of the Visconti as late as 1426. Vittorino no doubt had the use of the Gonzaga copy. Petrarch bought his copy at Mantua in 1350. Nolhac, *Pét.* p. 270.

[2] Bandini (*Cat. Codd. Lat.* iii. 417) notes the existence of a copy in the Library of S. Marco at Florence, which bears the words ' ...revisus et correctus fuit Mantuae sub clarissimo...Victorino '; and again, a second reading is recorded, under Vittorino, of the same book, which, the owner says, 'egregie emendatum inveni.'

[3] See the opinion of L. Bruni, below, p. 124.

[4] Barzizza's own academic addresses, Guarino's letters, Vergerius's Tract on Education, are examples of the *Selections* from modern Latinists which we know to have been very popular.

have been drawn from his allegiance to sound style by the idea that possessed some of his successors that Christian education required the employment of Christian rather than of pagan authors. But the list of Latin writers here given[1] is probably not a complete record of the texts which found a place in his school course.

To pass next to the Greek authors read. We shall notice that the Attic tradition was far less developed than the Ciceronian. Homer, described as 'oceano similis,' but, as a poet, inferior to Vergil, and Demosthenes, occupy a place corresponding to that of Vergil and Cicero in Latin. So soon as the preliminary stages in grammar and construing already described have been carefully passed through, the scholars, 'quasi lacte puro atque incorrupto imbuti' were introduced to the historians, Xenophon, Arrian[2], and Herodotus. Of Vittorino's interest in the first of these we have a significant illustration in the actual copy of Xenophon which he presented to Sassuolo da Prato his pupil, on his leaving Mantua, with an autograph inscription of the master[3]. A copy of Thucydides

---

[1] It is compiled from various notices of his pupils or correspondents; and may be compared with a similar list drawn up, from a far wider mass of material, by Prof. Sabbadini respecting Guarino's working library. *Museo Ital. di Antichità Class.*, Firenze 1887, tom. II. p. 373.

[2] The mediaeval interest in Alexander the Great (cf. the *Cento Novelle Antiche*) is illustrated by the fact that the first translation from the Greek into Latin due to the Revival was that of Arrian by Vergerius. Combi, *Epist. Verg.* p. xxi. The attempted version of the *Iliad* by L. Pilato does not count : as Prof. Borsa drily says : ' fu nè Omero, nè poesia, nè Latino,' *op. cit.* p. 73.

[3] This volume is preserved in the Laurentian Library at Florence, and is catalogued by Bandini, ii. 285–6. The inscription runs: 'Hunc librum Sassulo Pratensi, et discipulo et filio dono dedi, cum a me discederet, ut esset monumentum amoris nostri. Ego Victorinus Feltrensis manu propria scripsi et donum obtuli.' This MS. passed into the hands of Guarino, who seems to have tried to erase the name 'Sassulo'; who in extreme destitution probably was compelled to part with the book. Guasti, p. 30.

W. 4

was in the library, but we have no reference to its use in school. Plutarch, from the interest which the Biographies had in moral and historical teaching for all Humanists, occupied a prominent place. It was one of the first books acquired by Vittorino from Aurispa. In Oratory, next to Demosthenes stood Isocrates, as highly prized for 'perspicuity' as Demosthenes for 'energy.' Plato was read chiefly with the highest class: a fine copy of most of the Dialogues was bought about 1425. Amongst the dramatists, Vittorino valued Aristophanes as 'doctrina linguae, puritate sermonis Attici, ad formandum bonum virum, quod vitia insectaretur, aptum.' This is a curious estimate of Aristophanes, but shews the didactic method pursued by Vittorino with classical authors. Euripides was 'jucundus,' and full of weighty sentiments: and, whilst the admirable art of Sophocles appealed to Vittorino's taste, Aeschylus was his favourite dramatist, although the condition of the text at that time makes us doubtful how far he could have profitably used Aeschylus in class[1]. Hesiod was read for his 'practical reflections,' Pindar was valued for his wealth of metaphor and of epithet. It is probable that the orations of the Emperor Julian were used as a school text; we know that Chrysostom was translated as an exercise in Latin prose. Ambrogio saw a version from the Greek Father by one of the pupils and was delighted with it. We shall see that Vittorino had in his library other Greek authors of which he may have made some use in school.

Vittorino laid great stress upon the parallel teaching of Latin and Greek. At what age his scholars actually began Greek we are not told. But Cecilia Gonzaga was already learning the grammar at the age of seven; and rapidly became proficient[2]: and possibly her brother Gianlucido had begun

[1] The *Ed. Prin.* was published by the house of Aldus in 1518, which is fair evidence that Aeschylus was little read during the first century of Humanism.

[2] The rapidity with which Greek was learnt by pupils of Vittorino and

even earlier. It is repeatedly noted that Vittorino studied with great care the capacity, taste, and future career of each scholar, and adapted his method accordingly. But it is unlikely that in any instance did he regard Greek as an 'optional' subject, as Guarino[1] did. Indeed Prendilacqua[2] says that in the case of one pupil Vittorino devoted more attention to Greek than to Latin in the earlier years.

Vittorino himself was probably less sound as a Greek scholar than as a Latinist. We may recognise three degrees of Greek scholarship in Italy during the early decades of the fifteenth century. In the first rank are the three scholars who were natives of Greek lands, and the forerunners of a much larger group of men who after the fall of Constantinople are found scattered throughout Italy. These were Manuel Chrysoloras, whose presence in Western Europe lay between 1397 and 1415, Theodore Gaza of Salonica, and George of Trebizond. They were men of high attainments, and to Chrysoloras and Gaza are due the first Greek grammars compiled for Western students. The next class contains the Italian scholars who in their enthusiasm for the language undertook the perils of a residence in Greece or Constantinople. The chief of these, all of whom on their return were conspicuous as teachers, were Guarino, Aurispa and Filelfo. There is no doubt that scholars of this class were not a little prone to slight the knowledge of Greek possessed by Humanists who had not crossed the Adriatic. Aurispa, for instance, refers to Vittorino as 'Victorinus quidam ...litteras Graecas mediocriter eruditus[3].' The third degree of

Guarino is noted as especially deserving attention by Voigt i. 553. Greek was perhaps used conversationally, but the statement of Schmidt (*Gesch. d. Pädag.* ii. p. 404) that Cecilia spoke Greek fluently at the age of 10 rests upon a misreading of Ambrogio. Cf. B. Guarino, *De ordine docendi*, p. 167, inf.

[1] Voigt i. 552.

[2] Prendil. p. 45. Alessandro Gonzaga 'fu nella puerizia eccellentemente nutrito di Greche lettere, nell' adolescenza di Latine.'

[3] To Ambrogio, 'Bonon. vi Cal. Sep.'; no year, but, I conclude, in

scholarship was attained by those who had learnt Greek at the hands of one or other of the two classes of teachers just mentioned[1]. This was the nature of Vittorino's knowledge of Greek, gained originally from Guarino in Venice. A man of his intellectual sincerity was not likely to be under any illusion as to the immense advantage which a native Greek scholar had over one who, like himself, began the study of the language in his thirty-eighth year. But such native teachers were apt to be charlatans. Hence Vittorino kept careful watch for Greeks who could produce satisfactory evidence of ability and of character. Filelfo seems to have been the medium through which, in or about 1430, George of Trebizond (Georgius Trapezuntius) entered Vittorino's service. From a letter of Filelfo[2] to him dated July 1431 we find that he is already at work at Mantua. He had been for some years on bad terms with Guarino, from whom it was said that he learnt the first rudiments of Latin[3]. But his ability in Latin scholarship was, as we have seen, according to his own declaration, due to Vittorino. In return for this thorough training in Latin he taught Greek at the Giocosa. Although a man of perverse temper, his affection for Vittorino was deep and abiding. In 1426 he dedicated to him a little Tract, ' De generibus dicendi,' and again, about 1432, another ' De artificio Ciceron. orationis pro Q. Ligario,' in which he speaks of Vittorino as ' pater meus' and of himself as his son[4], though indeed he was far from inheriting the peace-loving spirit of his master[5]. With him

1424 or 1425 when Aurispa was professing Greek at Bologna just after his return (with a store of MSS.) from the East. Mart. et Dur. iii. 714. There are sufficient reasons why the date cannot be much later in any case.

[1] There were of course more who, like P. C. Decembri, simply taught themselves by help of Chrysoloras' *Erotemata* and one or two texts. See Prof. M. Borsa in *Arch. Stor. Lombard.* Mar. 1893, p. 69.

[2] Klette, *Beit.* iii. 105. Filelfo to George of Trebizond, July 1431.

[3] By Giovanni Pannonio. Cf. sup. p. 13.

[4] This is no doubt preserved in the anon. Tract, Ball. Coll. Oxon. MSS. cxxviii. (Coxe).

[5] His bitterest quarrels were with his fellow-scholars, Aleria, Gaza, and Perotti.

were associated three others of his fellow countrymen whom
Ambrogio found working in the school in 1432[1]. Ten or
twelve years later (1441) Vittorino engaged Theodore Gaza,
who had arrived in Italy in, or a little before, 1440[2]. He also,
introduced by Filelfo, learnt Latin from Vittorino, and his
excellence as a scholar, a teacher, and a copyist of MSS. made
him a most valuable acquisition to the Mantuan school. For
the Greek grammar of Gaza was the ablest of all the manuals
compiled by scholars during that century. Erasmus introduced
it at Cambridge, and in editing a version for his own use has
no hesitation in putting the work in the same high category in
which he includes the Latin grammar of Perotti, another pupil
of Vittorino[3]. Budaeus also found it the ablest book available
in his time. The merits of Gaza as a copyist and corrector of
Greek MSS. have long been recognised. He was much occupied
by this work at Mantua, and in the paucity of books, which was
one of the difficulties of Humanist education at that time, Gaza's
presence enabled Vittorino to extend the range of his Greek
reading with his scholars, and even to supply the need of
friends at a distance. By the help of Gaza also, we have no

[1] Cf. Castiglione, in Mehus, *Ambrog. Trav.* ccccviii. 'Semper aliquos
ex Graecia viros, nonnunquam tres quattuorve, domi habebat qui partim
nostros Graecas literas edocerent, partim ipsi Latinas docerentur, nonnullis
etiam pro librariis utebatur.'

[2] Gaza is seeking work as teacher of Greek in 1440, but his ignorance
of Latin stands in his way. Filelfo sent him to Vittorino, and he is at
work under him in 1441. Klette, *Beit.* iii. 63–4. He has left Mantua in
1444 for Ferrara, where he is the first public professor of Greek Letters.
Le Grand, *Bibl. Hellénique*, gives 1441 as the date of his arrival at
Mantua. But Sassuolo da Prato writes in 1443 'Nacti sumus nuper
Graecum hominem Thessalonicensem Theodorum, cum doctum, tum hac
aetate in sua lingua paene principem.' He stayed three years. See
Guasti, p. 40.

[3] Erasmus, *De Rat. Stud.* p. 521 C: 'the first place amongst Greek
grammarians belongs by common consent to Th. Gaza, the next to
C. Lascaris.' See also his Preface to his edition (Basil. 1513) of Gaza's
Instit. Grammat.

doubt, Vittorino himself continued to make further progress in Greek scholarship. For no characteristic is more noteworthy in the true Humanist teacher than his persistent attitude of a student. And Vittorino, humble and sincere in his passion for knowledge, was typical of the best of a group, worthy, not a few of them, in spite of many failings, of 'a Grammarian's Funeral.'

Vittorino was thus in a position to carry much farther than would otherwise have been possible the reading of Greek authors and the practice of Greek composition; possibly he included in certain cases the exercise of conversation in Greek. It may be safely affirmed that nowhere else in Italy was Greek so thoroughly and systematically taught; certainly not at Bologna, at Padua[1] or, until Gaza himself went there, at Ferrara. We could not have more striking evidence of the subordinate part played in the spread of Greek learning by the Universities as compared with the Courts, Societies and individual scholars[2] of northern Italy.

Interesting references to the method of teaching Composition, or Rhetoric in the strict sense, are preserved. The first steps were taken in speaking Latin and also in reading aloud, which Vittorino found helpful in acquiring vocabulary, and a sense of rhythm in prose not less than in verse. There were certain formal phrases, such as we find in Perotti's grammar[3] with the Italian equivalent, to be learnt by heart: then a book of exercises like Filelfo's, also in Italian and Latin, would be used. Very early Greek was introduced, a

---

[1] Padua had no public chair of Greek until after Vittorino's death in 1446.

[2] See Burckhardt's remarks in this connexion, *Ren. in Italy*, p. 212.

[3] 'Quo modo eleganter dicemus: 'Perche de la dicta litera io ho facilmente compreso e che tu sei sano e che tu non solamente me voi bene, ma me ami grandemente?' "Ex his enim facile intellexi te et valere et non modo me diligere sed etiam vehementer amare," (with other alternative renderings).

practice in which most leading schoolmasters[1] of the time coincided. Composition in the continuous form often now took the shape of a version from a simple Greek passage. Ambrogio[2] found nine of Vittorino's younger pupils who wrote Greek with an elegance which astonished him. Cecilia Gonzaga, now ten years old, in this facility surpassed his own pupils at Florence who were reaching manhood. The epistolary style was zealously cultivated. Original compositions in this form, and in oratory, were begun at the age of 11 or 12; and certain stiff and formal models were reproduced with accuracy. Latin passages were rendered into Greek, though there is no allusion to Greek verses. Latin verse was, in imitation of Vergil rather than Ovid, assiduously taught. Carlo Gonzaga at the age of fourteen recites before Ambrogio[3] portions of an original production in Hexameters upon the pageants at Mantua celebrated on the occasion of the Emperor's visit in 1432.

The whole subject was of the first importance in Vittorino's eyes. He invariably took it himself with one or other of the classes. Each exercise was individually corrected, and if necessary re-written, by Vittorino; and if any scholar thought to escape criticism by introducing some elaborately worded compliment to the Master, he was rudely undeceived. The three recognised marks of sound rhetorical composition had been thus laid down by Barzizza[4], and were accepted as canons of style: *compositio, elegantia, dignitas*; of which *compositio* was again divided into *iunctura* (or *nexus*), *ordo*, and *numerus* (or *rhythmus*). But Vittorino, we are expressly told, inculcated a plain direct style, which he used himself: 'nullo fuco aut ambitu orationis utens, quod plerumque ad

---

[1] Esp. Guarino and his son (cf. *De Ordine &c.*, p. 167, infra.).

[2] Mart. et Dur., iii. 553.

[3] Mart. et Dur., iii. p. 451. On Prosody and Verse Composition see inf. p. 165.

[4] Aen. Sylv. *Rhet. Praecept.*, (prologus), *opera*, p. 992.

iactationem ingenii ac doctrinae fieri consueverint.' Fine writing and the ostentation of learning he habitually discouraged. As the general rule for young Latin scholars his advice was 'A Cicerone nunquam discedendum.' He cultivated a fine taste in choice of words and in the arrangement of the sentence. He laid down as a factor of great moment in classical composition that the scholar must not set pen to paper until he has thought out the argument of the piece and determined the general form into which the matter should be thrown; and thereupon saturated himself with the reading of first-rate model passages from an ancient author. In the time of Vittorino, Rhetoric was not yet the elaborate art which it afterwards became in the hands of Perotti[1] and his followers, who by their formalism and minute analysis of style deprived Latin writing of all spontaneity. Oratorical ability and ease in writing and speaking Latin were arts of practical value for the youths of that day, especially for those who might fill professional or public positions. And with such practical aim it was taught by Vittorino or Guarino. Vittorino's ability as a Ciceronian and as a teacher enabled him to develope a sound Latinity in his pupils. George of Trebizond became one of the first Ciceronians of the century, an admitted superior to Guarino, and the author of the recognised treatise on Rhetorical style; Gaza, who in 1440 seems to have been all but entirely ignorant of Latin, could, after eighteen months of study under Vittorino, produce a version from the Greek worthy of dedication to a Medici. It is moreover significant that men like Valla, the finest Latinist of his day, Perotti, Ognibene da Lonigo[2], and other great masters were formed under the influence of Vittorino.

On the other hand he himself wrote nothing. Unlike most

[1] E.g. Perotti, after defining *Tropus* (figure), proceeds to divide it under thirteen heads: and this for beginners!

[2] See below, p. 87.

scholars[1] of his rank, he has left no 'elegant epistles'; he said that there was enough writing already in existence. His humility led him to conceal rather than display his great erudition and thorough scholarship; and in this way one aspect of his position in the history of learning has been overlooked.

That Vittorino fully realised the difficulties attending the use of some of the classical authors for school purposes has been indicated already. The question was frequently debated during the fifteenth century. Probably Vittorino was satisfied with the practice of Jerome and Basil; or with the principles laid down by Plutarch as to the care necessary in the choice of teachers, selection of matter, and the distinction to be drawn between literary form and moral content. We may remember that in the absence of printing, and in the consequent scarcity of texts, the lecturer had ample freedom in omissions[2]. Vittorino was we know more than ordinarily careful in all that concerned the morals of his scholars, and both in selection and in comment this consideration would be foremost in his mind. We hear nothing of any difficulty, which some teachers at least experienced, on score of the heathenism of the ancient writers;

---

[1] Guarino was very prolific in letters; Voigt rightly says that their formalism and want of living interest makes many of them a poor testimony to their writer's powers. Vittorino's letters to Ambrogio are lost; they were apparently of real personal interest. On Vittorino's *Pythagorean silence* see Prof. Brambilla, Prendilacqua, p. 92. On the other hand, it must be remembered that the letters most likely to be preserved were those of the formal and 'elegant' type which might be employed as models in composition. There are, however, not a few, still inedited, scattered throughout the libraries of Italy and southern Germany, of very great biographical value. From such neglected sources the reconstruction of the earlier history of Humanism is being slowly but surely attained by such scholars as Prof. Sabbadini.

[2] We must not forget the difference of standard of coarseness in humour, or of outspoken directness of expression between that age and our own.

for Vittorino's intense and living religious convictions enabled him to select truth and beauty, in example or in style, from pagan not less than from Christian writers, with a serene confidence that seems never to have been seriously embarrassed[1].

The classical scholar had two further interests besides literature and style, those namely of the History and the Philosophy of antiquity. The place of History in Education was not clearly defined by Humanist writers, and we have little light upon Vittorino's practice with respect to it. But his devotion to Livy has already been mentioned, and we learn that his interest was not confined to the text: he expressly refused to accept criticisms of the accuracy of the historian which were already mooted amongst scholars. Tacitus is never mentioned, Sallust, Curtius and Valerius Maximus were favourite authors. Plutarch was a favourite book of Gianfrancesco Gonzaga, as indeed of most public men with scholarly feeling, and several biographies were translated into Latin by pupils. Plutarch was the one historian of antiquity then popularly read; his use as a storehouse of moral and political wisdom is illustrated by every letter-writer and rhetorician. We have seen that Vittorino possessed the greater Greek historians. His pupil Perotti translated Polybius. Knowing the practical aim with which Vittorino had undertaken his post at Mantua, we are surprised, perhaps, that we do not find more stress laid upon the political value of ancient history. For, like Aeneas Sylvius and Erasmus[2], Vittorino seems mainly attracted to history for its moral and

---

[1] Guarino's experience at Ferrara was different: but then he was a man of far less sensitiveness in such matters than Vittorino, and could even commend *L'Ermafrodito* of Beccadelli.

[2] On Erasmus' view see Benoist, *De Puer. Instit.* p. 137, "forte hanc ei praecipuam utilitatem tribuit, ut praeclara apothegmata pulchrasque sententias philosophis suppeditaret."

anecdotal interest. A really broader and more modern view appears in Baptista Guarino's[1] treatise. But we must remember how little was as yet attained in the formation of either historical or critical method. Vittorino's contemporaries read Villani; nearly a century was to elapse before Guicciardini was possible.

As regards Philosophy, Vittorino treated Ethics, not from the speculative side, but as a guide to the art of living. We find Vittorino very soon after his arrival buying a set of Plato's dialogues[2]. He studied with the best light available the leading Greek philosophies, although we do not know which particular works of Aristotle he may have possessed. But Plato, Aristotle and the Stoics were taught at La Giocosa as a necessary part of the training of every educated man; 'for they are most important in forming the man and the citizen.' Younger scholars may learn their tenets from Cicero, who, as having absorbed the best elements in Greek Ethics, and having the truly practical temper of the Romans, is to be placed at the head of all philosophers useful in actual life. Sassuolo records that Vittorino himself took a select few of older pupils through a course of philosophy, using both Plato and Aristotle as his texts : that with this class 'every side of their teaching was handled with thoroughness.' Vittorino regarded this final course as the culmination of 'Letters,' affirming that those who then passed on to a career in Law, Medicine, Theology, or the public service, would find themselves equipped with the finest possible preparation for a life of dignity and usefulness in their several callings. In this conception of the place of Letters as preliminary to professional training we have the highest ideal of Humanist education whether in the fifteenth century or the nineteenth.

A few words must be added respecting the place accorded

---

[1] Cf. *De ord. docend. et stud.* infra, p. 169.
[2] Infra, p. 68.

to Dialectic or Logic. The attitude of the Humanists to this subject needs no lengthy exposition. Although one of the four[1] subjects included in the Arts course at the Universities, the Italian genius had never given to Logic the dominating place which it occupied in Paris or Oxford. "Quid est," asks Niccoli[2], "in Dialectica quod non britannicis sophismatibus conturbatum est? quid quod non ab illa vetere et vera disputandi via separatum et ad ineptias levitatesque traductum?" Vergerius, himself a Professor of Logic at Padua, had not proposed the exclusion of the subject from the new education. But he himself declares that he never taught Logic after the manner of other Logicians, but in such a way that it might serve as a guide and aid to the study of other sciences, especially of natural and of moral philosophy[3]. Now this coincides exactly with the judgement which is recorded of Vittorino. He valued Logic expressly on the ground of its use as an aid to exact thinking—in definitions, in classification, in inference, in the detection of fallacies. But the one aim to be kept in view is that of arriving at working truth in enquiry; mere clever fence, subtilty and verbal ingenuity, is banished as so much empty ostentation[4]. He would employ the Socratic questioning to expose conceit. He, however, laid stress upon Logic as of great service to a schoolmaster, enabling him to acquire the fundamental virtues of exposition, precision, connection, and clearness[5].

The use of Disputation was retained by the earlier Humanist

---

[1] Grammar, Rhetoric, Dialectic, Philosophy (Ethics).

[2] Klette, *Beit.* ii. 53. (The Dialogue of L. Aretino.)

[3] Gloria ii. 423; Combi, *Epistol. di Vergerio*, p. xlv. The actual letter, Ibid. *ep.* lxxiv. p. 100.

[4] This too had been Petrarch's position: he inveighed bitterly against the dialectic of the schools, but adds: 'scio quod...excitat intellectum, signat veri viam, monstrat vitare fallacias, denique, si nihil aliud, promptos et perargutulos facit.' Petr. *Ep. Fam.* i. vi. (ed. Fracassetti, i. p. 56).

[5] Bernardi.

teachers as a method of instruction in Classics[1]. Chrysoloras[2] had urged it as a process valuable only when conducted with straightforward simplicity upon a sound foundation of knowledge. The Humanist, with a wide unexplored field before him of positive realities of thought, literature and action, had no time to waste upon subjective puzzles, and the discipline associated with them fell into disrepute. Logic, as an honest aid to practical truth, had still its function to perform, but for the scholar of the Renaissance it could never claim a place of honour by the side of Letters.

Thus, whilst the curriculum of Vittorino covered the range of subjects constituting the Arts course as recognised in a University which, like Padua, was influenced by Humanist sympathies, the thoroughness and breadth of classical reading were probably far in advance of the standard usual for the degree of Master or Doctor. Scholars anxious for the University status might indeed proceed from Mantua to Pavia, Bologna, or Ferrara; and this step was indispensable in the case of those who entered upon Theology, Law or Medicine. For the project of Gianfrancesco Gonzaga, suggested possibly by Vittorino, of erecting a ' Studium Generale ' upon the foundation of the ' Gymnasium Palatinum ' was not carried beyond the stage of securing the necessary charter from the Emperor Sigismund in 1433[3]. We must however remember that in the Italian Revival the imprimatur of the University was generally of less

---

[1] For an instance of the form which Disputation sometimes assumed in Humanist hands, see the following title of such an exercise at the Studio of Florence (circ. 1440): 'Dialogus in quo fingit philosophos disputavisse cum Alexandro adeo suaviter, ut etiam Dii auscultarent descendentes et ut doctiores evaderent. [Begins,] Mercurius: Cur, O Charon infernas sedes relinquens' &c. Arund. MSS. in B. M. 138. 82.

[2] Klette, *Beit.* ii. 53.

[3] Dated Sep. 27. Renewed by Albert II. and by Frederic III. Lunig. iii. p. 1781. The diploma conferred 'all the privileges of Paris and Montpellier.' Mantua should be added to Mr Rashdall's list of ' paper Universities,' Rashd. *Univ.* vol. ii., p. 719.

importance to a student of Letters, even if he proposed to become a public Teacher, than the distinction of having been the pupil of a noted Humanist, who might be in the service of a Prince, or Municipality, in a city where no Studium existed. Hence it was possible for a school like that of Mantua to obtain a repute and an influence in the world of scholarship, which, so far as Letters were concerned, rendered its pupils largely independent of the University degree[1]. In Italy the great schools in no sense formed their curriculum upon the requirements of the Studium, as in France or England.

Vittorino taught for some seven or eight hours daily. His custom was to devote the early part of the day to work in class or lecture, and the evenings to tutorial preparation of individual scholars[2]. The school hours were probably shorter than the practice of the following century allowed; but the day no doubt began early. 'I remember,' writes Prendilacqua, 'that Vittorino, now well advanced in years, would of a winter's morning come early, candle in one hand and book in the other, and rouse a pupil in whose progress he was specially interested; he would leave him time to dress, waiting patiently till he was ready: then he would hand him the book, and encourage him with grave and earnest words to high endeavour.' Class teaching, as has been already said, took the form partly of dictation of text, notes and translation; partly of oral questioning. The 'running commentary' with its island of text surrounded by notes is a relic of the first, the second is illustrated by the form of all the earlier grammars. Many

[1] Northern Schools were more dependent on the University for the status of their scholars. Cf. Clerval, p. 439.

[2] Guarino's practice at Ferrara is described by Rosmini, *Guarino*, p. 85. 'La mattina facea pubblica lezione ai discepoli, poi passava a far la privata a Lionello. Il medesimo accadeva il dopo pranzo. Prima di sera ritiravasi in casa, la quale sino a notte era aperta ai discepoli che qualche dubbio propor volessero intorno alle cose insegnate.' With favourite pupils he would remain discoursing far into the night. Cf. Sabbadini, *Vita di Guarino*, p. 139.

contemporary woodcuts exist which shew us the Lecturer standing or seated at a high desk with pupils of varying ages, on comfortless benches, diligently taking down the master's comments[1]. The practice of declamation varied the monotony of the class lecture; but the especial feature of Vittorino's method was his careful individual work. He had, as we know, an ample staff, and this enabled him to devote much time to gaining that intimate knowledge of the tastes, capacity and industry of each scholar, which, with his readiness to adapt[2] thereto his choice both of subject and of treatment, secured the unique success for which his school was celebrated. He had an unaffected pride in his work, and a keen interest in the progress of each individual scholar; and with it all an unusual insight into the teaching art itself.

In actual methods of instruction, so far as our material enables us to speak, we notice the contrast with the teaching characteristic of mediaeval schools. Vittorino's attitude to his problem is altogether new: we have noticed the brightness which characterises the surroundings of his school, his cheerful personal relations with the boys; his serene hopefulness as to the possibilities of knowledge; his conviction of its influence upon life and character. This was partly due to the temper of the man; partly to the glow of Humanist enthusiasm which marked his age. But Vittorino had undoubted genius for teaching, and, in any Art, genius, as we know, often makes swift intuitions towards right method. So that modern Italian critics, such as Prof. Brambilla[3] or Dr Bernardi[4], are not, perhaps, exaggerating when they ascribe to Vittorino an unconscious

---

[1] The well-known monument to Cino Sinibaldi in the Duomo at Pistoia represents a similar subject dating from a somewhat earlier time.

[2] This is specially dwelt upon by all who watched his methods of teaching; there was clearly something unusual in this concern for individual capacity.

[3] Vid. his ed. of Prendilacqua, p. xii.

[4] Bernardi, *Vitt. da Felt. &c.*, p. 81.

anticipation of some of the more important doctrines of educational theory: such as the due alternation of subjects, the uniform development of the faculties, the dependence of mental upon physical conditions, the logical ordering of the lessons, the choice of stimulus, the careful observation of the child's mental powers. If he seems to have attached undue weight to memory, we must bear in mind the higher importance of accurate verbal recall in the absence of books, and its value in public life. The superiority of Vittorino to traditional methods has been by Ticozzi[1] ascribed to his study of the Pythagorean schools of Magna Graecia. Prof. Sabbadini[2] thinks that he learnt not a little from Guarino. It is difficult to find any evidence for this latter opinion; for in all that is truly characteristic of Vittorino, Guarino falls distinctly below him. We may however, viewing these two famous men together, safely claim for them that they rescued the function of the schoolmaster from the contempt[3] in which it was proverbially held. Petrarch's sarcastic comment upon the school teaching of his day henceforth ceased to represent educated opinion: 'Pueros doceant, qui maiora non possunt, quibus mens tardior, sanguis gelidus, animus lucelli appetens, negligens fastidii.' 'Let those,' he goes on, 'teach, who like disorder, noise, and squalor; who rejoice in the screams of the victim as the rod falls gaily, who are not happy unless they can terrify, flog, and torture. How then can teaching—be it of grammar or of any of the liberal arts—be a fit occupation for honourable age? Quit so debasing a trade while chance offers[4].' Vittorino was perhaps the first to prove that Humanism

---

[1] Ticozzi, p. 15.

[2] *Ciceronianismo*, p. 17.

[3] Cf. letter to Giov. da Ravenna (Conversino) in Voigt's *Die Brief-sammlungen Petrarca's*, p. 92. 'Quid enim indignius oro quam versari ingenium tuum...circa vilissimum exercitium omnium quae viderim ego, circa doctrinam scilicet puerorum...?' This letter is not from Petrarch.

[4] Petrarch, *Ep. Fam.* xii. 111 (ed. Fracas. ii. 176).

had not only made possible, but indeed demanded, a new ideal of a teacher of youth.

The important place which games and bodily exercises occupy in Vittorino's scheme of education is readily accounted for. For Vittorino was in one sense a continuator of the Court training which had held its place beside the municipal or ecclesiastical schools of the Middle Age. He was, we remember, preceptor in the first place to the family of a Condottiere prince; and a not inconsiderable proportion of his pupils were, like Frederic of Urbino, called to follow a career of arms. On the other hand Vittorino was a Humanist, and therefore derives part at least of his educational ideal from the example of Greece and Rome. The two influences combined to establish the training of the body as an integral element of a complete discipline. Indeed the highest level of Humanist culture was only attained when the full personality had received a cultivation duly proportioned to the three sides of human nature. So that it is not enough to say that Vittorino attached importance to the outdoor life as a means to brisk intellectual activity. No doubt this was in his mind. He always paid serious attention to the health of the scholars. Their life out of doors was carefully organised. Whatever the weather, daily exercise in some form was compulsory. There was ample space for games, riding, running, and all the athletic exercises then popular. We hear that he specially encouraged certain games at ball, leaping, and fencing. He prized excellence in sports as only less praiseworthy than literary power, for in such powers he found a sound corrective to self-indulgence and effeminacy. If we turn to three typical treatises upon education due to the Renaissance, those of Vergerius, of Castiglione, and of Milton, we see that each lays special stress upon the practice of martial exercises: each of them presents that union of the Courtly with the Humanist ideal to which reference has just been made. But although Vittorino undoubtedly kept such martial exercises in view, he seems to have taken generally a wider view of physical training, aiming rather at strengthening the frame, inducing habits of hardiness, and power of bearing fatigue, than at any special athletic skill. Thus he watched with peculiar care the health of the younger children, providing due supervision for them in their games and walks. In the summer heats he would take certain of them to the Castle of Goito, some twelve miles out of Mantua towards Verona. We know this pleasant spot where Sordello's youth was spent, and may wonder if Vittorino, who in his early Paduan days had had his lyrical moods, felt the associations of the place[1]. We find Ambrogio visiting him there one hot September day[2]. "Vittorino is staying at Goito in charge of the Gonzaga children. We found him at breakfast with them; he comes out to meet us, greeting us with tears of joy. He entertains us right royally. The children seem to be on the happiest terms with him. We talked together for several hours. Then one of the boys declaims some two hundred lines which he had composed upon the state entry of the Emperor Sigismund into Mantua. I was astonished by the taste and scholarship displayed not less than by the grace and propriety of delivery. Two younger[3] brothers and their sister were of the party, all bright and intelligent children......After a morning's most enjoyable intercourse several other youths of distinction were introduced, and after courteous greetings escorted us some distance on our way." The mountains above the Lake of Garda formed an accessible and favourite field for longer excursions, lasting several days, when Vittorino, wiry and active to the last, in company with his elder boys, explored that most striking of all the gateways of the Alps.

[1]   "just a castle built amid
      A few low mountains; firs and larches hid
      Their main defiles, and rings of vineyard bound
      The rest."   Browning's *Sordello.*

[2] 1435.   Mart. et Dur., iii. 451 (Ambrogio to Cosmo).

[3] Gianlucido, Alessandro and Cecilia.

In all this we see Vittorino consciously carrying out a definite aim of developing the physical not less than the intellectual side of his scholars. Free, on the one hand, from the sensuous cult of the body which marks a later stage of the Renaissance, he had even less sympathy with that neglect of all that concerns its vigour and grace which was still characteristic of much of the education of his time. Something of the finest temper of the antique world shews itself in this love of the simplicity of the open air and the tried discipline of the body.

But we must again remind ourselves of the depth of religious conviction upon which his own educational ideal ultimately rested. Reverence, piety and religious observance formed the dominant note of Vittorino's personal life. The dignity of human life was with him based upon its relation to the Divine. Hence the transparent sincerity of his religious teaching; the insistence upon attendance at the ordinances of the Church[1]; the inculcation of forgiveness and humility. He himself accompanied the boys to Mass; he set the example of regular Confession. Part of the religious instruction he himself took every day. Apart from the light that is thus thrown upon his personality, what is of chief interest in this aspect of Vittorino is its relation to his Humanism. This was with him no nominal reconciliation between the new and the old. Christianity and Humanism were the two coordinate factors necessary to the developement of complete manhood. There is no reason to suppose that Vittorino was embarrassed by a sense of contradiction between the classical and the Christian ideals of life. To him, and to men of his temper since, the thought and morals of the ancient world were identified with the ethical precepts of the Stoics and the idealism of Plato: and it was easy for them to point to the consistency of this teaching with the broader aspects of the Christian life.

---

[1] Mass was heard daily at the Duomo, which stood close to the Giocosa. Paglia, *op. cit.*, p. 156.

One special service rendered by Vittorino to scholarship must here be dwelt upon. He was one of the most generous of book owners. He readily allowed copies to be made from MSS. in his possession, and was addicted, even, to the doubtful habit of lending books, which in the fifteenth century led to more than one irremediable loss to literature. In his later years he found his kindness so much abused that he was obliged to issue, under official authority, a notice to the effect that delay in returning works borrowed from his library would lead to public penalties[1]. For Vittorino had found at Mantua a library much more important than he had anticipated. Three quarters of a century before, the Marquis of Mantua of the time had been a close friend and correspondent of Petrarch. Ludovic Gonzaga had acquired MSS. by his advice, certain of which were of decided rarity and of some critical importance. These books, in addition to a valuable series[2] of Romances, Vittorino found in the palace Library in 1423 : and he at once proceeded to add to their number. In 1425 we find him corresponding with Aurispa, then professor of Greek at Bologna, with this purpose. Aurispa, writing to Ambrogio, says[3], "I have received an offer from a correspondent named Vittorino who is attached to the Mantuan court and who appears to have some acquaintance with Greek. He proposes to pay fifty florins for two volumes of Plato and Plutarch. I happen to have these in duplicate : the Plutarch a very careful transcript of the Lives, the Plato containing all the Dialogues except the Laws, the Republic, and the

---

[1] The *Grida* was published in 1434, and read publicly and proclaimed by the Herald of the Municipio, 13 Oct. On Vittorino's death it was re-issued, declaring that persons detaining the books of the Marquis or of Vittorino would be ' riputati cometere furto e puniti per furto.' Ludovico, finding the decree only partly effective, committed its fuller execution to the ' Armorum Capitan.'

[2] Nolhac, *Pétrarque*, p. 414.

[3] Aurispa to Ambrogio, Bonon. vi. Cal. Sept. [1425], Mart. et Dur. iii. 714.

Letters. This latter MS. is as fine a one as I have ever seen."

Later on, Vittorino's library[1] has become a centre of interest to a wide circle of scholars. Filelfo sent him various MSS., some Greek codices which he had brought with him from Constantinople, others more complete copies of Latin authors already in the Library. Francesco Barbaro, the wealthy Venetian patrician, and the dear friend of the Paduan circle, added others of interest. Appended to the 'Grida' of 1434 was a significant clause: "that if any one possessed a copy of the book called 'De Genealogia Deorum,' and were prepared to part with it, he should at once offer it to Master Vittorino who will purchase it and will further regard such offer as a great personal favour[2]." We have other evidence of the direct interest taken in the Library by the Marquis, who seems to have been always most anxious to further the wishes of Vittorino for the welfare of the school. For instance, in 1444 Gian Francesco writes to Guarino now at Ferrara, "longo atque vehementi desiderio tenemur habendi in Graeco sermone Josephum de Antiquitate Judayca, totum et integrum"; he adds that a trusted friend of his starts immediately for Constantinople; can Guarino give him useful advice as to the right quarter for enquiries in that city? In sending instructions to this confidential agent, he adds "non curamo che libri siano ornati, nè di exquisita litera, pur che siano boni et ben correcti[3]." We gather that Vittorino's aim was to form a good sound working library, not merely a collector's cabinet of curiosities. There are further interesting notices of the school-books required for

---

[1] We cannot be sure whether Vittorino's personal library or the Palace library is referred to in the allusions made to his books. His own library was a good one.

[2] Luzio, *Cinque Lettere*, &c. in *Archiv. Veneto*, vol. 36 (1888), p. 339.

[3] Id., *op. cit.* 337, seq. Vittorino was ill during 1444, and the Marquis, possibly under his directions, undertook the correspondence regarding the Library.

the young princes: a Latin Psalter for Alessandro (aged 4), a Donatus, a Doctrinale of Alexander de Villa Dei, both manuals of accidence, for Cecilia (aged 6); and for her also, next year, (1432) a copy of the four Gospels in Greek. Vittorino attended both to the copying and the binding, and the cost was provided by Paola, the children's mother[1]. About the time to which these latter notices refer, and some seven years later than the date of the letter of Aurispa quoted above, Ambrogio paid a visit to Vittorino whom he found still at Mantua, although August was well advanced. He sees two sons of the Marquis and their sister Cecilia; there are also present two sons of neighbouring princes, about ten years of age. His introduction to Vittorino has come through Niccolo dei Niccoli, the distinguished Florentine collector, and to him Ambrogio reports upon his visit. "We saw and examined about seventy volumes[2], most of them however already known to us. We discussed Quintilian at some length: I saw Herodotus, Thucydides, Arrian, Plutarch's Lives; a long series of the poets; and what was new to me, a life of Homer by Herodotus. He shewed me also a treatise of Augustine 'De Musicâ,' and the 'Cathegoriae,' which are ascribed to him. He had also the Commentary of Accrius upon the Odes of Horace. There was, besides, the ' Mathesis' in eight books of Julius Firmicus, a copy of which I commissioned him to have made for myself: I also asked on your behalf for copies of the Orations of the Emperor Julian[3], the Life of Homer, the great Quintilian and the Bacchus. He was only too eager to oblige us in any way ; and regretted that you were not present in person to discuss these and other works

[1] Luzio, *op. cit.*, p. 331.

[2] Mart. et Durand, iii. 553. Ambrogio, *Hodoeporicon*, p. 34, describes his visit to the Library, when he was escorted by Vittorino, and the sons of the Marquis and some of their fellow-scholars: there 'expositam Graecorum voluminum struem evertimus,' which included all the best known philosophers, orators, historians and poets.

[3] 'Quattuor prolixas orationes,' he calls them: Mehus, *Ambros.*, p. 419.

at leisure. He sent after me to my lodging several Greek MSS., the Laws, the Republic and Epistles of Plato, a volume of Chrysostom, besides another work of St Augustine."

They were to become very dear friends, Ambrogio and Vittorino: "mecum est jugiter," says Ambrogio, "quantum per occupationes summas licet." This was their first meeting, and their intimacy ripened into cordial affection. The books thus commissioned for Niccolo were destined to form part of that most valuable collection of MSS. which passed into the hands of the Medici and so ultimately became the nucleus of the great Laurentian Library[1]. It is not possible however to identify any one of the volumes mentioned either from the Hand-list of 1536 or from Bandini. We see that within ten years Vittorino has become recognised as an important source from which texts may be secured. Niccolo himself had been on a visit to Vittorino a year before (1431) and writing to Ambrogio[2] tells him how deeply he is impressed by his host's learning and character. He had drawn from Vittorino a promise to spare one of the Greek copyists at work at Mantua for a similar position under Niccolo in Florence. But the true distinction of Vittorino's library would seem to date from the accession of Theodore Gaza to the staff in 1441[3], or early in 1442. Gaza was the finest transcriber of Greek MSS. Italy has ever known. He seems to have worked steadily at the editing of important authors, adding in some cases paraphrase or abstract as an aid to scholars. His scholarship enabled him to present a text far superior in accuracy to those produced during the previous five centuries; his services were much in

---

[1] Niccolo was the first to conceive the idea of a public library to be open to all students. He had always avowed his intention of placing it under the control of the Camaldolese monastery, of which Order Ambrogio was General.

[2] July 8, 1431. Mehus, *Ambr. Travers.*, p. 353.

[3] This date follows from the fact that he went to Ferrara in 1444: Sassuolo's 'nuper' must be interpreted in this case rather broadly.

request to supply the needs of the Mantuan School[1]. His
famous codex[2] of the Iliad 'cum perpetua paraphrasi inter-
lineari' in the Laurentian Library, and a Diodorus Siculus[3],
also in his hand, were produced for Filelfo[4], the friend who
had introduced him to Vittorino[5]. The catalogue of Vittorino's library was long preserved amongst the archives of the
Municipio of Mantua until it shared the fate of that invaluable
collection of documents, scattered, sold as waste paper or
destroyed, in 1830. Our record is, as has been seen, very
fragmentary. We should be glad to be able to compile such a
list of the books which he habitually used as we may form,
from his correspondence, of Guarino's[6] working library. The
books themselves Vittorino bequeathed to his pupil Jacopo
Cassiano[7] of Cremona, who for a time carried on the Mantuan
school in succession to its founder. But not a few appear to
have been carried off by his pupils as mementoes of the
Master, an appropriation sanctioned by opinion in that, as
perhaps also in a later, age[8].

[1] Sassuolo (Guasti, p. 40) speaks of the peculiar advantage of Vittorino's school accruing from Gaza's work as copyist.

[2] Described in Bandini, ii. 121. 2. This MS. was already in the
Medicean Library in 1534 (*Index Bibl. Med.*, p. 23).

[3] Bandini, ii. 677. 8.

[4] Upon the high value which Filelfo placed upon this precious possession, see Voigt, i. 400 and reff. there.

[5] Other MSS. in Gaza's hand are traced by Nolhac, *La Biblioth. de
F. Orsini*, p. 145.

[6] See Sabbad., *Museo Ital. di Antichità Classica*, Firenze, 1887, II. ii.
373 upon Latin Codices forming part of Guarino's library as inferred from
his letters. Nolhac has done the same, more elaborately, for Petrarch's
collection, 'la première bibliothèque de la Renaissance' (*Pétr. et l'humanisme*, Paris, 1892). This research into the notices of libraries and the fate
of MSS. is a necessity to the true history of scholarship, but much yet
remains unattempted.

[7] Platina, p. 25.

[8] Vittorino's creditors endeavoured to recover such borrowings, but
even with the aid of the Marquis scarcely succeeded. Giampietro, who kept
several books, was a man of the highest character. Luzio, *op. cit.*, p. 340.

The relations subsisting between Vittorino and the Gonzaga family have been already touched upon. From the outset Vittorino had demanded a position of independence and authority. The promises which then satisfied him seem to have been creditably fulfilled. Francesco Gonzaga was, no doubt, anxious to perpetuate the literary distinction which accrued to his House from its associations with Petrarch half a century earlier. He was also aware of the lustre which the presence of the most successful schoolmaster of the times brought to his court. Moreover, we know that his wife Paola di Malatesta[1], in spite of her ominous name, was a most devoted mother and a woman of deep religious feeling. The inner life of the palace was distinctly reputable. "I well remember," writes Corraro to Cecilia in 1443, "the surroundings amidst which you passed your childhood. I was an inmate of the palace at the time when you were born, and I had ample opportunity of knowing the affection, the care and the honourable example, amidst which you grew up. In the Palace no wanton luxury was permitted: self restraint was encouraged in all matters of food, of dress, and of habits of life. No parasites or flatterers found a place there, nor was immodest or indecorous amusement permitted[2]." We are able to form a very pleasant picture of the relations of Vittorino to the Marquis and the Lady Paola from a fragment of the correspondence which was in all likelihood regularly conducted between them in the frequent absence of Gianfrancesco, on his adventures in war or diplomacy, or on the occasions when Vittorino took his charges to Goito or Borgoforte, to escape the summer heats of Mantua. The Marquis, as we should expect, is of a bluff soldierly temper, very anxious for news of his boys, but leaving all details to his wife. When, however, Vittorino falls ill he evidently gives orders that everything

[1] She was daughter of Malatesta, Lord of Pesaro, and sister-in-law of Baptista di Montefeltro: see p. 119 below: and Vespasiano, iii. 296 (note).

[2] The letter, in Mart. et Durand, iii. 829 seq.

needful shall be most carefully supplied : when he is ill himself, and near to death, he writes from his sick-bed to Vittorino, 'Deum igitur pro recta valetudine nostra saepissime, ut scribitis, exorate, quoniam vestris orationibus plurimum fidei habemus' (Sept. 2, 1444)[1]. Again he is anxious for news of Alessandro, the delicate child of the family, and writes thanking Vittorino for his encouraging news[2], and for his care in devising special forms of exercise to suit the invalid. Several times we have notices of remissions of judicial penalties on Vittorino's intercession. And though there were boisterous fits[3], when Vittorino had occasion to make a decided protest against a dubious type of humour in which the Marquis could, like other soldiers of fortune, indulge himself at table, we may feel that Vittorino had, on the whole, good grounds for his respect for his patron.

It was natural, however, that Vittorino should in the matter of the young princes' progress come more into contact with the Marchioness Paola than with her husband. We have fortunately preserved to us a very few letters of Vittorino written to her, apparently in 1439[4], upon matters affecting the school. They are simple, straightforward letters, never intended for the public eye, and therefore far more interesting than formal epistles. We have in them, and in certain extracts from the Registri Economici, or household accounts of the

---

[1] Luzio, p. 337.

[2] Id., *l. c.* "placet nobis permaxime quod Alexander recte se habeat."

[3] Prendilacqua, who knew the house and family intimately, is careful to record the firmness with which Vittorino dealt with these lapses when his charges were present.

[4] One short note belongs to the year 1437, but refers only to the gift of a small property at Rivalta by the Marquis to Vittorino, (" Ex Burgoforti XXI. Martii"). Paola had apparently paid Vittorino the graceful compliment of making a copy in her own hand of the official deed. Another letter relates to acts of trespass committed by a neighbour on this property, which act of injustice he asks the Marchioness to see redressed in his own absence with the children. Luzio, p. 333.

palace, still surviving the disasters which have overtaken the Mantuan records, evidence of a direct personal concern in the details of the school. In the very first months of Vittorino's engagement (Dec. 1423) we find an entry of the cost of a 'mantello' given by his direction to Ognibene da Lonigo, of whom we shall speak again, one of the poor scholars from whom no fees were asked.

To Paola frequent reports are sent of the progress of the children, of whom Alessandro, the youngest, seems to have possessed the most marked intelligence and the finest type of character. There are allusions to affectionate concern for the safety of the Marquis engaged (1439) in a dangerous adventure against Venice. But we have also signs of a misunderstanding with the Lady Paola. Vittorino has quarrelled with the Matron, who was, we suppose, appointed by the Marchioness : and he says bluntly, " nec [illam] amplius pati possum, nec si possem volo." Vittorino regarded it as in some way essential to the welfare of the school that she should be discharged. Perhaps the Lady Paola demurred. But whatever the motive, we have from Vittorino a letter of respectful remonstrance. He has never taken thought of aught but his duty towards herself, the Marquis, their children, the School. He was deeply attached to them and their House. Had he been actuated by other aims, 'alia erat via uberior si illis animum applicare voluissem.' He is particularly anxious that the Marchioness should understand the grounds of his request, when he is confident she will agree to his wish. But the temper of these short letters is so frank and unaffected that we infer at once a relation of respect and confidence never seriously impaired on either side by passing difference of opinion. More than that, we are by them allowed a significant glimpse of the inner side of Court life at this period of the Renaissance, which contrasts pleasantly with the highly coloured and distorted pictures in which the Italy of that day is often portrayed.

Paola, moreover, was devoted to works of charity and piety
in the City; we are told[1] that she spent much time in personal
visitation of the sick and the poor, whom she consoled not by
word alone. Her deep sympathy for suffering made her a
warm supporter of the Observantia, or restored discipline of
the Franciscan Order as preached by San Bernardino of Siena,
and under her influence Mantua became one of its most
important centres[2]. In this work she found a co-adjutor in
Vittorino whose own feelings warmed readily to sickness or
distress. This tie of a common charity strengthened the
respect and confidence with which the mother of Cecilia
regarded Vittorino.

It was in relation to Cecilia that Vittorino's position in the
councils of the family was most strikingly illustrated. As her
girlhood advanced she manifested a strong desire to take the
veil. We must remember that apart from its attraction for a
devout spirit the religious life was still the one sure refuge to a
woman of studious instincts. There is no doubt that Vittorino
had watched the growth of this intention with at least silent
approval. He had lent to her a tractate[3] of Chrysostom 'In
vituperatores vitae monasticae,' probably knowing the intention taking shape in her mind. Perhaps no recorded fact
of his career throws so strong a light upon the religious temper
of Humanist education, as he understood it, than the part
he took in combating the objections of the Marquis to his
daughter's wish. In the spring of 1443 we find Vittorino
escorting the Lady Paola to Rome; he is staying in Florence,

---

[1] Castiglione, Mehus, *Ambrogio Traversari*, ccccix.

[2] Guarino was also very friendly towards the Observance: the Orders
seem to have left Vittorino in peace: although there was a strain of
opposition to him in Florence, perhaps amongst the Dominicans. Sassuolo
da Prato (ed. Guasti), p. 18.

[3] See the letters of Paul of Sarzana to Ambrogio (Mehus, *Amb. Trav.*,
p. 1037) in which he reports that he had sent this tract to Vittorino who
made a copy of it: 'is principis liberis et potissimum *cuidam adolescentulae*
Latinis Graecisque satis eruditae legere velle aiebat.' The translation was
the work of Ambrogio himself. Ball. Coll. MSS. cliv.

where he sees Vespasiano[1] and has a long conversation with him, and others took this rare opportunity of meeting one of whom they had heard so much. In all probability the visit to Rome had reference to Cecilia's determination which was strongly favoured by her mother. Corraro, the pupil of Vittorino to whom reference has just been made, was now an ecclesiastic of position, and at Florence held a conference with Paola upon the subject of her journey. At Vittorino's urgent request, 'assistebat namque illacrymans prae gaudio ut solet[2],' Corraro wrote to Cecilia consoling her in the conflict of duty. The journey to Rome, where Vittorino saw Eugenius IV. and was greeted by him in terms of honour and respect which shew that his fame had passed beyond the circle of scholars, was of no effect. But the Marquis died in the following year[3], and Cecilia thereupon carried out her desire.

Vittorino was confronted with another task scarcely less difficult in attempting to bring about a reconciliation between the Marquis Gonzaga and his eldest son Ludovico. Vittorino had had charge of the heir of the House since his tenth year and had discharged this responsible duty with much discretion but with unswerving firmness[4]. Vittorino himself had no difficulty in winning his confidence and affection which, in spite of the boy's quarrel with his father, he never lost. Ludovico, though the eldest son, was not regarded by his father as the soldier of the family and was in consequence usually left at home to represent the Marquis when the Condottiere was engaged in fighting, or more often, manœuvring,

---

[1] Sass. da Prato (ed. Guasti), p. 19. The little memoir of Vittorino by Vespasiano is interesting though of slight value. Vesp. da Bisticci, *Vite degli Uomini Illustri* (ed. 1893), ii. p. 222.

[2] The letter of Corraro quoted above, p. 73 ; Mart. et Dur., iii. p. 829.

[3] September, 1444. Paola and Cecilia both took the veil upon the death of Gianfrancesco.

[4] From a letter of Guarino addressed to Ludovico Gonzaga we may gather that the control under which the young prince had been trained before Vittorino's arrival was far from satisfactory. Sabbadini, *Guarino*, p. 75.

for his clients, the Venetian State. Carlo, the second son, was not seldom his father's companion, and the jealousy thus aroused drove Ludovico to seek service under Filippo Maria Visconti, who, though friendly with the Gonzaga, was none the less actually at war with Venice. This happened in 1436. Ludovico protested that he had no other intention but that of learning the art of war which his father so studiously closed against him. The appearance of bad faith in which Gianfrancesco was thus involved rendered him extremely bitter against his son. On his refusal to return to his home and to his allegiance the Marquis disinherited him with the Imperial consent, and even condemned him to death for contumacy and treason. Many were the expostulations addressed to the Gonzaga; amongst them letters from Poggio and Guarino full of classical allusions and virtuous maxims. But when neither friends, nor even wife and children could avail to reconcile the father to forgiveness, (for Ludovico had been easily brought by his old master to see and confess the error he had committed,) Vittorino, by firmly reproving the unnatural cruelty of his conduct and scorning all threats of consequences, won in the end a hard-earned consent from the Marquis to his son's return to favour[1]. The reconciliation proved sincere and final; it was a source of unaffected joy to Vittorino and in the eyes of all a signal triumph of his influence.

It is interesting to note the affectionate respect which Ludovico, who for the last eighteen months of Vittorino's life was head of the House, and his brothers, always manifested towards Vittorino. His advice or his reproof was never resented even if expressed in decided terms or in the presence of others. Carlo, the second son, had been as a boy severely

[1] There is a record of the affectionate zeal of Vittorino on behalf of Ludovico in one of his letters to Paola, in which he refers to some negotiation actually in progress with the Duke of Milan. The young wife of the exiled prince, Barbara of Brandenburg, was a pupil of Vittorino, and it is evident that she found in him a great support in her anxiety. Luzio, p. 336.

rebuked in the presence of the whole school for unbecoming speech—for such offences Vittorino had a swift discipline—but nothing seems to have disturbed the affectionate confidence with which all the young princes alike looked up to their master. For Alessandro, the youngest, his affection was deep-seated; in some ways the delicate, highly strung lad was his master's favourite pupil. The brothers are said by Platina to have been, at least during Vittorino's lifetime, singularly devoted to each other in spite of the estrangement of 1436, and this we may fairly ascribe in part to Vittorino's influence. The picture we have of them and of their master at Goito a few years earlier was no doubt typical of their relations with him. On the day of Vittorino's funeral the princes of the House were conspicuous amongst the crowd of sincere mourners gathered at his grave.

In the city of Mantua Vittorino was, we are told, held in profound veneration. He thoroughly identified himself with his adopted city. He had thrown open his school to ability without distinction of rank and provided an education free of all charges to many deserving boys. He treated all on one and the same footing and had no higher interest than their success. The poor he visited as a friend, and he aided distress so liberally that at his death he left no substance behind him that his heirs cared to claim. His gifts to churches were continuous, though made without ostentation, and often secretly. He was known to be a watchful power at Court on the side of mercy and good government: for he had never lost sight of the motive which had been prominent in bringing him to Mantua—that in moulding the character and guiding the conduct of a prince lay a sure opportunity of benefiting his fellow men. He was thus a practical example of the truest doctrine which actuated the Humanist teachers of the first period of the Revival. For it was manifest that Vittorino's ideal was the patriotic and the well-equipped citizen rather than the self-contained scholar, and we, as we read the memorials that have been left to us by men who knew him, realize not less clearly that, with Vittorino at least, scholarship was no excuse for aloofness from the common duties and sympathies of life.

Vittorino stands in contrast to other Humanists of his day in that his activity was confined to three cities, Padua, Venice, and Mantua. Partly as a consequence of this, his circle of acquaintances amongst scholars seems to have been a small one. He might easily have extended it had he encouraged the practice of literary correspondence. Guarino has left to us at least six hundred letters, some of which are to be found in manuscript in nearly every University library of Western Europe. Poggio, Ambrogio and Filelfo spent a large part of their working hours in elaborating tedious epistles, classical in form, if often somewhat empty of content, addressed to their friends or patrons[1]. Of Vittorino but six letters have been preserved: others, especially a series to Ambrogio[2], were highly prized by his friends in Florence, but they have disappeared. He avowed that he felt no call to add to the bulk of written matter, and we can certainly admit that, to judge from the correspondence of contemporary scholars which has been handed down to us, his reputation has suffered little from this self-restraint. His relations, however, with those scholars with whom he came in contact were of singular friendliness. In an age marked by the bitterness of its 'quarrels of authors,' Vittorino notoriously was never spoken of but in terms of respect or affection. It was in fact impossible to quarrel with Vittorino[3].

---

[1] Klette writes on this subject: 'We must not be surprised to find how much the formal expression of friendship, courtesy or adulation overshadows the element of actual fact in learned correspondence. Hence is explained the frequent want of dates' &c. *Beit.* iii. p. 9.

[2] Platina, p. 27.

[3] Castiglione is very emphatic, Mehus, *Amb. Trav.*, p. ccccix. : 'detestabatur plurimum quae ab aliis invective scribebantur.'

Niccoli, who offended nearly every one by his intolerable patronage, who in 1400 drove Chrysoloras from Florence[1], and embittered the temper of the mild-mannered Guarino[2], could hardly find words to express his veneration for the simple and earnest nature of Vittorino. He, indeed, it was who brought Ambrogio and Vittorino together, initiating a life-long friendship. Ambrogio Traversari, the Superior of the Camaldolese Order in Florence, was Vittorino's closest friend. He visited him, as we have seen, at Mantua and at Goito some three or four times between 1432 and 1435. He was attracted not less by his character than by his scholarship[3]; and in religious interests they had much in common. Ambrogio records the parting with Vittorino at the close of his first visit to him at Mantua. "We were on the point of starting. The sun had not yet risen, when Vittorino appeared at the gate, on horseback, with two or three young companions. He escorted us for the first three miles of our journey, during which he kept close by my side with all courtesy." In the words of Ambrogio, 'Totus illi sermo de literis, de probitate, de modestia, de religione, de viris nostrae aetatis illustribus'.

Ambrogio does not hesitate to ask his aid in recovering to the Order the buildings and endowments of a House which had been diverted from their founder's intention. He knows no one more likely to be interested in such a work of justice, no one whose influence with the Lord of Mantua (in whose territory it stood) would so certainly avail. Vittorino replies to him in a letter which is the only one of its kind which

---

[1] Klette, *Beit.* i. 52.

[2] Sabbad., *Epistolario*, p. 59. 'Il Niccoli era uomo impastato di invidiuzze di puntigli pretensiosi, di prepotenzuole, che finirono per seccar Guarino, il quale era molto prudente, molto paziente, ma si stancava anche lui.' It was due to Niccoli that Guarino left Florence in 1414.

[3] Vid. the letters already quoted, especially Mart. et Dur., iii. p. 353. "Condimentum humanitatis" is Ambrogio's expression respecting his learning. Cf. Ambrogio, *Hodoeporicon*, p. 34.

has come down to us and which may for its author's sake be given here.

Doleo equidem, praestantissime vir, cum tuarum vero literarum causa, quas augere in dies et sacris praeceptis ornare destitisti nunquam, dum tibi per otium licuit, ut jam ex Graecis hausta Doctoribus complura abs te edita volumina legantur. Doleo, inquam, te tantis nunc negotiis premi ut ad ea obeunda honestissima studia nihil tibi quidquam temporis supersit. Sed est quid me consoler, teque pariter tua prudentia consoleris, quod egregie praeter caeteros magnos et excellentes viros gerendis in rebus plurimum de virtute mereris, cum et Rhetoris nostri nunc quidem sententia virtutis laus omnis in actione consistat[1]. Sed haec ipse melius. Vellem sane is tibi videri posse cuius et auxilio et ministerio utereris. Neque enim praeceptis tuis desisterem sed in hac re tamen me id profecisse scias, ut hic domnus Jacobus Alborandus consentiat, ut cum Monachis sanctae Brigidae vestri Monachi disceptent quoniam id ipse facere haud sine dedecore possit ut illis, quod semel ratum fecerit, nunc solvere ac rumpere videatur. Quod si vos quidquam obtinueritis certissimum est itaque spondet hac de re quicquid ipse decernam, id omne firmare, modo si eadem conditio maneat, quae nunc hisce cum Monachis perstat, quod et ipse tuis literis procul dubio polliceris. Non enim illum possessione eiicere, sed ad proprios possessores possessionem traducere quaeris. Res ita acta est et hactenus deducta. Erunt tibi cetera curae. Ego tibi quantulumcumque possim pollicerer, sed tuam in me caritatem spero nulla ista pollicitatione indigere, quae jam diu fecit ut tibi omnis omnino deditus sim. Vale. Ex Mantua pridie Idus Dec.[2]

The correspondence of Poggio on the other hand reveals to us the irritable vanity, the pompous self-importance, which marked certain of the scholars who had reached celebrity.

---

[1] This expression of Cicero is not uncommon amongst Humanists : it is significant as an indication of the practical aim which most of them, at this period, set before their scholars. Cf. Aen. Sylv., *De Liber. Educ.* (Op., p. 989).

[2] Mitarelli, *Bibl. Codd. S. Michaelis* (Ven. 1779), p. 1207. It is a reply to the letters from Ambrogio given in Mehus.

We do not know when Vittorino and Poggio made personal acquaintance, but it was after 1436[1]. The quarrel between Gianfrancesco Gonzaga and his eldest son, which caused so much pain and anxiety to Vittorino, called forth a remarkable letter from Poggio to the Marquis of Mantua, upbraiding him, in irreproachable Latinity, with his conduct towards Ludovico. This he enclosed in a covering letter to Vittorino, whom he asked to present it formally to his patron. Now Vittorino was just as anxious to bring about a reconciliation as Poggio was to turn it to account for self-advertisement; so knowing the certain result of publicly reading to the Gonzaga a stilted pedantic tirade, of which the writer had already distributed sundry copies to scholars at neighbouring courts, Vittorino prudently, in the interests of Ludovico, kept back the letter. He thought it wiser to await the effect of his own more tactful intervention. This delay, which apparently he did not think it necessary to explain to his correspondent, produced intense irritation in Poggio, who thereupon wrote to Vittorino in the following strain[2].

Poggio to Vittorino.

" It is scarcely thoughtful or kind of you to have delayed so long in presenting my letter to the Marquis. It would have been an easy matter to have handed it to him with his other correspondence. For it is my habit to set forth plainly, on my own authority, convictions which I have formed : and you will hardly say that they are in this case lacking in sense, or inelegantly expressed. If you were afraid of the effect of my communication you might have at least returned it ; how else explain this long delay in putting it before your patron ? You

---

[1] This follows from certain expressions in Poggio's letter of remonstrance.

[2] I have used the copy contained in the MS. volume of letters of Poggio (p. 252) preserved in the Athenaeum Library, Liverpool. Portions only are given by Rosmini, *Vittorino da Feltre*, p. 223.

may, of course, allege the absence of fitting opportunity : or
you may have yielded to a base fear of some outburst of
temper on part of the Marquis. If that is the case, the
Marquis is not the man I had imagined him: nor can I
speak with respect of a man who resents out-spoken advice.
I should have thought his reading wide enough to have
shewn him the wisdom of following such an example as
that of Sulla, who recognised the literary merit of the satirist
even when smarting under his wit. For myself I do not lay
claim to learning nor to wisdom. But I have read much,
I have heard much, and I have seen much : and I am confident that I wrote nothing inconsistent with the proper pride
of the Marquis, nothing unworthy of myself. If he object to
read my letter, it will certainly be handed " (it had of course
been handed long ago !) " to others who will peruse it eagerly,
and will not think it undeserving of minute study. When
they hear that your patron declined the same task they will
assuredly abate something of their opinion of his judgement.
I may indeed say that no little credit has accrued to me from
this very letter already : without referring to any other critic,
the Pope has expressed himself much pleased with its style.

So I send you another copy, and with it three further
epistles, all addressed to the Marquis on the same subject,
on the chance that he may now have seen the error of his
previous conduct in declining my advice. I regret much
that I have been compelled to write to you in such terms.
But I, at least, have nothing to reproach myself with."

In spite of this correspondence Poggio had the highest
respect for Vittorino: he shewed it, as Platina tells us, by
confiding to his care one of his own sons, prizing both the
watchful care and sound instruction which he thereby secured[1].

The same course was followed by Filelfo[2], another difficult

---

[1] Supra p. 30.

[2] I am unable to give either the name of the son, or the date.

subject. He had probably made acquaintance with Vittorino, his senior by some years, when acting as deputy for Gasparino Barzizza in 1416 or 1417. We know that at a later period he was instrumental in establishing Theodore Gaza, and possibly also George of Trebizond, at Mantua. With the latter he kept up a regular correspondence during his residence with Vittorino as master of Greek. This, and his close relations with Gaza, gave him ample opportunity of realising the greatness of Vittorino as a man and as a teacher. We have no record of their meeting, but friendly messages[1] came through others to Vittorino from Filelfo, who, when his son was growing up, could find no master to whom he would entrust him more readily[2]. There must, however, have been much in Filelfo's character which had little attraction for Vittorino.

It will be enough now to refer to his friendship for Guarino. The acquaintance of the two men dated, as we have seen, at least from the time of Guarino's residence at Venice in 1414[3]. Guarino referred[4] in later years to the intercourse which subsisted between them at that period when they read Greek and Latin authors together with mutual benefit. Guarino did not hesitate to write in the highest terms to Gonzaga of Vittorino's character and powers: he congratulated Ludovico on the noble temper of his preceptor. Whether these two famous school-masters, who were near neighbours for a large part of their lives—Guarino's work after 1418 lay always at

---

[1] E.g. through Trapezuntius: 'ἀσπάσαι Οὐικτορῖνον ὡς φίλτατα,' Klette, iii. 105.

[2] Supra p. 30.

[3] Probably indeed much earlier; Guarino had been at Padua during the earlier years of Vittorino's residence there: and was occasionally at the University after his return from Constantinople in 1408.

[4] Sabbadini, *Guarino*, quotes from a letter to Ludovico Gonzaga, 1424. 'If he calls me his master it is more than I have a right to, and it proceeds from the goodness and gratitude of his nature. I taught him but little, though he loves to dwell upon the service I rendered him.' *Vita di Guar.* p. 75.

Verona or Ferrara—carried on any active correspondence we do not know[1]; it is however unlikely: nor have we any definite ground for thinking that they co-operated in any way in editing books or texts[2]. But Guarino, himself a scholar and eager to train up his sons in learning, sent his boy Gregorio to Vittorino; and this we may safely regard as a further piece of expert testimony to Vittorino's ability.

Allusion has already been made to the impress which Vittorino left upon such scholars of the latter half of the fifteenth century as had been his pupils. I would refer especially to the men who were chiefly active in Latin scholarship. The Ciceronian tradition securely established by Barzizza at Padua and Milan was definitely accepted by Vittorino. George of Trebizond was in Latin learning a typical pupil of Vittorino, and we may confidently say that he was an abler scholar than Guarino and that his work on Rhetoric[3] had a profound influence upon the teaching of style. Valla was one of the first pupils[4] of Vittorino. His Latin scholarship was undoubtedly distinguished and his services in furthering it are perhaps as yet scarcely estimated aright. It was Valla[5] who definitely displaced the inaccurate

[1] A letter, hitherto unnoticed, (Brit. Mus. Harl. MSS. 2570 f. 175) from Guarino to Karolus Brugnolus, a pupil of promise to whom Vittorino gave special private instruction, contains an affectionate greeting to Vittorino.

[2] Prendilacqua says that they did so: but no particulars are given and we have no confirmation of the statement from any source. Certainly nothing of the kind has survived.

[3] On the repute of G. of Trebizond as a Rhetorician, see the letter of Porcia (Comes Purliliensis) *Epist. Famil.* vi. ci., written towards the very end of the 15th century: "ut reliquos rhetoricae artis scriptores in praesentia omittam, Ciceronem, Quintilianum, Aristotelem et Trapezuntium."

[4] The presence of Valla at the School of Vittorino rests upon the authority of Platina alone : and the fact is doubted by the biographer of Lorenzo Valla, Mancini, *Vita di L.V.*, p. 12, who admits that he cannot explain how Platina with his intimate knowledge of the School could have made the mistake.

[5] On the influence of Valla and Perotti on the teaching of Latin, Benoist, *De puer. erud.*, p. 71, may be read in confirmation of what is urged in the text.

and incomplete grammar books of mediaeval Latinists (such as Alexander de Villa Dei) from the new schools. But he did not himself write a grammar. That was the work of Nicholas Perotti who had been one of the later pupils of the Mantuan school[1], and who had so brilliant a subsequent career first as Professor of Rhetoric at Bologna and later as Pontifical secretary. In 1468 after completing his translation of Polybius he wrote his great manual of Latin Grammar which was printed through the agency of his friend and fellow pupil, John, Bishop of Aleria, by Sweynheym and Pannarzt at Rome in 1473— a magnificent folio. Grammar and Rhetoric are now combined and the main lines of Latin Grammar, accidence, syntax, prosody, as understood for centuries afterwards, were for the first time determined. Grammar[2] is now defined: 'est ars recte loquendi recteque scribendi, scriptorum et poetarum lectionibus observata.' 'Quattuor sunt partes grammatices: Littera: syllaba: dictio: et oratio.' Grammar thus defined is 'initium et fundamentum omnium disciplinarum.' It is important to notice that Erasmus[3] has no hesitation in praising the Grammar of Perotti as the most complete manual extant in his day. Perotti wrote also a tractate[4], 'De puerorum eruditione,' which has never been printed, and which has perhaps altogether disappeared. It would be interesting to us as giving the experience of one trained under Vittorino at his best[5].

Ognibene da Lonigo, who became a school-master, and from 1449—1453 occupied Vittorino's place at Mantua[6], wrote a

---

[1] Perotti entered the School in 1443.   [2] These are taken from the second page of the *Grammatices Rudimenta*.   [3] *Erasmi Opera*, i. 521 C.

[4] Vid. Fabricius (J. A.), *Bibl. Lat.* (ed. Mansi, Patav. 1754) v. 124. I have not been able to trace a reference to a copy in any Library. The British Museum contains an Elizabethan (1598) list of books upon Education which includes Perotti 'De puerorum eruditione': Harl. MSS. 4043. f. 16. I have not found any other reference to the work except that of Fabricius, who does not give his source of information, and the statement of the Nuremberg Chronicle (1493, f. 232 *v.*) that Perotti wrote such a tract.

[5] Perotti was for a time in the service of Card. Bessarion, and forms thus a personal link between Vittorino and the great patron of Greek learning.   [6] Davari, *Notizie Storiche*, p. 8.

small Grammar[1] which he dedicated to Francesco Gonzaga. It was a school book and was drawn up on the lines of Vittorino's oral method of Grammar teaching.

But the most interesting figure of all is that of John, Bishop of Aleria. The position which he occupies in the history of scholarship is unique. For to him fell a lot whose distinction can again happen to no one: he prepared for the great Roman press the Editiones Principes of the chief monuments of Latin literature. In one year, 1469, he edited the works of Caesar, Aulus Gellius, Livy, Lucan and Vergil. Then followed in 1470 the Epistles of Cicero: a volume of his Orations, and Ovid, appeared in 1471. This was by no means the limit of his scholarly activity. But the mere recital of these names exhibits the distinction which belongs to Aleria in the history of learning, and at the same time confirms our respect for the Master to whom he so affectionately attributes whatever capacity in scholarship he possessed[2].

Vittorino, absorbed always in the many sided work of the school, became thus, unconsciously perhaps, one of the most powerful formative influences of the Renaissance. La Giocosa was at once a centre of erudition, a school of wide and varied training, the seat of a noble discipline of manners and of character. Another " Accademia," Castiglione named it : so marvellous a combination of wisdom and learning, of

[1] *De octo partibus orationis.* Padua, 1473, is the date of the first edition. In his preface he refers to Vittorino: ' aetatis huius tam sanctitate vitae quam doctrina praestantissimum '...'ut litterarum magister esset simul et vivendi praeceptor.' One half of the book, which is very elementary, is in form of question and answer.

[2] The only scholar of Vittorino who forms in any sense a link between him and our own country was Antonio Beccaria, who on leaving Mantua entered the service of Duke Humphrey. On the fall of his patron he returned to Italy, much the poorer, in pocket at least, for his experience. After the fashion of the time he translated Plutarch into Latin ; he did the same for the Ethics of Aristotle. But he was chiefly known for his elegies of an amorous sort. He seems to have been a rather fierce controversialist on the Humanist side. Vid. Prendil., p. 54.

skill in teaching, of self-devotion, of bright and attractive surroundings had no parallel since ancient times. To Vittorino's school was first applied, in modern days, the well-known simile of the Trojan horse giving forth its hidden band of heroes. Originally spoken of the school of Isocrates at Athens, the comparison was a favourite one with the Humanists, who used it to describe the school of Guarino at Ferrara, Colet's school at St Paul's and many others.

As old age drew on, Vittorino won more and more the affection of his scholars and the respect of his fellow Humanists. Gianfrancesco Gonzaga was dead. Ludovico his son accorded to his old Master no less confidence than his father had done, tinged with a certain veneration alike graceful and sincere. We can picture to ourselves the spare ascetic figure, perhaps below the middle height, active still and vigorous, the keen straight glance, the dress plain and simple as became a scholar, the 'tonaca' of sombre cloth or common fur, the plain sandals. In spite of the severe strain of work and the rigid discipline of body, from which, even in the fiercest extremes of climate, he never swerved, his health had been until 1444 uniformly good. He rarely left home except for his yearly visit to Goito or the Lake of Garda. He took no little pride in his ownership of a small property outside the city walls given to him probably by the Gonzaga: for it contained within its bounds the site venerated as marking the very birthplace of Vergil himself. We cannot well imagine any one to whom such an association would have appealed more powerfully than to Vittorino.

Vittorino's health had been poor during the autumn of 1444, and in 1445 he was seized with the low-fever which then as now haunted the valley of the Mincio. The attack was a severe one, but his constitution, fortified as it was by lifelong habits of temperate self-restraint, enabled him to throw off the malady. Early in the following year, however, the fever recurred with graver symptoms. He was now nearly 69 years of age. Conscious that his work was over, he resigned himself to contemplation, and so awaited the end. He died on February the second, 1446. According to his express wish no ceremonial pomp was observed at his burial. His body was placed in the church of San Spirito, by the side of his mother, who, it would seem, had spent her last days near her famous son. The princes of the House and a great concourse of pupils and of citizens attended to mourn the loss of one who had been, to some amongst them at least, the truest friend and the most powerful influence for good which their lives had known.

Scholars scattered throughout Italy and beyond, knew that a great loss had befallen not themselves only but the whole world of learning. 'Non uni civitati...sed universae Graeciae atque Italiae mors haec acerba et lamentabilis,' says Platina[1]. For Vittorino had lived as he had indeed desired to live, a truly devoted life. His unselfishness, his contempt for vulgar reputation or merely material success, which distinguished him from most of his fellow scholars, was manifest in all that he did. It was found after his death that his promises of help for needy scholars or for pious works had mortgaged even the income which he had not lived to receive.

Thus passed away one of the most attractive of all the personalities which meet us in an age conspicuous, above all things, for its manifold types of activity and character. In an age of bitter rivalries he made no enemy. With ample opportunity of self indulgent ease he remained always, as his pupils boasted, 'divitiarum contemptor.' In an atmosphere of moral upheaval, here and there, indeed, of semi-pagan licence, he kept a high standard of personal purity and of religion. The courage, sincerity and simplicity of his nature struck all who came to know him. Even Filelfo, envious, sarcastic as he was, could but speak of him as καλὸς κἀγαθὸς[2]—a high minded

---

[1] Platina, p. 21.

[2] To George of Trebizond : July 28, 1431: τὸν καλὸν κἀγαθὸν Οὐικτορῖνον ἀσπάσαι ὡς φίλτατα. Klette, *Beit*. iii. p. 105 (ep. 5).

gentleman. Platina[1] laments the character, the piety, the lofty earnestness which are in Vittorino's death lost to the world, never in the same measure to be replaced. To John of Aleria[2] he is 'pater pauperum studiosorum, honestatis specimen, bonitatis exemplum.' Ambrogio[3] has nothing to add to this simple judgement: 'Meliorem illo virum, ausim dicere, nescio an unquam viderim.'

I have endeavoured to indicate the place of Vittorino da Feltre in the history of learning and of education. It is perhaps doubtful whether future research will add materially to the sources of our knowledge of the man and his work. But we can already see that the importance of his position lay partly in his own scholarship and reading, but more in the genius which he manifested in reducing the vast body of re-discovered literature to the service of a new education. It is hard for us to realise, even remotely, the bewildering effects of the stores of ancient learning so suddenly uncovered to view during the century which ended with Vittorino's death. The old ideal of knowledge, the growth of centuries, was replaced, almost within a generation, by a new one, which should correspond in some way with a deeper sense of national continuity, and of the breadth of human interests. But this ideal, hopeful and inspiring as it was, was as yet indefinitely grasped: and the education which should express it was tentative and uncertain. The relation of the new hope to the old faith; the balance between literary form and moral content; the conflict of the Greek ideal of the body and the asceticism of the Church,—here were some of the graver problems which pressed for attention. And side by side with them were questions of practical procedure. Wherein lay the true canon of literary excellence? What was the true function of Logic in education? or what claim to education could be allowed to

---

[1] 'nostri seculi unicum praesidium et ornamentum.' Plat., p. 28.
[2] Praefatio in Livium: Botfield, p. 95.
[3] Ambrogio to Niccoli. Mart. et Dur., iii. 553.

women ? How should a teacher reduce to educational method
and apparatus that ancient learning which, imposing as it was,
was but slowly yielding up the secret of its own criticism and
interpretation ? When in the first years of the fifteenth century
Vittorino began to teach at Padua, questions such as these
were taking shape in the minds of scholars. At his death in
1446 each of them was advancing rapidly and surely to the
solution which satisfied the educated opinion of Western Europe
for the next four hundred years. And if this solution was reached
partly in direct imitation of the practice of the antique world, it
was due in much larger degree to the activity of a very few
men who worked their way to the light by actual experience,
enforced by genius, by strong personality, and by untiring
zeal. Amongst them stands out preeminent in each of these
three main qualities of a great Teacher, the figure of Vittorino.
As in Petrarch we recognise, in M. Renan's words, 'the first
modern Man,' so with no less truth may we claim for the
founder of the Mantuan School the significant title of 'the
first modern Schoolmaster.'

THE TREATISE *DE INGENUIS MORIBUS*
BY PETRUS PAULUS VERGERIUS.

VERGERIUS has been referred to above, p. 14 seqq., in connection with Humanism at Padua during the period when Vittorino da Feltre was residing there.

Vergerius was born at Capo d' Istria in 1349: after spending some years at Padua he removed to Florence, where he taught Logic, and studied Civil and Canon Law. In 1391 we find him again in Padua, as 'Doctor Artium,'[1] as 'Doctor Medicinae,'[2] and as professor of Logic[3]. In his teaching of this latter subject he has broken away from scholastic method, and already gives evidence of an essentially modern treatment of Dialectic, in which he was followed by Vittorino[4]. But he had already at Florence, if not earlier, imbibed the full Humanist enthusiasm. In or soon after the year 1404[5], he composed the Treatise *De ingenuis moribus*[6], for the use of Ubertinus,

[1] Gloria, *Mon. Pad.* ii. 491.

[2] Ibid.

[3] Ibid., p. 493. But Voigt (i. 432) is wrong in saying that he taught at Padua between July 1397 and June 1400 : his name never occurs during those years in the University records. Gloria, ii. 492.

[4] Supra, p. 60. See the important letter in Prof. Combi, *Epist. Verg.* p. 100 and Gloria, ii. 493.

[5] The date fixed by the allusion of Vergerius to the siege of Brescia, 1403 : inf. p. 113. Sabbadini, *La Scuola* &c. p. 29. Rösler, *Kardinal Johannes Dominicis, u.s.w.* p. 75, agrees with Combi in giving 1392 as the date. Combi, p. 40. Novati gives 1399.

[6] The full title given in the earliest editions and in most MSS. runs :

son of Francesco Carrara, the lord of Padua.   This work,
which has been too much overlooked by later students of
the Renaissance[1], was for a century and a half after its
appearance amongst the most widely read of all the productions of the Revival of Letters.   In the sixteenth century
it was diligently studied in schools, as Paulus Jovius[2] records.
Bembo prized it as 'digna philosopho,' Sabellico finds it
'gravissimis respersa sententiis, utpote qui philosophiae prius
operam dedit quam ad scribendum venisset.'   Brucker is
astonished at the knowledge of human nature, and at the
lofty view of the Teacher's function, so much in advance
of that age, which the work reveals.   Prof. Combi[3], the
latest and most ardent student of Vergerius, affirms that he
is 'one of the most illustrious of the long series of Italian
educators, and the first to approach the subject upon the
new lines, and with the larger scope, rendered possible by
the Revival and demanded by the altered conditions of
society.   In this Treatise we find, for the first time, systematically urged and defended, subjects and methods of
instruction hitherto neglected or indeed forbidden.'

Vergerius was a thorough Humanist of the finer type.
His Latinity, natural and unaffected, proves this, as does his
intimacy, revealed by his Letters, with the scholars and
public men who were at the head of the new movement,
Salutato, Barzizza, Zabarella: so too, his wide acquaintance
with classical texts[4]; or the privilege unanimously accorded to
him of composing the epitaph upon the grave of Chrysoloras

'Petri Pauli Vergerii Justino-Politani ad Ubertinum Carariensem de
ingenuis moribus opus praeclarissimum.'   Some MSS. (e.g. Harl. 2678)
have the additional words, 'et liberalibus studiis.'

[1] No edition seems to have been printed after 1700: the only translation I have traced is the Italian one by Prof. E. Michele (1878).

[2] Paolo Giovio, *Elog. Clar. Virorum*, Venet. 1546, p. 68.

[3] *Epistol. di P. P. Vergerio*, p. xix.

[4] Id., p. xlviii.

at the Monastery in Constance; or the denunciation of Carlo Malatesta on his destruction of the statue of Vergil at Mantua[1]. But his most important contribution to classical learning was undoubtedly this Treatise, the main characteristic of which lies in that union of Classical enthusiasm with Christianity[2] which has been the ideal of Humanist education ever since.

The Contents of the Tract fall naturally under the following heads:

§ 1. Introduction. The purport of the Treatise.
§ 2. Concerning Character and its Discipline.
§ 3. Concerning Liberal Studies.
§ 4. Concerning the Manner of Study.
§ 5. Concerning Bodily Exercises and Training in the Art of War.
§ 6. Concerning Recreation.
§ 7. Conclusion.

[1] In full in Combi, *Verg.* p. 113. Cf. p. xxii.
[2] Combi, p. xlvii, and supra, p. 15.

[The history of the earlier editions of Vergerius *De Ingenuis Moribus* is obscure. Combi says that at least twenty editions appeared before 1500; and he examined twenty more of later date. The first edition has latterly been ascribed, by Combi and Michele, to 1472, possibly one of those printed at Brescia. Hain, *15987*, is probably 'Roma, 1473.' Colle is in any case wrong (*Storia dell' Univ. di Pad.* iv. 46) in giving 'Milano, 1474' as the earliest. Dr Copinger, however, informs me that he believes that the *Ed. Pr.* was printed at Venice by Adam de Ambergau in 1470, a copy of which is in his own possession. The Treatise was printed in Louvain in 1485, and in Paris in 1494. The MS. copies are very numerous: it is found generally in conjunction with Plutarch's treatise, as translated by Guarino, and with that of St Basil, in Bruni's version.]

P. P. VERGERIUS TO UBERTINUS OF CARRARA.

§ 1. Your grandfather, Francesco I., a man distinguished for his capacity in affairs and for his sound judgment, was in the habit of saying that a parent owes three duties to his children. The first of these is to bestow upon them names of which they need not feel ashamed. For not seldom, out of caprice, or even indifference, or perhaps from a wish to perpetuate a family name, a father in naming his child inflicts upon him a misfortune which clings to him for life. The second obligation is this: to provide that his child be brought up in a city of distinction, for this not only concerns his future self-respect, but is closely connected with the third and most important care which is due from father to son. This is the duty of seeing that he be trained in sound learning. For no wealth, no possible security against the future, can be compared with the gift of an education in grave and liberal studies. By them a man may win distinction for the most modest name, and bring honour to the city of his birth however obscure it may be. But we must remember that whilst a man may escape from the burden of an unlucky name, or from the contempt attaching to a city of no repute, by changing the one or quitting the other, he can never remedy the neglect of early education. The foundation, therefore, of this last must be laid in the first years of life, the disposition moulded whilst it is susceptible and the mind trained whilst it is retentive.

This duty, common indeed to all parents, is specially incumbent upon such as hold high station. For the lives of men of position are passed, as it were, in public view; and are fairly expected to serve as witness to personal merit and capacity on part of those who occupy such exceptional place amongst their fellow men. You therefore, Ubertinus, the bearer of an illustrious name, the representative of a house for many generations sovereign in our ancient and most learned city of Padua, are peculiarly concerned in attaining this excellence in learning of which we speak. Our name, our birth-place, are not of our own choice. Progress in learning, on the other hand, as in character, depends largely on ourselves, and brings with it its own abiding reward. But I know that I am urging one who needs no spur. Can I say more than this?—continue as you have begun; let the promise of the future be consistent with your performance in the past.

To you, therefore, I have addressed this tractate upon the principles of Learning and of Conduct: by which I intend the subjects and the manner of study in which youth may be best exercised, and the actions which it behoves them to pursue, or to avoid, in the course of their daily life. Although addressed to you, it is intended for all who, blessed by nature with quickened minds and lofty aims, desire to shew by their lives their gratitude for such gifts. For no liberal mind will readily sink into mere sloth or become absorbed in the meaner side of existence.

§ 2. In *judging character* in youth, we recognise, first of all, that it is a mark of soundness in a boy's nature that he is spurred by desire of praise: upon this rests Emulation, which may be defined as rivalry without malice. Next we notice the quality of willing and ready obedience, which in itself is full of promise for future progress, whilst, combined with the love of approbation, it suggests the possibility of the highest excellence. For, as yet, the boy is not of an age to be stimulated by the dictates of reason, which would be, doubtless, (as Plato and Cicero said) the surest motive, but emulation, going along with obedience, supplies that which reason is as yet too weak to give. Again, we prize every sign of alertness, of industry, of thoroughness, in the growing character. As in a horse the mettle which needs neither whip nor spur, so in a boy eagerness for learning, marks a temper from which much may be hoped. Where all these qualities are found united we need have little anxiety as to character at large. Again, we may feel confidently about a boy who shews signs of due shame at punishment or disgrace, or who respects his master in spite of it. The boy, too, who is naturally of a friendly disposition, forgiving, sociable, taking all that is said and done in good part, gives good promise for the future. Perhaps we may add, with Aristotle, that excessive physical energy rarely goes with keen intellectual tastes. Arguments drawn from physiognomy I prefer to leave to others. But we have said enough to shew how bent of character may be recognised in early years. And we may admit that there is often a relation between dignity of mien and loftiness of temper. Socrates suggested that boys should be encouraged to regard themselves in a mirror, that the boy of dignified bearing may feel himself bound to act worthily of it, the boy of less attractive form braced to attain an inner harmony to compensate for his defect. Perhaps, however, we gain surer stimulus from contemplating others than from the reflection of our own selves: as Scipio, Fabius and Caesar kept before their eyes the images of Alexander or other heroes of the past.

If, however, it is helpful to contemplate the outward form of a dead hero, how much more shall we gain from the example of living worth? For it is with character as with instruction: the 'living voice' is of far more avail than the written letter; the life we can observe, the character actually before us, affect us as no other influence can. Let, then, the examples of living men, known and respected for their worth, be held up for a boy's imitation. And, moreover, let those of us who are older not forget so to live that our actions may be a worthy model for the youth who look up to us for guidance and example.

As to the *moral discipline* of the young, we must remember, first, that each age has its peculiar dangers, and next that these are due, in part, to natural bent, in part, to defective training or to inexperience of life. For instance, a boy will be of open-handed and generous disposition, just as he is by virtue of his years of warm and sanguine habit of body : and such a temper we prefer to parsimoniousness. But yet a habit of squandering money thoughtlessly, from indifference to its value, or careless-ness as to the character of those upon whom it is bestowed, must be checked. Again, the same superabundant vitality which, rightly directed, inspires a young man to high endeavour, may, without such guidance, generate a spirit of arrogance, or intoler-able self-conceit. Herein lies that great danger to character, a habit of boasting, which in turn gives rise to a disregard of truth in all relations of life, a fault apt to become ingrained as years roll by. Nothing so injures a young man in the eyes of serious people as exaggeration and untruthfulness. Indeed a master will be well-advised to inculcate generally a habit of speaking little, and seldom, and of answering questions rather than asking them. For a youth who is silent commits at most but one fault, that he *is* silent ; one who is talkative probably commits fifty. Looseness of conversation must be vigorously dealt with, remembering the poet's warning, repeated by St Paul : the natural sense of shame may be successfully appealed to in this matter. Once more, if boys are credulous we may ascribe it to inexperience ; if they change their tastes or opinions, it is due to the flux of the bodily humours, caused by excess of natural heat. This, moreover, produces also that intensity or passion in all that they do which scarcely admits of precepts of moderation, and certainly not of harsh condemna-tion, for it belongs to their age, and has its proper function in early years. To this same natural tendency we may attribute the fickle character of their first friendships.

Children, although for the most part under the unwritten discipline of home, are not to be regarded as outside the control of public regulation. For the education of children is a matter of more than private interest ; it concerns the State, which indeed regards the right training of the young as, in

certain aspects, within its proper sphere. I would wish to
see this responsibility extended. But to come to detail. It
is especially necessary to guard the young from the temptations
natural to their age. For, as has been said, every period of life
has its own besetting sins. Manhood is the age of passion:
middle-life of ambition: old age of avarice. I speak, of course,
in general terms. So, too, we find faults common to boyhood,
which are obvious subjects for Regulations. In order to
maintain a high standard of purity all enticements of dancing,
or suggestive spectacles, should be kept at a distance: and the
society of women as a rule carefully avoided. A bad companion
may wreck the character. Idleness, of mind and body, is a
common source of temptation to indulgence, and unsociable,
solitary temper must be disciplined, and on no account encouraged. Harmful imaginations in some, moroseness and
depression in others, result from want of healthy companionship. Tutors and comrades alike should be chosen from
amongst those likely to bring out the best qualities, to attract
by good example, and to repress the first signs of evil. All
excess in eating and drinking, or in sleep, is to be repressed:
though we must not forget the differing needs of individuals.
But our physical nature should be satisfied only, not pampered.
In the matter of allowing wine to children I should prohibit
its use, except in the smallest quantities, and even then carefully
diluted, with water in the larger proportion. But in no case
is it allowable to eat, drink or sleep up to the point of complete
satisfaction; in all bodily pleasures we must accustom our children
to retain complete and easy control of appetite. Above all, respect for Divine ordinances is of the deepest importance; it should
be inculcated from the earliest years. This reverential temper,
however, must not be forced in such a way that it pass into
unreasoning superstition, which engenders contempt rather
than faith. Profane language is to be held an abominable
sin; and disrespect towards the ceremonies of the Church or
vain swearing must be sternly repressed. Reverence towards

elders and parents is an obligation closely akin. In this, antiquity offers us a beautiful illustration. For the youth of Rome used to escort the Senators, the Fathers of the City, to the Senate House: and awaiting them at the entrance, accompany them at the close of their deliberations on their return to their homes. In this the Romans saw an admirable training in endurance and in patience. This same quality of reverence will imply courtesy towards guests, suitable greetings to elders, to friends and to inferiors. For right bearing in these points is always attractive; and in none more than in the son of a Prince, who must unite in his carriage a certain dignity with a becoming and natural ease. And these details of personal bearing can be learnt by observation, aided by wise guidance. This, indeed, must often take the form of correction, and will, perhaps, be most needed by those who are to be called to the sovereignty of a city or a state. The reproofs of our friends may be likened to a faithful mirror: and he who wilfully refuses to listen to them flings himself thereby into the arms of flatterers. For it is little short of a miracle that a man of wealth, of birth and of station, brought up amidst luxury and ease, should prove himself on all occasions wise and strong; the allurements of pleasure, and the evil influence of parasites, with every opportunity of self-indulgence, leave scarcely a chink by which reason and integrity may force an entrance. Plato, in the *Gorgias*, specially commends the man who in such surroundings can resist temptation. I would have you note that one special source of danger lies in the weak indulgence of parents, which undermines the moral strength of their children; and this is often seen the more conspicuously when the father's stronger hand has been taken away. Therefore I strongly approve of the system under which children liable to such dangers are educated abroad; or if in their own city, in the house of relatives or friends. For as a rule the sense that they are not in their own house checks self-will and imposes a healthy restraint upon boys, and removes, at least, some of the

hindrances which stand between them and full devotion to
those liberal studies which I must now set forth.

§ 3.   We call those studies *liberal* which are worthy of a
free man; those studies by which we attain and practise virtue
and wisdom; that education which calls forth, trains and
develops those highest gifts of body and of mind which
ennoble men, and which are rightly judged to rank next
in dignity to virtue only.   For to a vulgar temper gain and
pleasure are the one aim of existence, to a lofty nature, moral
worth and fame.   It is, then, of the highest importance that
even from infancy this aim, this effort, should constantly be
kept alive in growing minds.   For I may affirm with fullest
conviction that we shall not have attained wisdom in our later
years unless in our earliest we have sincerely entered on its
search.   Nor may we for a moment admit, with the unthinking
crowd, that those who give early promise fail in subsequent ful-
filment.   This may, partly from physical causes, happen in
exceptional cases.   But there is no doubt that nature has
endowed some children with so keen, so ready an intelligence,
that without serious effort they attain to a notable power of
reasoning and conversing upon grave and lofty subjects, and
by aid of right guidance and sound learning reach in manhood
the highest distinction.   On the other hand, children of modest
powers demand even more attention, that their natural defects
may be supplied by art.   But all alike must in those early
years,

'Dum faciles animi iuvenum, dum mobilis aetas,'

whilst the mind is supple, be inured to the toil and effort of
learning.   Not that education, in the broad sense, is exclusively
the concern of youth.   Did not Cato think it honourable to
learn Greek in later life?   Did not Socrates, greatest of
philosophers, compel his aged fingers to the lute?

Our youth of to-day, it is to be feared, is backward to learn;
studies are accounted irksome.   Boys hardly weaned begin

to claim their own way, at a time when every art should be employed to bring them under control and attract them to grave studies. The Master must judge how far he can rely upon emulation, rewards, encouragement ; how far he must have recourse to sterner measures. Too much leniency is objectionable ; so also is too great severity, for we must avoid all that terrifies a boy. In certain temperaments—those in which a dark complexion denotes a quiet but strong per-sonality—restraint must be cautiously applied. Boys of this type are mostly highly gifted and can bear a gentle hand. Not seldom it happens that a finely tempered nature is thwarted by circumstances, such as poverty at home, which compels a promising youth to forsake learning for trade : though, on the other hand, poverty is less dangerous to lofty instincts than great wealth. Or again, parents encourage their sons to follow a career traditional in their family, which may divert them from liberal studies : and the customary pursuits of the city in which we dwell exercise a decided influence on our choice. So that we may say that a perfectly unbiassed decision in these matters is seldom possible, except to certain select natures, who by favour of the gods, as the poets have it, are unconsciously brought to choose the right path in life. The myth of Hercules, who, in the solitude of his wanderings, learned to accept the strenuous life and to reject the way of self-indulgence, and so attain the highest, is the significant setting of this profound truth. For us it is the best that can befall, that either the circumstances of our life, or the guidance and exhortations of those in charge of us, should mould our natures whilst they are still plastic.

In your own case, Ubertinus, you had before you the choice of training in Arms or in Letters. Either holds a place of distinction amongst the pursuits which appeal to men of noble spirit; either leads to fame and honour in the world. It would have been natural that you, the scion of a House ennobled by its prowess in arms, should have been content to

accept your father's permission to devote yourself wholly to
that discipline. But to your great credit you elected to
become proficient in both alike : to add to the career of arms
traditional in your family, an equal success in that other great
discipline of mind and character, the study of Literature.

There was courage in your choice. For we cannot deny
that there is still a horde—as I must call them—of people who,
like Licinius the Emperor, denounce learning and the Arts
as a danger to the State and hateful in themselves. In reality
the very opposite is the truth. However, as we look back
upon history we cannot deny that learning by no means expels
wickedness, but may be indeed an additional instrument for
evil in the hands of the corrupt. To a man of virtuous
instincts knowledge is a help and an adornment; to a Claudius
or a Nero it was a means of refinement in cruelty or in folly.
On the other hand, your grandfather, Jacopo da Carrara, who,
though a patron of learning, was not himself versed in Letters,
died regretting that opportunity of acquiring a knowledge
of higher studies had not been given him in youth ; which
shews us that, although we may in old age long for it, only in
early years can we be sure of attaining that learning which we
desire. So that it is no light motive to youthful diligence that
we thereby provide ourselves with precious advantages against
on-coming age, a spring of interest for a leisured life, a
recreation for a busy one. Consider the necessity of the
literary art to one immersed in reading and speculation : and
its importance to one absorbed in affairs. To be able to speak
and write with elegance is no slight advantage in negotiation,
whether in public or private concerns. Especially in admini-
stration of the State, when intervals of rest and privacy are
accorded to a prince, how must he value those means of
occupying them wisely which the knowledge of literature
affords to him ! Think of Domitian : son of Vespasian though
he was, and brother of Titus, he was driven to occupy his
leisure by *killing flies !* What a warning is here conveyed

of the critical judgments which posterity passes upon Princes! They live in a light in which nothing can long remain hid. Contrast with this the saying of Scipio: ' Never am I less idle, less solitary, than when to outward seeming I am doing nothing or am alone': evidence of a noble temper, worthy to be placed beside that recorded practice of Cato, who, amid the tedious business of the Senate, could withdraw himself from outward distractions and find himself truly alone in the companionship of his books.

Indeed the power which good books have of diverting our thoughts from unworthy or distressing themes is another support to my argument for the study of letters. Add to this their helpfulness on those occasions when we find ourselves alone, without companions and without preoccupations—what can we do better than gather our books around us? In them we see unfolded before us vast stores of knowledge, for our delight, it may be, or for our inspiration. In them are contained the records of the great achievements of men; the wonders of Nature; the works of Providence in the past, the key to her secrets of the future. And, most important of all, this Knowledge is not liable to decay. With a picture, an inscription, a coin, books share a kind of immortality. In all these memory is, as it were, made permanent; although, in its freedom from accidental risks, Literature surpasses every other form of record.

Literature indeed exhibits not facts alone, but thoughts, and their expression. Provided such thoughts be worthy, and worthily expressed, we feel assured that they will not die: although I do not think that thoughts without style will be likely to attract much notice or secure a sure survival. What greater charm can life offer than this power of making the past, the present, and even the future, our own by means of literature? How bright a household is the family of books! we may cry, with Cicero. In their company is no noise, no greed, no self-will: at a word they speak to you, at a word they are still:

to all our requests their response is ever ready and to the point. Books indeed are a higher—a wider, more tenacious—memory, a store-house which is the common property of us all.

I attach great weight to the duty of handing down this priceless treasure to our sons unimpaired by any carelessness on our part. How many are the gaps which the ignorance of past ages has wilfully caused in the long and noble roll of writers! Books—in part or in their entirety—have been allowed to perish. What remains of others is often sorely corrupt, mutilated, or imperfect. It is hard that no slight portion of the history of Rome is only to be known through the labours of one writing in the Greek language: it is still worse that this same noble tongue, once well nigh the daily speech of our race, as familiar as the Latin language itself, is on the point of perishing even amongst its own sons, and to us Italians is already utterly lost, unless we except one or two who in our time are tardily endeavouring to rescue something —if it be only a mere echo of it—from oblivion.

We come now to the consideration of the various subjects which may rightly be included under the name of 'Liberal Studies.' Amongst these I accord the first place to History, on grounds both of its attractiveness and of its utility, qualities which appeal equally to the scholar and to the statesman. Next in importance ranks Moral Philosophy, which indeed is, in a peculiar sense, a 'Liberal Art,' in that its purpose is to teach men the secret of true freedom. History, then, gives us the concrete examples of the precepts inculcated by philosophy. The one shews what men should do, the other what men have said and done in the past, and what practical lessons we may draw therefrom for the present day. I would indicate as the third main branch of study, Eloquence, which indeed holds a place of distinction amongst the refined Arts. By philosophy we learn the essential truth of things, which by eloquence we so exhibit in orderly adornment as to bring conviction to differing minds. And history provides the light of experience—

a cumulative wisdom fit to supplement the force of reason and the persuasion of eloquence. For we allow that soundness of judgment, wisdom of speech, integrity of conduct are the marks of a truly liberal temper.

We are told that the Greeks devised for their sons a course of training in four subjects : letters, gymnastic, music and drawing. Now, of these drawing has no place amongst our liberal studies ; except in so far as it is identical with writing, (which is in reality one side of the art of Drawing), it belongs to the Painter's profession : the Greeks, as an art-loving people, attached to it an exceptional value.

The Art of Letters, however, rests upon a different footing. It is a study adapted to all times and to all circumstances, to the investigation of fresh knowledge or to the re-casting and application of old. Hence the importance of grammar and of the rules of composition must be recognised at the outset, as the foundation on which the whole study of Literature must rest : and closely associated with these rudiments, the art of Disputation or Logical argument. The function of this is to enable us to discern fallacy from truth in discussion. Logic, indeed, as setting forth the true method of learning, is the guide to the acquisition of knowledge in whatever subject. Rhetoric comes next, and is strictly speaking the formal study by which we attain the art of eloquence ; which, as we have just stated, takes the third place amongst the studies specially important in public life. It is now, indeed, fallen from its old renown and is well nigh a lost art. In the Law-Court, in the Council, in the popular Assembly, in exposition, in persuasion, in debate, eloquence finds no place now-a-days : speed, brevity, homeliness are the only qualities desired. Oratory, in which our forefathers gained so great glory for themselves and for their language, is despised : but our youth, if they would earn the repute of true education, must emulate their ancestors in this accomplishment.

After Eloquence we place Poetry and the Poetic Art, which

though not without their value in daily life and as an aid to oratory, have nevertheless their main concern for the leisure side of existence.

As to Music, the Greeks refused the title of ' Educated ' to anyone who could not sing or play. Socrates set an example to the Athenian youth, by himself learning to play in his old age; urging the pursuit of music not as a sensuous indulgence, but as an aid to the inner harmony of the soul. In so far as it is taught as a healthy recreation for the moral and spiritual nature, music is a truly liberal art, and, both as regards its theory and its practice, should find a place in education.

Arithmetic, which treats of the properties of numbers, Geometry, which treats of the properties of dimensions, lines, surfaces, and solid bodies, are weighty studies because they possess a peculiar element of certainty. The science of the Stars, their motions, magnitudes and distances, lifts us into the clear calm of the upper air. There we may contemplate the fixed stars, or the conjunctions of the planets, and predict the eclipses of the sun and the moon. The knowledge of Nature —animate and inanimate—the laws and the properties of things in heaven and in earth, their causes, mutations and effects, especially the explanation of their wonders (as they are popularly supposed) by the unravelling of their causes—this is a most delightful, and at the same time most profitable, study for youth. With these may be joined investigations concerning the weights of bodies, and those relative to the subject which mathematicians call ' Perspective.'

I may here glance for a moment at the three great professional Disciplines : Medicine, Law, Theology. Medicine, which is applied science, has undoubtedly much that makes it attractive to a student. But it cannot be described as a Liberal study. Law, which is based upon moral philosophy, is undoubtedly held in high respect. Regarding Law as a subject of study, such respect is entirely deserved : but Law as practised becomes a mere trade. Theology, on the other hand, treats of themes removed from our senses, and attainable only by pure intelligence.

§ 4. The principal 'Disciplines' have now been reviewed. It must not be supposed that a liberal education requires acquaintance with them all : for a thorough mastery of even one of them might fairly be the achievement of a lifetime. Most of us, too, must learn to be content with modest capacity as with modest fortune. Perhaps we do wisely to pursue that study which we find most suited to our intelligence and our tastes, though it is true that we cannot rightly understand one subject unless we can perceive its relation to the rest. The choice of studies will depend to some extent upon the character of individual minds. For whilst one boy seizes rapidly the point of which he is in search and states it ably, another, working far more slowly, has yet the sounder judgment and so detects the weak spot in his rival's conclusions. The former, perhaps, will succeed in poetry, or in the abstract sciences ; the latter in real studies and practical pursuits. Or a boy may be apt in thinking, but slow in expressing himself ; to him the study of Rhetoric and Logic will be of much value. Where the power of talk alone is remarkable I hardly know what advice to give. Some minds are strong on the side of memory : these should be apt for history. But it is of importance to remember that in comparison with intelligence memory is of little worth, though intelligence without memory is, so far as education is concerned, of none at all. For we are not able to give evidence that we know a thing unless we can reproduce it.

Again, some minds have peculiar power in dealing with abstract truths, but are defective on the side of the particular and the concrete, and so make good progress in mathematics and in metaphysic. Those of just opposite temper are apt in Natural Science and in practical affairs. And the natural bent should be recognized and followed in education. Let the boy of limited capacity work only at that subject in which he shews he can attain some result.

Respecting the general place of liberal studies, we remember that Aristotle would not have them absorb the entire interests of life : for he kept steadily in view the nature of man as a citizen, an active member of the State. For the man who has surrendered himself absolutely to the attractions of Letters or of speculative thought follows, perhaps, a self-regarding end and is useless as a citizen or as prince.

In acquiring our knowledge we should be careful to go to the best teachers even for the Rudiments ; in choosing our authors to take only those of the first rank. Thus Philip entrusted Alexander to Aristotle even for the Alphabet ; the Romans used Vergil as the first reading book. Rightly in both cases : for that which is early implanted in the growing mind will strike deep roots. If, therefore, instead of sound methods and right examples, wrong principles and perverse standards be set before the beginner in any subject, he has a twofold difficulty to overcome. The story of Timotheus, the Spartan teacher of music, illustrates what I mean. He was accustomed to charge double fees to those pupils who came to him with a knowledge of music already acquired. For he said that he had to spend one course in teaching them to forget what they had previously learnt, before he could begin to give them his own special instruction.

Two faults, in particular, whether in the school master or in the student, seem to call for stringent correction. The first is the habit of attempting too much at once. For as the digestion refuses its task upon ill-assorted or excessive food, so the memory cannot retain an undue burden, and the mind ill-nourished becomes feebler instead of stronger with manhood. The remedy for this is to limit the number of subjects in hand at one time so that the memory may fully overtake each of them, and daily revision make our acquisition secure. The second fault is that of hastily passing from one subject to another, which is destructive of all steady progress. For there is an Italian proverb which warns us that 'Wine not allowed to rest turns sour.' And so we shall do well to put our heart into one subject at a time, and to repress a superficial curiosity. There is an order in studies which should be obeyed. A habit of irregular reading, or dipping into books, here the beginning, here the end, here the middle, is responsible for much useless study. On the other hand, wide reading concentrated round one special subject is often conducive to a thorough acquaintance with it.

Again, we must remember that mental endowments differ. There is the eager intellectual temper, which is apt to be soon discouraged by difficulties unless spurred by question or discussion. Where there is real capacity behind, success seems generally to reward patient guidance. And there is the brilliant genius, daunted by nothing, which attacks the gravest problems, and refuses to admit defeat. But here keen insight and swift acquisition often go with poor retentiveness. To boys thus gifted I would urge the adoption of sóme such plan as that of Cato, who, whatever he had done, seen, read during the day, reviewed it in the evening, when he would account, not only for his working hours, but for his leisure also. So a regular revision of all new knowledge, at least of that which strikes us as most important in it, will be a great help to memory. So, too, a habit of discussing our subject with a fellow student will aid us alike in understanding, in expressing, and in remembering, what we have gained. This indeed is the valuable effect of disputation as an educational instrument. Once more, the practice of teaching what we have learnt is a certain way of securing our own knowledge of the subject. Moreover, any exercise by which we may learn to distrust our own attainments, and so increase our diligence and our modesty is to be prized. For the temptation to exhibit their prodigious erudition besets many young students: and we may admit that a man deceives no one so readily as himself. It is perhaps the first essential of real progress to be sceptical of our own powers, and to discard that presumption of our own ability or knowledge which tempts us to make light of the need for thoroughness.

It will always happen that a beginner meets with difficulties of matter or expression in the subject, whatever it may be, upon which he is engaged. Perhaps he blames the book he is using or its author, whilst the fault lies, of course, in his own ignorance, which is only to be overcome by quiet perseverance in the particular study. To give a fixed time each day to reading, which shall be encroached upon under no pretext whatsoever, is a well tried practice which may be strongly recommended. Alexander read much even on campaign; Caesar wrote his Commentaries, and Augustus recited poetry, whilst commanding armies in the field. With such examples what distractions of peaceful city life can be pleaded as excuse for neglect of daily study? Nay, many leisure hours now wasted may be saved by devoting them to the recreation of lighter reading. Some wisely arrange a course of Readings during dinner; others court sleep, or banish it, amidst books, although physicians are, no doubt, right in condemning the abuse of this latter practice. In every Library let a clock be so placed that it may catch the eye of the reader, to warn him by the swift lapse of time of the need of diligence, and, I would add, let the Library be used for no other purpose whatsoever than that for which it is designed.

§ 5.   In what I have written thus far upon the choice of studies I have had regard more particularly to those whose temperament inclines them to Learning rather than to War. But where an active frame is conjoined to a vigorous intellect a true education will aim at the efficient training of both—the Reason, that it may wisely control, the Body, that it may promptly obey. So that if we be involved in arms we may be found ready to defend our rights or to strike a blow for honour or power. Especially must the education of a Prince accord a high place to instruction in the art of war, not less than to training in the arts of peace. Alexander the Great, himself a prince conspicuous in arms, and also a constant student of Homer, preferred to every other line of the Poet that one in which he speaks of Agamemnon as a great king *because* a valiant warrior, holding him thus typical of every true ruler of men.

Now war involves physical endurance as well as military skill. So that from his earliest years a boy must be gradually inured to privations and grave exertion, to enable him to bear strain and hardship when he reaches manhood. The institutions of Minos and Lycurgus ordained that the youth of Crete and Sparta should be exercised in activity and courage by feats of strength, or dangers of the field; in endurance by bearing heat and cold, hunger and thirst. For as luxury enervates mind and body alike, so exertion fortifies both. Nor could I find, even in antiquity, a more significant example than that of your own father Francesco, who always declared that this stedfastness under hardship and bodily strain was the quality of which he felt most proud. Endeavour to shew yourself a worthy son in this most important quality. This physical power, also, is accompanied by a contempt of death and by a consequent invincible courage. For all ought to regard life as of less moment than noble action. If we hold it our first duty to live honourably and bravely, whether in peace or war, we shall not over-rate the blessing of long life, as so many do. If death comes we shall meet it manfully, and, if need be, go to welcome it cheerfully. Even if it seem to come untimely, we shall still have had our opportunities. Scipio Africanus, the hero of the Second Punic War, hardly more than a boy at the time, had at the battle of the Ticino the glory of saving his father under the very feet of the enemy. Aemilius Lepidus is another instance of conspicuous bravery rewarded by the highest distinction of his fellow citizens. Nor have you yourself been backward in the field, as you shewed lately at Brescia against the German hordes, winning there the highest admiration of friend and foe alike.

So, I repeat, it is of greatest importance that boys should

be trained from childhood in feats of courage and endurance. The Lacedaemonian discipline was indeed severe. The boys were trained to be of such a temper that in their contests they could not yield nor confess themselves vanquished; the severest tests produced no cry of pain, though blood might flow and consciousness itself give way. The result was that all antiquity rehearses the deathless courage of the Spartans in the field; their arms were to them part of their very selves, to be cast away, or laid down, only with their lives. What else than this same early and most diligent training could have enabled the Romans to shew themselves so valiant, so enduring, in the campaigns they fought? Wherefore, whether a boy be trained in Arms or in Letters (for these are the two chief liberal Arts and fittest therefore for a prince), so soon as he be able to use his limbs let him be trained to Arms : so soon as he can rightly speak let him be trained to Letters. Further, it will be easy and it will be of great benefit to a boy to alternate the study of letters with bodily exercises : and, indeed, at whatever age he may be, the same practice is to be commended. Theodosius, we are told, spent the day in martial exercises, or in the business of the state ; the evening he devoted to books.

In choice of bodily exercises those should be adopted which serve to maintain the body in good health and to strengthen the limbs : and thus it will be necessary to consider to some extent the case of each individual boy. For some boys are of a soft and humid bodily habit: they will need to be dried and hardened by vigorous exercises ; or those whose blood mounts too readily will be best practised in restraint if they be exercised in the full heat of the sun. In childhood much care must be taken lest the growth be hindered, or the nerves of the body be strained, by severe exertion ; but as youth develops this may be slowly increased. The order, perhaps, to be observed is this : in childhood, learning first ; in youth, morals; with physical exercises, varying in degree, for all.

The importance attached by the Romans to systematic and scientific training in arms is illustrated by the example of Caius Marius, who, according to Plutarch, was present every day at the Camp, in which his son was quartered as a Cadet. In spite of his years and his high position, the great soldier himself took his place habitually at drill. To P. Rutilius is due the introduction of methodical training in the handling of the sword, especially in the art of the thrust and parry; so that swordsmanship became thenceforward a matter, not merely of muscle and daring, but of elaborate skill. So, too, our youth must learn the art of the sword, the cut, the thrust and the parry; the use of the shield; of the spear; of the club; training either hand to wield the weapon. Further, swimming, to which Augustus rightly attached so great importance, running, jumping, wrestling, boxing, javelin-throwing, archery, thorough horsemanship, in sport or in war,—these are all needful to the full training of the soldier. Particularly will it be necessary that he be practised in the drill of the heavy man-at-arms. Arms and methods of warfare change from age to age. The chariot of the Homeric Greeks, the legion of the Romans, have both disappeared; the chief arm of to-day is cavalry. But whatever the method or the weapon of the time, let there be ample practice for our youth, with as great variety of exercises as can be devised, so that they may be ready for combat hand to hand or in troop, in the headlong charge or in the skirmish. We cannot forestall the reality of war, its sudden emergencies, or its vivid terrors, but by training and practice we can at least provide such preparation as the case admits. So, with Horace, we may say:

> Angustam amice pauperiem pati
> robustus acri militia puer
>   condiscat et Parthos ferocis
>   vexet eques metuendus hasta
> vitamque sub divo et trepidis agat
> in rebus.   *Odes,* iii. 2.

8—2

Further, it will be desirable to include the wider aspects
of the art of war, by which I mean the principles of generalship:
strategy and tactics; discipline; supplies; and the ordering of
camps and winter quarters.   For the commander must be
prepared to bear a heavy responsibility.   If he be not calm
and confident, as one who has truly learnt his art, the forces
under him will not support the day; and the discredit of
failure will, fairly or not, attach to him alone.   The art of
war, indeed, can only be rightly acquired by constant experience
in the field, but such books as have been written by great
soldiers upon their calling must not be overlooked.   Your
father, too, is more capable than any other of giving you
wise instruction in these subjects, more especially concerning
the use of engines of war.   Indeed, your own family to-day
supplies you with notable instances of warlike skill, and to
them (your father Francesco and your uncle Jacopo in particular) you will turn repeatedly, with that respect and filial
affection which is ever due from youth to age, and is the
true corner stone of orderly communities of men.

§ 6.   But as we are not so constituted that we are able to bestow ourselves all day long upon our ordered tasks, I will now set
forth the true place of recreation.   First of all, it imports that
boys engage in no debasing games, or such as cannot develop
bodily gifts or powers of Will.   We cannot, therefore, accord a
high place to that practice which found favour with Scipio and
Laelius, namely, of seeking rest for exhausted minds in aimless
walks along the shore, picking up pebbles and shells as they
went.   Scaevola, on the other hand, was wiser: he spent
wearisome days in the Courts, and found in the sharp exertion
of ball-play the best refreshment alike for jaded spirits and
for bodily fatigue.   So, too, others seek recreation in hunting,
hawking, or fishing; and so keen is their enjoyment, that
the severe efforts which these pursuits demand are cheerfully
borne.

" The labour we delight in physicks pain" :

so to render the well known line of Horace[1]. If these be too strenuous a relaxation for those who are exhausted by study, it may suffice to seek it in quiet repose, in gentle riding, or in pleasant walks. Wit and comely humour may find a place, as Lycurgus allowed. Nor will it be unbecoming to have recourse to music and to song. Did not the Pythagoreans approve this? nay, Homer himself shews us Achilles refreshing his spirit after the fight by singing, though his songs were not of love but of heroic deeds. Then we may choose such measures as shall be best suited to our moods. The Sicilian measures conduce most to restful calm; the Gallic, on the other hand, stir us to energy and movement; the Italian hold a middle place. To accompany oneself in singing is less dignified than to sing to the accompaniment of another; whilst to watch dancing girls, or to dance ourselves to music, is altogether unworthy; though some may defend the latter as a form of exercise in spite of its tendency to lasciviousness and vain conceit. The game of "tabulae" which Palamedes is said to have invented during the Trojan war to keep his soldiers occupied during wearisome inaction, is free from all such objections. Dice-playing is to be utterly condemned. It is either a base form of money-getting, or an effeminate excitement; though a game of skill, in which chance plays but a small part, is allowable. Claudius, the Emperor, wrote a book on dice-playing, which the vicious have found a useful argument for their indulgence.

Those whose time is occupied in Letters may find sufficient relaxation in change of subject. But it must not be forgotten that it is sometimes needful, in the interests of our work, to do absolutely nothing for a while. For the string ever stretched will end by breaking. I know, indeed, that to the wise man nothing is so laborious as doing nothing. We know of some who divide their day into three parts, one of which is given to

---

[1] 'Molliter austerum studio fallente laborem,' *Sat.* II. ii. 12.

sleep, one to recreation and to meals, one to liberal studies. On such a point I cannot pronounce: but this at least I can safely say, that the larger the place we can allot to learning, the richer, the fuller, is the life we thereby secure to ourselves.

Lastly, I must add a word upon attention to personal habits. In this matter we must not be neglectful: for whilst we may not bestow too much thought upon our outward appearance, which is effeminacy, we must have due regard to our dress, and its suitability to time, place, and circumstance. Perhaps we ought not to be too severe if a young man verging on manhood seem to spend undue care upon his person; something may be forgiven him, provided he does not carry his foible into the more serious years of life.

§ 7. In offering this Treatise to you, Ubertinus, I end as I began. You do not need my insistence; follow the instincts of your best self, and you will be found worthy. If I seem to flatter you, it is that I look confidently to see you fulfil the promise of your youth. Should you prove me a true prophet, you will reap the praise of men, not of your own day alone, but, if my pen avail, of days far distant. Should you, however, disappoint my hopes, there is one, at least, who will be forced to admit, with sorrow, that nothing was lacking to you but yourself.

THE TRACTATE OF LIONARDO BRUNI D'AREZZO,
DE STUDIIS ET LITERIS.

THIS short Treatise, cast as usual in the form of a Letter, is probably the earliest humanist tract upon Education expressly dedicated to a Lady; just as Baptista di Montefeltro, to whom it is addressed, may stand as the first of the succession of studious women who were a characteristic product of the Renaissance.

Baptista was the younger daughter of Antonio, Count of Urbino, who died in 1404. She was then twenty-one years of age, and was married, on June 14, 1405, to Galeazzo Malatesta, the heir to the lordship of Pesaro. The marriage was a most unhappy one. The worthless husband was so hated as a ruler that, after two years of power (1429–1431), he was driven from his city. His wife thereupon found a welcome refuge in her old home at Urbino. She lived for some twenty years a widowed and secluded life; she died, as a Sister of the Franciscan Order of Santa Chiara, in 1450.

Even before her marriage she had cultivated a taste for poetry and was powerfully attracted by the passion for the ancient literature which marked the close of the 14th century. Her husband's father, the reigning lord of Pesaro, is known to us as "Il Malatesta degli Sonetti," and he aided and shared the literary tastes of his young daughter-in-law. They interchanged *canzoni* and Latin epistles, many of which are preserved in MS. collections[1]. The Emperor Sigismund passing through Urbino in 1433 was greeted by her in a Latin oration[2], which half a century later was still thought worthy of print. To her Lionardo Bruni, at the time probably Apostolic Secretary, addressed the Letter which is here given in English form. The date of its composition cannot now be determined. But we may fairly assume from the tenor of the opening words that it was written not much later than the year of her marriage (1405).

The interest of the tractate lies chiefly in the fact that it reveals, at an early stage in the history of Humanism, a concern for classical study on the part of the more thoughtful and earnest of the great ladies of Italy. Baptista is the forerunner of the Nogarola of Verona[3], of Cecilia Gonzaga, of Ippolita Sforza, and of her own more fortunate and distinguished descendants, Costanza and her daughter, another Baptista (1447–1472), the wife of the great Duke Federigo of Urbino.

There is evidence also, I think, of the bitterness with which the New Learning was regarded in Florence by the Dominicans of Santa Maria Novella, which had lately found expression in the work of Giovanni Dominici[4], who denounced the growing

---

[1] Two *Canzoni* by Baptista of a religious cast and a Letter from her to Martin V. are printed in Dennistoun, *The Dukes of Urbino*, i. 409.

[2] We remember that Gianlucido Gonzaga composed an hexameter poem of two hundred lines on the emperor's visit to Mantua soon afterwards.

[3] Upon the sisters Isotta and Ginevra Nogarola, who were pupils of Guarino, see Sabbad. *Vita di Guarino*, p. 123. In them, he says, 'L' umanismo si sposa alla gentilezza femminilè.'

[4] *Regola del Governo di Cura Familiare*, dal B. Giovanni Dominici: ed. Salvi, Fir. 1860. This work is the most important protest, in literary form, against the revival of ancient learning which has come down to us. Giovanni was Vicario of the Convent of Sta Maria Novella, and his book set the temper of the Dominicans for the next century. Its publication fell within the years 1400—1405. Bruni's version of the Homily of S. Basil was intended as a direct retort to Giovanni: and Humanists were always glad to defend the reading of the classics by the authority of this Father. See Aen. Sylv. *De Liberor. Educ.*, inf. p. 150.

absorption of the intelligence of his day in pagan thought and letters. Bruni, however, as became his position, and in accord moreover, with all that we read of the ideals of the highest training of women during this century, in mapping out a course of reading for his correspondent holds fast by the supreme worth of morals and religion. He is anxious to shew the connection between the ancient world and the Christian standards of life. Hence the paragraph[1] upon the relation of profane learning to the art of noble living is very significant. It expresses with precision what we feel to have been the aim of Vittorino da Feltre in his education of Cecilia and Barbara, and it coincides in principle with the judgments on the education of girls laid down in the treatise of Maffeo Vegio[2]. The main features of this course of study best adapted to a woman seem to be these. Religion, as a subject of study not less than as a personal quality, demands the first place: morals, as recognised by the best intelligence of the ancient world, as well as by the Church, stand in close relation to Faith. Philosophy, disputation, the art of clever conversation and discussion, history, as a body of illustration of moral precepts, all these follow closely. Literature, in a broad sense covering the range of Latin antiquity and the greater Fathers, must be studied both for its matter and its form. The importance of this last is hardly to be exaggerated. For taste and fluency of expression are among the finer marks of distinction accepted by educated opinion.

It cannot be said that the study of Letters by women, in spite of some pedantry and occasional display, was, judging from the more prominent instances of which we have intimate knowledge, unfavourably regarded by social opinion, or that it established a new standard of womanly activity. Women, indeed, at this

---

[1] Infra, p. 133.

[2] *De Educatione Liberorum*, the work often attributed, wrongly, to Filelfo. Vid. Lib. iii. § 12, 13, for his judgment upon the education of girls.

epoch seem to have preserved their moral and intellectual balance under the stress of the new enthusiasm better than men.   The learned ladies were, in actual life, good wives and mothers, domestic and virtuous, women of strong judgment, and not seldom of marked capacity in affairs.   The duchess Baptista, great in scholarship, was even more distinguished for her needlework.   At the same time, before the century was out, Chairs at the Universities, both in Italy and in Spain, were occasionally occupied by women[1].

[Hain, *1571*, gives the Cologne edition as the earliest, but no date is suggested (? 1472).   A Florentine edition appeared in April 1477, which from its Prefatory Letter would seem to be the first current in that city.   This was followed by a Roman issue.   Two others, Padua, 1483, and Munich, 1496, were printed during the century.   Very few editions are noted of later date.]

[1] Dennistoun, op. cit. ii. 123.

LIONARDO D'AREZZO CONCERNING THE STUDY OF LITERATURE,—A LETTER ADDRESSED TO THE ILLUSTRIOUS LADY, BAPTISTA MALATESTA.

I AM led to address this Tractate to you, Illustrious Lady, by the high repute which attaches to your name in the field of learning; and I offer it, partly as an expression of my homage to distinction already attained, partly as an encouragement to further effort. Were it necessary I might urge you by brilliant instances from antiquity: Cornelia, the daughter of Scipio, whose Epistles survived for centuries as models of style; Sappho, the poetess, held in so great honour for the exuberance of her poetic art; Aspasia, whose learning and eloquence made her not unworthy of the intimacy of Socrates. Upon these, the most distinguished of a long range of great names, I would have you fix your mind; for an intelligence such as your own can be satisfied with nothing less than the best. You yourself, indeed, may hope to win a fame higher even than theirs. For they lived in days when learning was no rare attainment, and therefore they enjoyed no unique renown. Whilst, alas, upon such times are we fallen that a learned man seems well-nigh a portent, and erudition in a woman is a thing utterly unknown. For true learning has almost died away amongst us. True learning, I say: not a mere acquaintance with that vulgar, threadbare jargon which satisfies those who devote themselves to Theology, but sound learning in its proper and legitimate sense, viz., the knowledge of realities—Facts and Principles—united to a perfect familiarity with Letters and the art of expression. Now this combination we find in Lactantius, in Augustine, or in Jerome; each of them at once a great theologian and profoundly versed in literature. But turn from them to their successors of to-day: how must we blush for their ignorance of the whole field of Letters!

This leads me to press home this truth—though in your case it is unnecessary—that the foundations of all true learning must be laid in the sound and thorough knowledge of Latin: which implies study marked by a broad spirit, accurate scholarship, and careful attention to details. Unless this solid basis be secured it is useless to attempt to rear an enduring edifice. Without it the great monuments of literature are unintelligible, and the art of composition impossible. To attain this essential knowledge we must never relax our careful attention to the grammar of the language, but perpetually confirm and extend our acquaintance with it until it is thoroughly our own. We may gain much from Servius, Donatus and Priscian, but more by careful observation in our own reading, in which we must note attentively vocabulary and inflexions, figures of speech and metaphors, and all the devices of style, such as rhythm, or antithesis, by which fine taste is exhibited. To this end we must be supremely careful in our choice of authors, lest an inartistic and debased style infect our own writing and degrade our taste; which danger is best avoided by bringing a keen, critical sense to bear upon select works, observing the sense of each passage, the structure of the sentence, the force of every word down to the least important particle. In this way our reading reacts directly upon our style.

You may naturally turn first to Christian writers, foremost amongst whom, with marked distinction, stands Lactantius, by common consent the finest stylist of the post-classical period. Especially do I commend to your study his works, ' *Adversus*

falsam Religionem,' '*De via Dei,'* and '*De opificio hominis.'*
After Lactantius your choice may lie between Augustine,
Jerome, Ambrose, and Cyprian ; should you desire to read
Gregory of Nazianzen, Chrysostom, and Basil, be careful as to
the accuracy of the translations you adopt. Of the classical
authors Cicero will be your constant pleasure : how unap-
proachable in wealth of ideas and of language, in force of style,
indeed, in all that can attract in a writer ! Next to him ranks
Vergil, the glory and the delight of our national literature. Livy
and Sallust, and then the chief poets, follow in order. The
usage of these authors will serve you as your test of correctness
in choice of vocabulary and of constructions.

Now we notice in all good prose—though it is not of course
obtrusive—a certain element of rhythm, which coincides with
and expresses the general structure of the passage, and consequently gives a clue to its sense. I commend, therefore, to you
as an aid to understanding an author the practice of reading
aloud with clear and exact intonation. By this device you will
seize more quickly the drift of the passage, by realising the
main lines on which it is constructed. And the music of the
prose thus interpreted by the voice will react with advantage
upon your own composition, and at the same time will improve
your own Reading by compelling deliberate and intelligent expression.

The art of Writing is not limited to the mere formation of
letters, but it concerns also the subject of the diphthongs, and
of the syllabic divisions of words ; the accepted usages in the
writing of each letter, singly and in cursive script, and the
whole field of abbreviations. This may seem a trivial matter,
but a knowledge of educated practice on these points may
fairly be expected from us. The laws of quantity are more
important, since in poetry scansion is frequently our only
certain clue to construction. One might ask, further, what
capacity in poetic composition or what critical ability or taste
in poetical literature is possible to a man who is not first of all

secure on points of quantity and metre? Nor is prose, as I have already hinted, without its metrical element; upon which indeed Aristotle and Cicero dwelt with some minuteness. A skilful orator or historian will be careful of the effect to be gained by spondaic, iambic, dactylic or other rhythm in arousing differing emotions congruous to his matter in hand. To ignore this is to neglect one of the most delicate points of style. You will notice that such refinements will apply only to one who aspires to proficiency in the finer shades of criticism and expression, but such a one must certainly by observation and practice become familiar with every device which lends distinction and adornment to the literary art.

But the wider question now confronts us, that of the subject matter of our studies, that which I have already called the realities of fact and principle, as distinct from literary form. Here, as before, I am contemplating a student of keen and lofty aspiration to whom nothing that is worthy in any learned discipline is without its interest. But it is necessary to exercise discrimination. In some branches of knowledge I would rather restrain the ardour of the learner, in others, again, encourage it to the uttermost. Thus there are certain subjects in which, whilst a modest proficiency is on all accounts to be desired, a minute knowledge and excessive devotion seem to be a vain display. For instance, subtleties of Arithmetic and Geometry are not worthy to absorb a cultivated mind, and the same must be said of Astrology. You will be surprised to find me suggesting (though with much more hesitation) that the great and complex art of Rhetoric should be placed in the same category. My chief reason is the obvious one, that I have in view the cultivation most fitting to a woman. To her neither the intricacies of debate nor the oratorical artifices of action and delivery are of the least practical use, if indeed they are not positively unbecoming. Rhetoric in all its forms,—public discussion, forensic argument, logical fence, and the like—lies absolutely outside the province of woman.

What Disciplines then are properly open to her? In the first place she has before her, as a subject peculiarly her own, the whole field of religion and morals. The literature of the Church will thus claim her earnest study. Such a writer, for instance, as St Augustine affords her the fullest scope for reverent yet learned inquiry. Her devotional instinct may lead her to value the help and consolation of holy men now living; but in this case let her not for an instant yield to the impulse to look into their writings, which, compared with those of Augustine, are utterly destitute of sound and melodious style, and seem to me to have no attraction whatever.

Moreover, the cultivated Christian lady has no need in the study of this weighty subject to confine herself to ecclesiastical writers. Morals, indeed, have been treated of by the noblest intellects of Greece and Rome. What they have left to us upon Continence, Temperance, Modesty, Justice, Courage, Greatness of Soul, demands your sincere respect. You must enter into such questions as the sufficiency of Virtue to Happiness; or whether, if Happiness consist in Virtue, it can be destroyed by torture, imprisonment or exile; whether, admitting that these may prevent a man from being happy, they can be further said to make him miserable. Again, does Happiness consist (with Epicurus) in the presence of pleasure and the absence of pain: or (with Xenophon) in the consciousness of uprightness: or (with Aristotle) in the practice of Virtue? These inquiries are, of all others, most worthy to be pursued by men and women alike; they are fit material for formal discussion and for literary exercise. Let religion and morals, therefore, hold the first place in the education of a Christian lady.

But we must not forget that true distinction is to be gained by a wide and varied range of such studies as conduce to the profitable enjoyment of life, in which, however, we must observe due proportion in the attention and time we devote to them.

First amongst such studies I place History: a subject which

must not on any account be neglected by one who aspires to true cultivation. For it is our duty to understand the origins of our own history and its development; and the achievements of Peoples and of Kings.

For the careful study of the past enlarges our foresight in contemporary affairs and affords to citizens and to monarchs lessons of incitement or warning in the ordering of public policy. From History, also, we draw our store of examples of moral precepts.

In the monuments of ancient literature which have come down to us History holds a position of great distinction. We specially prize such authors as Livy, Sallust and Curtius; and, perhaps even above these, Julius Caesar; the style of whose Commentaries, so elegant and so limpid, entitles them to our warm admiration. Such writers are fully within the comprehension of a studious lady. For, after all, History is an easy subject: there is nothing in its study subtle or complex. It consists in the narration of the simplest matters of fact which, once grasped, are readily retained in the memory.

The great Orators of antiquity must by all means be included. Nowhere do we find the virtues more warmly extolled, the vices so fiercely decried. From them we may learn, also, how to express consolation, encouragement, dissuasion or advice. If the principles which orators set forth are portrayed for us by philosophers, it is from the former that we learn how to employ the emotions—such as indignation, or pity—in driving home their application in individual cases. Further, from oratory we derive our store of those elegant or striking turns of expression which are used with so much effect in literary compositions. Lastly, in oratory we find that wealth of vocabulary, that clear easy-flowing style, that verve and force, which are invaluable to us both in writing and in conversation.

I come now to Poetry and the Poets—a subject with which every educated lady must shew herself thoroughly familiar

For we cannot point to any great mind of the past for whom the Poets had not a powerful attraction. Aristotle, in constantly quoting Homer, Hesiod, Pindar, Euripides and other poets, proves that he knew their works hardly less intimately than those of the philosophers. Plato, also, frequently appeals to them, and in this way covers them with his approval. If we turn to Cicero, we find him not content with quoting Ennius, Accius, and others of the Latins, but rendering poems from the Greek and employing them habitually. Seneca, the austere, not only abounds in poetical allusions, but was himself a poet; whilst the great Fathers of the Church, Jerome, Augustine, Lactantius and Boethius, reveal their acquaintance with the poets in their controversies and, indeed, in all their writings. Hence my view that familiarity with the great poets of antiquity is essential to any claim to true education. For in their writings we find deep speculations upon Nature, and upon the Causes and Origins of things, which must carry weight with us both from their antiquity and from their authorship. Besides these, many important truths upon matters of daily life are suggested or illustrated. All this is expressed with such grace and dignity as demands our admiration. For example, how vividly is the art of war portrayed in Homer: the duties of a leader of men : the chances of the field : the varying temper of the host ! Wise counsel, too, is not wanting, as when Hector upbraids Aeneas for too rashly urging the pursuit. Would, indeed, that in our own day our captains would deign to profit by this ancient wisdom, to the security of the common-wealth and the saving of valuable lives ! Consider, again, how fitly Iris, descending upon Agamemnon in his sleep, warns against the sloth of rulers—could Socrates, Plato or Pythagoras more pointedly exhibit the responsibility of a king of men ? There are the precepts also, not fewer nor less weighty, which pertain to the arts of peace. But it is time to pass to our own Poets, to Vergil, who surpasses, it seems to me, all philosophers in displaying the inner secrets of Nature and of the Soul :

w.   9

> " Know first, the heaven, the earth, the main,
>   The moon's pale orb, the starry train,
>   Are nourished by a soul,
>   A bright intelligence, whose flame
>   Glows in each member of the frame
>   And stirs the mighty whole.
>   Thence souls of men and cattle spring,
>   And the gay people of the wing,
>   And those strange shapes that ocean hides
>   Beneath the smoothness of the tides.
>   A fiery strength inspires their lives,
>   An essence that from heaven derives,
>   Though clogged in part by limbs of clay
>   And the dull ' vesture of decay[1].' "

Nor can we deny a certain inspiration to a poet who, on the very eve of the Redeemer's birth, could speak of ' the Virgin's return,' and ' the Divine offspring sent down from on High.' So thought Lactantius, who held that the Sibyl here alludes directly to the Saviour. Such power of reading the future is implied in the name ' vates,' so often given to the true poet, and we must all recognise in such one a certain ' possession,' as by a Power other and stronger than himself.

We know, however, that in certain quarters—where all knowledge and appreciation of Letters is wanting—this whole branch of Literature, marked as it is by something of the Divine, and fit, therefore, for the highest place, is decried as unworthy of study. But when we remember the value of the best poetry, its charm of form and the variety and interest of its subject-matter, when we consider the ease with which from our childhood up it can be committed to memory, when we recall the peculiar affinity of rhythm and metre to our emotions and our intelligence, we must conclude that Nature herself is against such headlong critics. Have we not often felt the sudden uplifting of the Soul when in the solemn Office of the

---

[1] Vergil, *Aeneid* VI. (Conington's version).

Mass such a passage as the ‘Primo dierum omnium’ bursts upon us? It is not hard for us, then, to understand what the Ancients meant when they said that the Soul is ordered in special relation to the principles of Harmony and Rhythm, and is, therefore, by no other influence so fitly and so surely moved. Hence I hold my conviction to be securely based; namely, that Poetry has, by our very constitution, a stronger attraction for us than any other form of expression, and that anyone ignorant of, and indifferent to, so valuable an aid to knowledge and so ennobling a source of pleasure can by no means be entitled to be called educated. If I seem to have dwelt at undue length upon this matter, please believe that my difficulty has rather been to restrain myself, so keenly do I feel upon it. I do not forget that one of your own House has expressly taken up a position in a contrary sense. He, indeed, justly commands the respect of all. But there are disputants of another class. Their attitude is merely this : ‘the themes of the ancient poets are chosen from stories of love and sin.’ But I point to the tale of Penelope and Ulysses, of Alcestis and Admetus, which are but typical of many others, and I ask, ‘Where can you find nobler examples of constancy and devotion, or more pointed lessons in the highest virtues of womanhood?’ ‘True,’ it is replied, ‘but there are stories of a different kind, of Phoebus and Danae, of Vulcan and Venus.’ But who can fail to understand that such fictions are not to be read literally, that such episodes are insignificant in number as compared with that great array of noble figures which stand forth from the pages of Vergil and Homer, and that it is unjust criticism to ignore the beauties of any work of art and to call attention only to its blemishes? ‘Yes, but, like Cato, we are willing to sacrifice the beauties so we be not soiled by the blots : hence we would neither read the poets ourselves nor put them into the hands of others.’ Plato and Aristotle, however, studied the poets, and I decline to admit that in practical wisdom or in moral earnestness they yield to our modern critics. They were not Christians, indeed, but consistency of life and abhorrence of evil existed before Christianity and are independent of it. Suppose we turn to the Scriptures. We must admit that they contain not a few narratives which compare unfavourably with any treated by the poets, but we do not for that reason prohibit the Bible. When I read the loves of Aeneas and Dido in the *Aeneid* I pay my tribute of admiration to the genius of the poet, but the matter itself I know to be a fiction, and thus it leaves no moral impression : and so in other instances of the kind, where literal truth is not the object aimed at. The Scriptures, on the other hand, whose literal accuracy no one questions, not seldom cause me misgivings on this head.

But I am ready to admit that there are two types of poet : the aristocracy, so to call them, of their craft, and the vulgar, and that the latter may be put aside in ordering a woman's reading. A comic dramatist may season his wit too highly : a satirist describe too bluntly the moral corruption which he scourges : let her pass them by. Vergil, on the other hand, Seneca, Statius, and others like them, rank with the noblest names, and may, nay must, be the trusted companions of all who aspire to be called cultivated.

To sum up what I have endeavoured to set forth. That high standard of education to which I referred at the outset is only to be reached by one who has seen many things and read much. Poet, Orator, Historian, and the rest, all must be studied, each must contribute a share. Our learning thus becomes full, ready, varied and elegant, available for action or for discourse in all subjects. But to enable us to make effectual use of what we know we must add to our knowledge the power of expression. These two sides of learning, indeed, should not be separated : they afford mutual aid and distinction. Proficiency in literary form, not accompanied by broad acquaintance with facts and truths, is a barren attainment ; whilst information, however vast, which lacks all grace of expression, would seem to be put under a bushel or partly thrown away.

Indeed, one may fairly ask what advantage it is to possess profound and varied learning if one cannot convey it in language worthy of the subject. Where, however, this double capacity exists—breadth of learning and grace of style—we allow the highest title to distinction and to abiding fame. If we review the great names of ancient literature, Plato, Democritus, Aristotle, Theophrastus, Varro, Cicero, Seneca, Augustine, Jerome, Lactantius, we shall find it hard to say whether we admire more their attainments or their literary power.

But my last word must be this. The intelligence that aspires to the best must aim at both. In doing so, all sources of profitable learning will in due proportion claim your study. None have more urgent claim than the subjects and authors which treat of Religion and of our duties in the world ; and it is because they assist and illustrate these supreme studies that I press upon your attention the works of the most approved poets, historians and orators of the past.

THE TREATISE OF AENEAS
SYLVIUS PICCOLOMINI, AFTERWARDS PIUS II,
DE LIBERORUM EDUCATIONE.

WRITTEN FOR LADISLAS, KING OF BOHEMIA
AND HUNGARY. 1450.

LIKE the Treatise of P. P. Vergerius, this Tractate of
Aeneas Sylvius was primarily addressed to the scion of a ruling
House. Ladislas, the young King of Bohemia, was born after
the death (1439) of his father, Albert II, and his ward-ship
was one of the many responsibilities which awaited the new
Emperor, Frederick III, on his election in the following year.
Ladislas remained in the charge of the Emperor until 1452,
and died at the age of 18 in November 1457. It may be said
that his short life hardly gave promise of much capacity or
strength of character.

Aeneas Sylvius, after his experiences at the Council of
Basel, had entered the service of the Emperor, as Secretary, in
1442. He was thus thrown into close contact with the child,
who for political reasons was never allowed to be far from the
Court. In 1446 Aeneas took Holy Orders and next year was
preferred to the Bishopric of Trieste. His many gifts led to
his employment upon missions demanding delicacy of touch,
and he thus attained a position of trust and authority in the
household and Chancellery of the Emperor. His relations
with Ladislas seem to have been inspired by a genuine interest
in the boy ; and when he had reached the age of ten years the

Bishop addressed to him, in formal shape, his general views upon the education desirable in a Prince.

Aeneas Sylvius, as an Italian of good circumstances, had been brought up in the atmosphere of Humanism. He regarded it as his function to prepare a way by which the new light might reach even the barbarous people amongst whom his career now lay. But he was not a scholar in the strict sense; his Latinity was fluent rather than 'elegant'; he knew very little Greek. Translations, however, already supplied, in part, the needs of the superficial student of Greek thought and letters. Moreover, Aeneas was naturally of active tastes, life rather than study was his main interest; and he was of too practical bent and too clear-headed to be misled by the affectations and self-conceit which disfigured some even of the abler humanists of his time. It is therefore evidence of the hold which the new educational ideal had already secured that a man whose interests lay in practical life, and who had few illusions as to the ultimate power of literature, should yet treat Letters as the indispensable foundation of Education. We may wonder that one who showed elsewhere so broad and rational a concern in history and geography should have dwelt so briefly on these subjects; his main purpose seems to be to warn his correspondent, for reasons of style[1], against the study of the history of his own country[2].

[The first edition known to bibliographers is that of W. Zell, *Colon. s.a.*, but *circ.* 1475. No other is noted as of the fifteenth century. It was included in the collected edition of the works of Pius II printed at Basel 1551. This was reissued with additions in 1571; the *Tract on Education* has never been since reprinted.]

---

[1] See p. 152.

[2] On the position of Aeneas Sylvius in the Revival of Learning see Voigt, Enea Silvio, ii. p. 248 seqq.

AENEAS SYLVIUS PICCOLOMINI TO LADISLAS, KING OF BOHEMIA AND HUNGARY.

§ 1. IN addressing ourselves to the question of the education of a boy in whom we are interested, we must first of all satisfy ourselves that he is endowed by Nature with a good and a teachable disposition. Now this is a gift, not an acquirement; although a gift which has been not sparingly granted. For, as Quintilian rightly says, if flying is instinctive with birds, or galloping with horses, so an eager and forward temper is the natural mark of a child. The educator, therefore, is generally entitled to assume a native bent towards mental activity on part of his charge, although, to be productive of real progress, this innate energy needs to be developed by methodical training and experience; nature, training, practice—these seem to be the three factors of all education.

Now both mind and body, the two elements of which we are constituted, must be developed side by side. At what age intellectual education should be definitely begun need not here be discussed. You have already reached boyhood, and the instruction I now offer has regard to your own particular case. Yet I have not yourself only in mind, but your Masters also may with profit heed what I here lay down. Socrates, indeed, is said to have visited the negligence of a pupil upon the head of his teacher; Seneca is blamed by some for the crimes of Nero; Plutarch records the public reprimand of schoolmasters for faults of their scholars. So important a matter, even in the earliest stages of education, is the choice of Teachers that we stand amazed at the carelessness which is daily exhibited in their selection. The example of Philip of Macedon, in committing Alexander to the care of Aristotle, not to mention the ancient story of Peleus and Phoenix, may serve as sufficient rebuke to such indifference.

A conceit of knowledge in a master is only less injurious to his efficiency than looseness of character. Bad example may easily lead to habits which no efforts in later life will enable a man to shake off. The master, therefore, must be intellectually able and sincere, of wide experience, and of sound morals. In demeanour he should avoid austerity without falling into vulgar familiarity. A master thus qualified will be competent to fulfil his duty, which is to fence in the growing mind with wise and noble precept and example, as a careful gardener hedges round a newly-planted tree. For in right training of the boy lies the secret of the integrity of the man. But this training must be enforced by friendly but effective authority, and should require no recourse to the rod. For, as Quintilian and Plutarch taught, a boy must be won to learning by persuasive earnestness, and not be driven to it like a slave. For whilst praise must never degenerate into flattery, so on the other hand correction which takes the form of personal indignity gives rise to hatred for teacher and subject alike. In fine, the master, as Juvenal says, does in reality exercise a parental function towards his pupil and should not be satisfied unless he attract a corresponding filial affection.

§ 2. As regards a boy's physical training, we must bear in mind that we aim at implanting habits which will prove beneficial through life. So let him cultivate a certain hardness which rejects excess of sleep and idleness in all its forms. Habits of indulgence—such as the luxury of soft beds, or the wearing of silk instead of linen next the skin—tend to enervate both body and mind. Too much importance can hardly be attached to right bearing and gesture. Childish habits of playing with the lips and features should be early controlled. A boy should be taught to hold his head erect, to look straight and fearlessly before him and to bear himself with dignity whether walking, standing, or sitting. In ancient Greece we find that both philosophers and men of affairs— Socrates, for instance, and Chrysippus, or Philip of Macedon— deemed this matter worthy of their concern, and therefore it may well be thought deserving of ours. Games and exercises which develope the muscular activities and the general carriage of the person should be encouraged by every Teacher. For such physical training not only cultivates grace of attitude but secures the healthy play of our bodily organs and establishes the constitution.

Every youth destined to exalted position should further be trained in military exercises. It will be your destiny to defend Christendom against the Turk. It will thus be an essential part of your education that you be early taught the use of the bow, of the sling, and of the spear; that you drive, ride, leap and swim. These are honourable accomplishments in everyone, and therefore not unworthy of the educator's care. Ponder the picture which Vergil gives of the youth of the Itali, skilled in all the warlike exercises of their time. Games, too, should be encouraged for young children—the ball, the hoop—but these must not be rough and coarse, but have in them an element of skill. Such relaxations should form an integral part of each day's occupations if learning is not to be an object of disgust. Just as Nature and the life of man present us with alternations of effort and repose—toil and sleep, winter and summer—so we may hold, with Plato, that it is a law of our being that rest from work is a needful condition of further work. To observe this truth is a chief duty of the Master.

In respect of eating and drinking the rule of moderation consists in rejecting everything which needlessly taxes digestion and so impairs mental activity. At the same time fastidiousness must not be humoured. A boy, for instance, whose lot it may be to face life in the camp, or in the forest, should so discipline his appetite that he may eat even beef. The aim of eating is to strengthen the frame; so let vigorous health reject cakes or sweets, elaborate dishes of small birds or eels, which are for the delicate and the weakly. Your own countrymen, like all northern peoples, are, I know, sore offenders in this matter of eating and drinking. But I count upon your own innate self-respect to preserve you from such bad example, and to enable you to despise the sneers and complaints of those around you. What but disease and decay can result from appetite habitually over-indulged? Such concession to the flesh stands condemned by all the great spirits of the past. In Augustus Caesar, in Socrates, we have instances of entire indifference in choice of food. Caligula, Nero and Vitellius serve as sufficient examples of grossly sensual tastes. To the Greeks of the best age eating and drinking were only means to living—not the chief end and aim of it. For they recognized, with Aristotle, that in this capacity for bodily pleasures we are on the same level with the lower creatures.

As regards the use of wine, remember that we drink to quench thirst, and that the limit of moderation is reached when the edge of the intellect is dulled. A boy should be brought up to avoid wine; for he possesses a store of natural moisture in the blood and so rarely experiences thirst. Hence highly diluted wine alone can be allowed to children, whilst women are perhaps better without it altogether, as was the custom in Rome. The abuse of wine is more common amongst Northern peoples than in Italy. Plato allowed its moderate enjoyment as tending to mental relaxation, and, indeed, temperance in the true sense is hardly consistent with the absolute prohibition of all that might seduce us from our virtuous resolutions. So that a young man's best security against excess may be found to lie in a cautious use of wine,

safeguarded by innate strength of will and a watchful temper.
There is no reason why social feastings should not be dignified
by serious conversation and yet be bright and gay withal.
But the body, after all, is but a framework for the activities of
the mind; and so we hold fast to the dictum of Pythagoras—
that he who pampers the body is devising a prison for himself.
Even if we had not the support of the Ancients, it is evident to
the serious mind that food and clothing are worthy of regard
only so far as they are indispensable to the vigorous activity of
body and spirit: all beyond that is triviality or effeminacy.
But this is not to exclude that care for the outward person
which is, indeed, demanded from everyone by self-respect, but
is peculiarly needful in a prince.

§ 3.   We must now hasten on to the larger and more
important division of our subject, that which treats of the most
precious of all human endowments, the Mind.   Birth, wealth,
fame, health, vigour and beauty are, indeed, highly prized by
mankind, but they are one and all of the nature of accidents;
they come and they go.   But the riches of the mind are a
stable possession, unassailable by fortune, calumny, or time.
Our material wealth lies at the mercy of a successful foe, but,
as Stilpho said, 'war can exact no requisition from personal
worth.'   So too, you will remember the reply of Socrates to
Gorgias, applying it to your own case : 'How can I adjudge the
Great King happy, until I know to what he can truly lay claim
in character and in wisdom?'   Lay to heart the truth here
conveyed : our one sure possession is character : the place and
fortune of men change, it may be suddenly, profoundly; nor
may we, by taking thought, cunningly hedge ourselves round
against all the chances of life.   As Solon long ago declared,
no sane man dare barter excellence for money.   Nay rather,
it is a function of true wisdom, as the Tyrants found by their
experience, to enable us to bear variations of fortune.   Philosophy, or, in other words, the enquiry into the nature of Virtue,
is indeed a study specially meet for princes.   For they are

in a sense the arbitrary embodiment of Law; a responsibility which may well weigh heavily upon them. Truly has it been said that no one has greater need of a well-stored mind than he whose will counts for the happiness or misery of thousands. Like Solomon he will rightly pray for wisdom in the guidance of the State.

Need I, then, impress upon you the importance of the study of Philosophy, and of Letters, without which indeed philosophy itself is barely intelligible? By this twofold wisdom a Prince is trained to understand the laws of God and of man, by it we are, one and all, enlightened to see the realities of the world around us. Literature is our guide to the true meaning of the past, to a right estimate of the present, to a sound forecast of the future. Where Letters cease darkness covers the land; and a Prince who cannot read the lessons of history is a helpless prey of flattery and intrigue.

Next we ask, at what age should a boy begin the study of Letters? Theodosius and Eratosthenes regarded the seventh year as the earliest reasonable period. But Aristophanes, followed by Chrysippus and Quintilian, would have children from the very cradle begin their training under nurses of skilled intelligence. In this matter of nurses the greatest care is necessary, so subtle are the influences which affect the growing mind. But above all other safeguards stands the unconscious guidance of the mother, who, like Cornelia of old, must instil by example a refined habit of speech and bearing.

In Religion, I may assume from your Christian nurture that you have learnt the Lord's Prayer, the Salutation of the Blessed Virgin, the Creed, the Gospel of St John, and certain Collects. You have been taught in what consist the chief Commandments of God, the Gifts of the Spirit, the Deadly Sins; the Way of Salvation and the doctrine of the Life of the world to come. This latter truth was, indeed, taught by Socrates, as we know from Cicero. Nor can any earthly interest have so urgent a claim upon us. We shall not value this human existence which has been bestowed upon us except in so far as it prepares us for the Future State. The fuller truth concerning this great doctrine is beyond your years : but you may, as time goes on, refer to what has been laid down by the great Doctors of the Church ; and not only by them, for, as Basil allows, the poets and other authors of antiquity are saturated with the same faith, and for this reason deserve our study. Literature, indeed, is ever holding forth to us the lesson 'God before all else.' As a Prince, moreover, your whole life and character should be marked by gratitude for favours showered upon you for no merit of your own, and by reverence, which, in all that concerns the services, the faith, and the authority of the Church, will lead you to emulate the filial obedience of Constantine and Theodosius. For although the priesthood is committed to the protection of kings, it is not under their authority.

In the choice of companions be careful to seek the society of those only whose example is worthy of your imitation. This is indeed a matter which closely concerns your future welfare. We are all, in youth especially, in danger of yielding to the influence of evil example. Above all, I trust that your Tutors will keep you clear of that insidious form of flattery which consists in agreeing with everything we may affirm or propose. Extend your intimacy only to those of your own years who are frank and truthful, pure in word and act, modest in manner, temperate and peaceful. Seize every opportunity of learning to converse in the vulgar tongues spoken in your realm. It is unworthy of a prince to be unable without an interpreter to hold intercourse with his people. Mithridates could speak with his subjects of whatever province in their own language ; whilst neglect of this plain duty lost to the Empire and its German sovereigns its fair province of Italy. The ties that bind monarch and people should be woven of mutual affection, and how is this possible where free and intelligible communication cannot exist? As

Homer says, silence is becoming in a woman, but in a man, and that man a king standing before his people, it is rather a shame and a disgrace.

§ 4. But further: we must learn to express ourselves with distinction, with style and manner worthy of our subject. In a word, Eloquence is a prime accomplishment in one immersed in affairs. Ulysses, though a poor warrior, was adjudged worthy of the arms of Achilles by virtue of his persuasive speech. Cicero, too, admonishes us to the same effect: "let arms to the toga yield." But speech should ever follow upon reflection; without that let a boy, nay, a man also, be assured that silence is his wiser part. Such orators as Pericles or Demosthenes refused to address the Assembly without opportunity for careful preparation. A facile orator speaks from his lips, not from his heart or his understanding; and forgets that loquacity is not the same as eloquence. How often have men cause to regret the gift of too ready speech, and 'the irrevocable word' of which Horace warns us. Still there is a middle course; a moderation in speech, which avoids alike a Pythagorean silence and the chatter of a Thersites; and at this we should aim. For without reasonable practice the faculty of public speech may be found altogether wanting when the need arises. The actual delivery of our utterances calls for methodical training. The shrill tremulous tone of a girl must be rigidly forbidden, as on the other hand must any tendency to shout. The entire word must in every case be uttered, the proper value given to each syllable and each letter, with especial attention to the final sound. Words must not, as it were, linger in the throat, but be clearly emitted, both tongue and lips taking duly their respective parts. Your master will arrange as exercises words in which the form or connexion of syllables demands peculiar care in their enunciation. You remember the device by which Demosthenes trained his voice to reach a crowded assembly.

To express yourself, then, with grace and distinction is a

proper object of your ambition; and without ambition excellence, in this or other studies, is rarely attained. But if speech be, as Democritus said, the shadow, of which thought and conduct are the reality, you will be warned by corrupt conversation to avoid the corrupt nature from which it proceeds. We know that Ulysses cunningly guarded his comrades from the song of the Sirens; and that St Paul quotes Menander upon the mischief wrought by 'evil communications.' But this by no means implies that we must be always at the extreme of seriousness in social intercourse. In conversation, kindliness and courtesy are always attractive: pertinacity or pretentiousness are odious: a turgid affected style arouses contempt. Insincerity or malice are, of course, not mere defects in form but positive sins. So let your address be frank, outspoken, self-respecting, manly.

Nature and circumstances thus provide us with the general material of speech, its topics, and the broader conditions of their treatment. When, however, speech is considered as an art, we find that it is the function of Grammar to order its expression; of Dialectic to give it point; of Rhetoric to illustrate it; of Philosophy to perfect it. But before entering upon this in detail we must first insist upon the overwhelming importance of Memory, which is in truth the first condition of capacity for Letters. A boy should learn without effort, retain with accuracy, and reproduce easily. Rightly is memory called 'the nursing mother of learning.' It needs cultivation, however, whether a boy be gifted with retentiveness or not. Therefore let some passage from poet or moralist be committed to memory every day.

§ 5.   Grammar, it is allowed, is the portal to all knowledge whatsoever. As a subject of study it is more complex and more fruitful than its name would imply, and it yields its full profit only to such as enter early and zealously upon its pursuit. The greatest minds have not been ashamed to shew themselves earnest in the study of Grammar. Tully, Consul and defender of the state, Julius Caesar, the mighty Emperor, and Augustus his successor, gave evidence in their writings of skill in this fundamental branch of learning, and no prince need feel it unworthy of him to walk in the steps of so great exemplars. I have already said that learning is a necessary equipment of Kings, and this the Royal Prophet of old enforces, when he declares:

'Be wise now therefore, O ye Kings; be learned, ye that are judges of the earth.'

But how, in our day, can a man be learned and acquire wisdom unless first he master that which is the very foundation of all knowledge, viz. Grammar?

Now the term *Grammar*, as Quintilian says, is identical with *Literature* (γράμμα i.e. litera), and this art of Grammar falls naturally into three parts, the first being the art of right speech, or eloquence, the second that of composition in prose and verse, the third that of the epistolary style. Grammatical correctness in speaking signifies the right choice both of vocabulary and of construction. As regards the former point, the usage of words and the source from which they are derived have to be carefully noted. For words are either of native or of foreign origin; they are either simple or compound; they may bear a natural and direct, or a metaphorical and transferred, sense; or, once more, we may distinguish between words of accepted usage and invented words. For instance, all words of Italian origin are *native*; *foreign* words have many sources, as Gaul (e.g. reda), Spain (e.g. gurdi, i.e. stolidi), Germany (marchio); but, of course, Greece provides us with far the greater number. In the use of words of Greek origin it is right to choose the Latin form of inflexion, though Vergil's usage justifies the preference of the Greek form in verse. Of *simple* words 'amo,' 'lego,' are sufficient instances; 'per-lego,' 'im-probus' we call *compound*: and there are, again, more complex forms, 'im-per-territus,' 'male-volus,' 'Antichristus.' By a word in its *natural* sense we mean one which retains its original direct application : 'flumen' (fluo), for instance, is simply a 'flowing body of water'; but 'durus' as referring to a man's disposition is obviously used in a *metaphorical* sense. As a literary artifice this use of words in a transferred sense is common enough, as we speak of 'lumen orationis,' 'contentionum procellae,' or say of a parrot, 'monetare voces,' when he imitates the human voice. But when such employment of metaphor obscures the plain meaning of discourse, it ceases to be an ornament and becomes a weariness. If long drawn out, this affectation of figure tends to allegory or to mere verbal puzzles. By accepted words we mean those which form the recognised vocabulary of the language, and upon these only ought we to rely. To very few, the great creators of a tongue, is it given to coin new words with impunity. But in all composition one controlling rule must be observed. Secure euphony, indeed, and grace, wherever you may be able, but first and foremost choose the word which will most exactly express the sense you wish to convey.

Having thus grasped the characteristics of words generally, you will go on to study inflexions, diminutives and other derived forms; examples of the latter are 'scabellum,' 'bipennis,' 'excido.' Inflexional changes expressing the modifications of case, mood, or tense are sufficiently exhibited in the Grammars and must be carefully learnt; so too the distinctions of gender, and the forms by which they are expressed. The right order of words in the sentence and the methods of connecting subordinate clauses are of even greater importance.

In speaking Latin, barbarisms of all kinds need to be avoided with great care. The term 'barbarism' includes a variety of faults, partly against taste, partly against the standard usage of the best writers. It is, for example, a 'barbarism' to employ foreign words not recognised in Roman speech, such as German importations. Again, exaggerated or violent delivery comes under the same heading. Ignorant or perverse changes in the usual forms of words or inflexions, pardonable, perhaps, in verse, if metre requires, disfigure prose. A false quantity in the same way is a decided 'barbarism.' Solecism is another, but closely-allied, type of grammatical error; such as the mis-use of gender, or of case; the wrong force of the preposition; the confusion of 'an,' 'ne,' and 'non'; the employment of such forms as 'nex,' 'mortes,' and others unknown to the best writers. Care must be taken to distinguish apparent solecisms; 'equulus grandis' is to be avoided but it is not a solecism. So 'Ludi floralia'; 'Catalina,' 'Galba,' and other masculine names in -a, and 'Glycerium' and others in -um, though they seem incorrect, are all in order. Real may be distinguished from apparent solecisms by falling back upon four canons: Reason, Antiquity, Authority, Usage.

By Reason we may mean, first, analogy, and analogy implies comparison of similars. So we compare a word whose use is doubtful with another, parallel in certain respects, whose use is definitely settled. Secondly, reason rests upon etymology, but neither derivation nor analogy may determine the form of a word in contradiction to fixed Usage; thus we do not say 'audaciter,' nor 'conire': and indeed analogy alone will often lead us astray, as we may see from the declension of 'domus.' Etymology is the enquiry into the origin of words, but too ingenious guesses tend to bring the science into contempt: such an one as that which derives 'homo' from 'humus' (as a being sprung from the ground), 'stella' from 'stilla' (a drop of light); 'caelebs' from 'caelum' (as one who is free from the heaviest burden of existence, i.e. a wife). Even the great Varro errs in connecting 'ager' with 'ago' (as a place where work is done). Nor should etymology, even when sound in itself, induce you to tamper pedantically with the spelling accepted by the best writers. Antiquity and Authority demand our respect, for they carry with them a certain dignity of their own not to be lightly regarded. At the same time, nothing is worse in a young writer than affectation; beware, therefore, of the forced imitation of an older style, and abstain from introducing words and expressions, now obsolete, into speech whose cast is of to-day.   As said Phavorinus to a pupil—you will find the anecdote in Aulus Gellius—'Copy the virtues of the great men of old, but let their archaisms die with them.'   Speech should above all things be intelligible, and without pretension.   Who would now use 'nox' as an ablative, or 'im' as an accusative for 'eum'?   Yet the 'Twelve Tables' exhibit both.

The Authority to which we appeal must be that of orators and historians, in the first place; of poets, only in the second, owing to their dependence upon metrical limitations.   But one and all must be drawn from the best age, when oratory was marked by perspicuity of matter and style.

Authoritative usage, then, affords the final canon to be obeyed in all composition; and no argument from analogy, from venerable antiquity, or from opinion can set this aside. Now, to determine this usage is not so simple a matter as it may seem.   For in style as in more important matters we may not take usage to be merely the practice of the majority, as Quintilian warns us.   Eloquence, like wisdom, like nobleness of life, is a gift of the minority.   The usage of the commonalty degrades Latin; 'erit cito venire' would be a popular version of 'he will come.'   So we must look for a higher standard for our usage, and we shall find it.   For as in Conduct we agree to take as our norm the customary motive and action of *good* men, so by usages in style we mean only such as are exhibited in the uniform practice of scholars and men of education.

§ 6.   Let this stand as a sketch or suggestion—it is nothing more—of the first of the three functions of Grammar above alluded to, viz., that which concerns correct speech and eloquence.   But, as the study of Letters forms in reality one complete whole, the second function of grammar, as the art of written composition in prose and verse, is illustrated by what has been written above upon the spoken language.   So I repeat that skill in composition can only be attained by close and copious reading of the standard authors in oratory, history and poetry, in which you must direct your attention not only to the vocabulary employed by them, but also to their method of handling their subject-matter. Following ancient precedent, Homer and Vergil, the masters of the Heroic style, should be your first choice in poetry. The loftiness of theme and the romantic spirit of the *Iliad* and the *Aeneid* mark them out, as Augustine held, as an inspiring training for boys. But this advice implies the study of Greek in which you are unlikely to find a competent tutor. Still, the immense advantage of this branch of Letters should urge you to seek for one if opportunity offers : for, as King of Hungary, you will reign over not a few descendants of that ancient race. Moreover, true freedom in the use of the Latin tongue can only be assured by a simultaneous study of the older language. I cannot forget the authority of Cato in this respect, although I feel I am offering a counsel of perfection to one living in remote Pannonia. Meanwhile we will confine ourselves to the speech and literature of Rome.

Now I meet an objection. You will be confronted by the opposition of the shallow Churchman. 'Why waste precious time in studying such sources of corruption as the pagan poets?' They will quote Cicero and Plato, Jerome and Boethius, and will cry out for the banishment of the very names of the ancient poets from the soil of your country. To this your answer can only be : 'If this tirade indeed represents the serious opinion of my people, I can but shake off the dust from my feet and bid farewell to a land shrouded in darkness so appalling.' Happily, however, there are in Hungary not a few to whom the poets of antiquity are a precious possession. You will have no difficulty in quoting classical precedent for honouring them as they deserve. Nay the Fathers themselves, Jerome, Augustine, Cyprian, did not hesitate to draw illustrations from heathen poetry and so sanctioned its study.

Further, if we are to reject the great writers of antiquity

for the errors they contain, how shall we treat the masters of theology? From them proceeded the heresies. Shall we, then, expel them and their writings, as once the Romans banished doctors because they made mistakes? Finally, it is enough to remember that Paul the Apostle availed himself of Epimenides or Menander to enforce a doctrine. Is not this a sufficiently strong position: 'you despise Paul's authority; can you ask us then to respect yours'?

But I do not assert that all the poets are suited to the youthful mind; nor, I would add, are all the theologians suited to the Christian student. The crucial question is: how do you use your authors? Basil has left us a clear guidance on the matter: we leave on one side their beliefs and superstitions, their false ideas of happiness, their defective standard of morals; we welcome all that they can render in praise of integrity and in condemnation of vice. Consider the habits of the bees. Other creatures enjoy the colour, or the scent, of the flower; they, however, are wise to extract its lurking sweetness. Thus they choose where they will settle, and are content with just that fruition of their choice which serves their end. So, as Jerome says, in reading the ancient poets we absorb the things of life and beauty, leaving that which is but idolatry, error, or lust, to pass to its natural decay. Herein is laid down an admirable principle by which we may be guided in reading all authors of antiquity. Wherever excellence is commended, whether by poet, historian or philosopher, we may safely welcome their aid in building up the character. For with the young the early impressions of moral worthiness are usually the most enduring. To quote Horace[1]:

> 'After long years the scent will still imbue
> The jar of that which seasoned it when new.'

Thus morals and learning are alike forwarded by the judicious use of Literature in education.

[1] *Epist.* i. II. 70 (Sir Theodore Martin's version).

In making our selection of individual authors, we must consider not poets only, but historians, philosophers and orators. Christian writers I leave for the present. As regards the poets, amongst the Latins the first place belongs of perpetual right to Vergil. So noble is the music of his language, so enduring his fame, that here, at least, praise can no further exalt, nor criticism detract. Let the scholar observe his varying style, now terse, now abounding, now severe, now luxuriant. Lucan dignifies his historical theme and Statius, less impressive, is yet worthy of a place beside him. Ovid, pathetic, appealing, wanton, is best read in his *Metamorphoses.* Of other poets of the heroic vein, scarcely fit to rank as *poets,* Claudian and the poet of the Argonauts may be preferred. Horace holds a place only next to Vergil: the charm of style and of subject graces each variety of his work. But here, once more, we must choose what is fit for youthful study. This is even more necessary in the case of the other great Satirist, Juvenal, in spite of his moral earnestness and severity of judgment. In handling Martial one cannot gather the roses for the thorns. Persius is helpful only to one who can master his obscurities.

The Elegiac poets are one and all unsuited for boys' reading: all are enervating. Plautus and Terence must be studied for diction; in Tragedy, a most valuable discipline, we have Seneca alone. In Speech we aim at dignity and grace. Tragedy presents us with the one, Comedy with the other. Moreover in reading the Dramatists let the master win his pupil to judge characters and situations, with grave warnings against all pleadings in favour of wrong-doing.

Of Orators, with Cicero at their head, there is no small choice. Frank and straightforward in style he is always intelligible. To read his book *De Officiis* is not merely a useful exercise but an absolutely necessary one. St Ambrose wrote, in imitation of it, a work which may be wisely read to supplement his model, and so Cicero's teaching made good on the Christian side. Lactantius, Augustine and Jerome have each a polished style; and Gregory may be profitably used. Of our own contemporaries, Lionardo Aretino, Guarino, Poggio and Ambrogio exhibit a chaste diction which is valuable for study.

Among historians Livy and Sallust take the first rank; though Justin, Quintus Curtius, Valerius Maximus, and Arrian, in a translation, may be read by boys; Suetonius I exclude. Under this same head of history I strongly urge that portions of the Old and New Testaments, such as extracts from the books of Genesis, the Kings, the Maccabees, Judith, Esdras and Esther; and parts of the Gospels and Acts of the Apostles be taught. History, as Cicero says, is the living witness of the past, the lamp of truth; it is our guide to the days that are now, because it exhibits those that are gone. It is most important, therefore, to be thoroughly versed in the works of the chief historians and from their study learn practical wisdom in affairs. But I would add here a most serious caution. Beware of wasting time over such a subject as the history of Bohemia or the history of Hungary. For such would be but the productions of mere ignorant Chroniclers, a farrago of nonsense and lies, destitute of attraction in form, in style, or in grave reflections. For boys must from the earliest be made familiar only with the *best*, if we look for them to develope a sound judgment in their later years.

§ 7. The third part of Grammar is concerned with the art of Letter-writing. This, too, is an art which a Prince may by no means regard as beneath his attention. Apart from the fact that correspondence is to him a duty of importance, a regular habit of composing in this style is helpful to the study of authors. Several of the great Caesars of the early Empire were conspicuous for their powers as letter-writers. So too were the late Pontiff Nicolas V. and his predecessor. Further, a Prince may, perhaps, not write very often, but let him learn to write legibly. It was no credit to the great Alfonso that his signature was most like the traces of a worm crawling over the paper. It is worth while to be careful over so small a thing as the shape of the letters; let round letters be round, looped letters shew their loops, and so on. Both neatness and accuracy in writing should be cultivated. The ancient style of hand-writing was neater, more legible, than ours, and was more like that of the Greeks, from whom indeed it was derived. But whatever be the style adopted care must be taken to provide good models. Moreover, in choosing writing copies select useful and elevating subjects, for instance moral maxims from famous prose writers or poets, so that unconsciously the scholar absorb ennobling thoughts. As to spelling, rules may indeed be laid down but the real method is that of practice in writing combined with observant reading of good authors; in the case of poetry prosody aids the spelling. I will now add a few words on Orthography. In dealing with compound words (e.g. those with 'ad-' as prefix) usage will be the safest guide, as the same compound may be differently written with equal authority. The rules for doubling the consonant in compo-sition need attention. For since *x* is equivalent to *cs*, or *gs*, 'ex-surgo' should be written 'exurgo,' 'ex-sanguis,' 'exanguis.' Notice the usage as to compounds of 'iacio'; and the more important modifications of prepositions in composition. In a word borrowed from the Greek retain the spelling *ph* for ϕ. With Quintilian distinguish *cum* the preposition from *quum* the conjunction. Purists write 'Caius' but pronounce 'Gaius.' From this we observe that the written form has not always preserved for us the true phonetic value: though Quintilian tells us that 'Caius' is a man, 'Gaius' a woman. Other doubtful cases are 'quidquid' or 'quicquid,' 'id-circo' or 'icirco.' Consonants are sometimes inserted for euphony, e.g. 'si-*c*-ubi'; 'em-*p*-tum'; 'am-*b*-io'; 'ob-*s*-curus'; 'ob-*l*-iquus.' *K* is a redundant letter, always to be replaced by *c*, in spite of usage which supports '*K*alendas,' '*K*arolus.'

Usage, indeed, has practically determined spelling in the majority of cases and we must be careful in our own practice to abide by the standard of the best scholars and writers of the past.

The use of the aspirate in the two words containing the Greek letter ρ, *Rh*enus and *Rh*odanus, indicates that in earliest times both Germans and Gauls made use of Greek letters and that these rivers derived their names from the Greeks.   In other adopted words the right rule of the aspirate must be observed.   No Latin consonant is aspirated, unless with Servius we except "pulcher."   Hence we should write 'mihi,' 'nihil,' and probably 'incoo,' 'sepulcro.'   Other aspirated consonants met with in Latin are Greek derivatives: 'rhetor,' 'archiepiscopus,' 'monarcha'; and so we correctly write 'Phoebus,' 'Orpheus.'   We note as an exception 'fama' from 'φήμι,' 'filius' from 'φίλος,' 'fero' from 'φέρω.'   'Yerusalem' is wrongly spelt: the first syllable consists of the simple vowel sound I.   So too are 'autumpnus,' 'contempno,' where euphony does not require ρ: but we write 'contempsi.'   Latin superlatives are written regularly in -ssimus: not -ximus.   'Nixus' (from nitor) implies physical, 'nisus' mental, effort.   So far for general rules of orthography; the spelling of individual words can only be learnt, as already said, by observation of usages in your own reading.

§ 8.   Between Grammar and Rhetoric there is of necessity the closest connection; for it is by means of Rhetoric that the author, whether historian or poet, displays his literary style and artifice, and derives the form in which he casts his judgments of men and things, or the Orator exhibits his appeals and his conclusions.   Both poet and historian have habitual recourse to the rules of Rhetoric, for which you will do wisely to betake yourself exclusively to the great authorities, to Cicero, Quintilian and Aristotle, whose *Rhetoric* has lately appeared in a translation.   You, indeed, are not destined to the career of an orator, but to the responsibilities of Kingship; yet a sound knowledge of the usages of Rhetoric will be of no small gain to you, even though in actual life a moderate skill in oratory is all that circumstances may require or admit of.

Nor can you neglect Dialectic, which in its turn has so near relation with Rhetoric; for both alike aim at convincing the reason. Logic, indeed, has no profit except it serve as a direct aid to clear and precise thinking and expression, enabling us to recognise in our reasonings the fundamental difference between certain, probable, and manifestly false steps in argument. But beware of logicians who waste time and ingenuity in mere verbal subtleties, in whose hands Logic is a thing, not of living use, but of intellectual death. You will remember that Cicero reproached Sextus Pompey for too great devotion to Geometry, and affirmed that far too much time was spent in his day upon Civil Law and Dialectic. His reason was that the true praise of men lies in *doing*[1], and that consequently all ingenious trifling, however harmless in itself, which withdraws our energies from fruitful activity, is unworthy of the true Citizen.

If that be so, we must ask whether we are to include Music amongst pursuits unsuited to a Prince? The Romans of the later age seem to have deprecated attention to this Art in their Emperors. It was, on the other hand, held a marked defect in Themistocles that he could not tune the lyre. The armies of Lacedaemon marched to victory under the inspiration of song, although Lycurgus could not have admitted the practice had it seemed to him unworthy of the sternest manhood. The Hebrew poet-king need be but alluded to, and Cicero is on his side also. So amidst some diversity of opinion our judgement inclines to the inclusion of Music, as a subject to be pursued in moderation under instructors only of serious character, who will rigorously disallow all melodies of a sensuous nature. Under these conditions we may accept the Pythagorean opinion that Music exerts a soothing and refreshing influence upon the mind.

---

[1] Vittorino urges the same sentiment to Ambrogio (supra p. 82). Both of these men shared the strong practical instincts which marked the best side of the new Learning. With all three Literature was a means rather than an end in itself.

Geometry is peculiarly fitted to the earlier stages of a boy's
education. For it quickens alike the perceptive faculty and
the reasoning powers. Combining with this subject Arithmetic
your Masters will certainly include the two in your course of
training. The value of Geometry may be proved by the case
of Syracuse, which city prolonged its defence simply by virtue
of the skill of the geometrician Archimedes. Further the study
of Geometry provides us with a more exact method of reasoning
than is always supplied by Dialectic; for many apparently just
assumptions are corrected by the strict observation of the truths
of Geometry. For instance, the most perfect form of the line,
which is the circle, is that which encloses the largest space: and
the equilateral triangle contains more than the scalene: although reason, apart from the aid of geometrical method,
would not suggest these truths. At the same time, though an
attractive study, Geometry should not be allowed to become too
absorbing. A prince must not be ignorant of Astronomy,
which unfolds the skies and by that means interprets the
secrets of Heaven to mortal men. Did not the greatest rulers
of antiquity hold this wisdom in high esteem? Pericles and
Sulpicius both alike restored the day in a crisis in the field by
their ready use of this lore. Dion and Nicias are examples of
the gain and the loss which may be involved in the right or
wrong study of eclipses. And one may fairly ask how without
a knowledge of astronomy we can understand the many allusions to the Heavens contained in the ancient Poets. On
these grounds let the young Prince include this science in his
courses.

But we must here interpose a caution. There is a danger
lest in our interest in natural, or external, objects we find but a
lower place for those weightier things which concern character
and action. Two difficulties confront us, that of the choice of
subjects and methods of instruction, and that of the risk we
run of overburdening the learner's mind by too great a variety
of study. But we must bear in mind that the thinking faculties

find relief from strain in this very variety, just as the digestion is aided by succession in diet. So that I have no fear lest your mind should suffer from alternations in subjects or change of masters. Therefore let grammar, dialectic and other subjects occupy you in turn, due regard also being had to the place which physical training must occupy in your education.

§ 9. So far we have touched upon studies by which we may attain enlightenment of the mind. We have not yet however directly considered how we may most surely distinguish the true and the just from the base and degrading in our Reading and in Life : and what as a consequence must be imitated and what avoided. The poets, the orators and the historians, suggest, perhaps, rather than enforce, the Virtues : hence we must look for final guidance to a higher source, viz. to Philosophy. Now Philosophy signifies desire for wisdom ; and wisdom includes more than is contained within the limit of the seven Liberal arts, for it enquires into the causes of all things human and divine. To Thales philosophy meant Natural Science ; Socrates followed, and brought the divine laws of morality from heaven to man : Plato completed Philosophy by adding the science of mind. For the truths of conduct, then, we send our scholar to Moral Philosophy, a truly indispensable study. For here he will more exactly learn the duty he owes, in the first place, to the Deity; to his parents, to his elders, to strangers ; to the civil and military powers, and to his fellow-citizens; he will learn what becomes him towards wife, towards friend, towards tenant and slave.

Moreover Philosophy will teach you to despise avarice— that lust for wealth which Sallust tells us the truly wise never feel. Respect towards women, affection for children and for home ; pity for the distressed, justice towards all ; self-control in anger, restraint in indulgence, forbearance in success : contentment, courage, duty—these are some of the virtues to which philosophy will lead you. In order that from early youth this true wisdom may be duly inculcated I would prescribe the study of books, carefully prepared and attractive in style, specially adapted to this end. I have already alluded to one or two works suited to this purpose; to them I would add all the writings of Cicero which touch upon moral duty, as the treatises on *Old Age*, *Friendship*, and others; the Letters of Seneca, Boethius upon *Consolation*; others of later date may be advised, provided always that the Master restrict the choice to works recognised by good judges as sound both in matter and in style.

THE TREATISE OF BATTISTA GUARINO,
DE ORDINE DOCENDI ET STUDENDI.

BATTISTA GUARINO was the youngest son[1] of Guarino
Veronese, and was born in 1434 during his father's residence
at Ferrara, where Guarino held the post of tutor to the heir of
the House, Leonello d'Este[2], and kept school. We gather
that he was the only one of the sons of Guarino who shewed
any genuine taste for scholarship, and that his father built high
hopes upon his abilities. As a boy he was brought up and
educated under the immediate direction of Guarino, who was
led, by his early promise, to entrust him with a share in
the private tuition of the students resident in the Master's
house (*contubernales*). It was Guarino's purpose in this way to
secure a continuity for his methods.

In 1455, when only twenty-one years of age, Battista was
elected to the chair of Rhetoric at Bologna, which is decisive
evidence of his reputation for scholarship. This he held for
two years, when he returned to join his father at Ferrara. He
had become an expert in textual emendation and devoted
much time to the study of the MSS. of Catullus. He wrote
the treatise *Upon the method of Teaching and of Reading the
Classical Authors* at the age of twenty-five, probably at his
father's suggestion ; for we have no recognised publication

---

[1] Sabbadini, *Epistol. Guar.* p. 81.

[2] Guarino, like Vittorino, associated many other pupils with the princes
forming his immediate charge. The University of Ferrara was founded in
1436, when Guarino was made Professor of Rhetoric.

upon the educational art from the elder Guarino, if we except
such a Letter as that addressed by him to Leonello d'Este[1].
The date of the Treatise is given as October 1459; Guarino
Veronese died in December of the following year. We may
take it, then, that the tract represents, as it claims to do, the
general principles which guided the teaching at the School at
Ferrara.   On the death of his father, Battista was unanimously
elected his successor in the Professorship in the University.

The Treatise is narrower in scope than that of Vergerius
or of Aeneas Sylvius.   It contains no reference to subjects
outside Ancient Literature ; History, by which of course Livy
and Plutarch are intended, has a sympathetic paragraph, but
Logic or Ethics seem to be regarded mainly as illustrations of
Cicero.   The Greek authors, however, occupy an important
place; and it is evident that this Tract marks the time
when the claim to be considered an educated gentleman will
only be allowed to one who is familiar with both the ancient
Literatures.   This standard of culture is upheld and defended in formal terms for the first time in this Treatise[2].

[The Treatise bears date 'Verona xv Kal. Martii, 1459.
Hain, *8128, is the earliest (apparently) edition recorded, but no
place, date, nor printer, is given.   The Heidelberg edition of
1489 (Hain *8131) and the Modena edition of 1496 (Hain
8129) are the only others of the century so far distinguished.
It is not met with in later collections of such Tracts published
in the sixteenth and seventeenth centuries in Paris or
Amsterdam[3].]

[1] Sabbadini, *Epistolario*, no. 373: 'prima di 1441'; the letter itself,
nearly in full, in Rosmini, *Guarino*, i. 113.

[2] The practice of Vittorino da Feltre was, we know, in advance of
general opinion, and I believe that, in reality, at the Mantuan School far
more weight was attached to Greek than at the School of Guarino at
Ferrara.

[3] Rösler is wrong as to date of First Edition (Strassb. 1514).   A later
one is recorded : Jena 1704.   Rösler, *Johan. Dominicis*, &c. p. 142 n.

BATTISTA GUARINO TO MAFFEO GAMBARA, OF BRESCIA,

CONCERNING THE ORDER AND THE METHOD TO BE OBSERVED IN TEACHING AND IN READING THE CLASSICAL AUTHORS.

In offering this short Treatise for your acceptance, I am fully aware that you need no incentive to regard the pursuit of Letters as the most worthy object of your ambition. But you may find what I have written a not unwelcome reminder of our past intercourse, whilst it may prove of use to other readers into whose hands it may fall. For I have had in view not only students anxious for guidance in their private reading, but masters in search of some definite principles of method in teaching the Classics. Hence I have treated both of Greek and of Latin Letters, and I have confidence that the course I have laid down will prove a thoroughly satisfactory training in literature and scholarship. I should remind you that the conclusions presented in this little work are not the result of my own experience only. It is indeed a summary of the theory and practice of several scholars, and especially does it represent the doctrine of my father Guarino Veronese; so much so, that you may suppose him to be writing to you by my pen, and giving you the fruit of his long and ripe experience in teaching. May I hope that you will yourself prove to be one more example of the high worth of his precepts?

Let me, at the outset, begin with a caution. No master can endow a careless and indifferent nature with the true passion for learning. That a young man must acquire for himself. But once the taste begins to develope, then in Ovid's words 'the more we drink, the more we thirst.' For when the mind has begun to enjoy the pleasures of learning the passion for fuller and deeper knowledge will grow from day to day. But there can be no proficiency in studies unless there be first the desire to excel. Wherefore let a young man set forward eagerly in quest of those true, honourable, and enduring treasures of the mind which neither disease nor death has power to destroy. Riches, which adventurers seek by land and sea, too often win men to pleasure rather than to learning ; for self-indulgence is a snare from whose enticements it is the bounden duty of parents to wean their children, by kind word, or by severity if need arise. Perchance then in later years the echo of a father's wise advice may linger and may avail in the hour of temptation.

In the choice of a Master we ought to remember that his position should carry with it something of the authority of a father : for unless respect be paid to the man and to his office regard will not be had to his words. Our forefathers were certainly right in basing the relation of teacher and pupil upon the foundation of filial reverence on the one part and fatherly affection on the other. Thus the instinct of Alexander of Macedon was a sound one which led him to say that, whilst he owed to his father Philip the gift of life, he owed to his tutor Aristotle an equal debt, namely, the knowledge how to use it. Care must be taken therefore from the outset to avoid a wrong choice of master : one, for instance, who is ill-bred, or ill-educated. Such a one may by bad teaching waste precious years of a boy's life ; not only is nothing rightly learnt, but much of that which passes as instruction needs to be undone again, as Timotheus[1] said long ago. Faults, moreover,

---

[1] For the anecdote, see p. 110, above.

imbibed in early years, as Horace reminds us, are by no means easy to eradicate. Next, the master must not be prone to flogging as an inducement to learning. It is an indignity to a free-born youth, and its infliction renders learning itself repulsive, and the mere dread of it provokes to unworthy evasions on the part of timorous boys. The scholar is thus morally and intellectually injured, the master is deceived, and the discipline altogether fails of its purpose. The habitual instrument of the teacher must be kindness, though punishment should be retained as it were in the background as a final resource. In the case of elder boys, emulation and the sense of shame, which shrinks from the discredit of failure, may be relied upon. I advise also that boys, at this stage, work two together with a view to encouraging a healthy spirit of rivalry between them, from which much benefit may be expected. Large classes should be discouraged, especially for beginners, for though a fair average excellence may be apparently secured, thorough grounding, which is so important, is impossible. In the case of more advanced pupils, however, numbers tend rather to stimulate the teacher.

§ 2. As regards the course of study. From the first, stress must be laid upon distinct and sustained enunciation, both in speaking and in reading. But at the same time utterance must be perfectly natural; if affected or exaggerated the effect is unpleasing. The foundation of education must be laid in Grammar. Unless this be thoroughly learnt subsequent progress is uncertain,—a house built upon treacherous ground. Hence let the knowledge of nouns and verbs be secured early, as the starting point for the rest. The master will employ the devices of repetition, examination, and the correction of erroneous inflexions purposely introduced.

Grammar falls into two parts. The first treats of the rules which govern the use of the different Parts of Speech, and is called therefore 'Methodice,' the second includes the study of continuous prose, especially of historical narrative[1], and is called 'Historice.'

Now these Rules can be most satisfactorily learnt from the Compendium[2] written by my father which briefly sets out the more important laws of composition. In using this or a similar text-book the pupil must be practised both in written and in oral exercises. Only by rapid practice in oral composition can fluency and readiness be gained. And this will be further secured if the class is accustomed to speak in Latin. Certain general Rules of a crucial nature must be early learnt, and constantly practised, by the whole class. Such are those by which we recognise the differences between active, passive and deponent verbs, or between those of transitive or intransitive meaning. It is most important that each boy be required to form examples in illustration of the main rules of accidence and syntax, not only with accuracy but also with a certain propriety of style, as for instance with due attention to the order of words in the sentence. In this way the habit of sound and tasteful composition is imbibed during the earliest stages of education. A master who is properly qualified for his work will be careful to use only such transcripts of texts as can be relied upon for accuracy and completeness. The work just referred to has been much disfigured by additions and alterations due to the ignorance or conceit of the would-be emendator. As examples of what I mean you may turn to the rule as to the formation of the comparative of adjectives of the second declension where an inept correction is added in some copies ('vowel before a vowel' is turned into 'vowel before -us'); and in another place the spelling 'Tydites' is substituted for my father's (and, of course, the correct) form 'Tydides.'

---

[1] This would take the form of Delectus, Extracts, or continuous reading of an easy historical author in Greek or Latin.

[2] The *Regulae Guarini*, a very popular manual of accidence, intended to be learnt by heart.

But to return. Let the scholar work at these Rules until they are so ingrained, as it were, into the memory that they become a part and parcel of the mind itself. In this way the laws of grammar are accurately recalled with effort and almost unconsciously. Meanwhile rules of quantity and metre have been entered upon. This branch of Letters is so important that no one who is ignorant of it can claim to be thought an educated man. Hence it is significant that so much attention was paid to the subject by the ancients; even Augustine, that great pillar of the Church, did not disdain to publish a tract upon Scansion[1]. In reading the Poets a Knowledge of Prosody is indispensable to the enjoyment, nay even the understanding, of their works. An acquaintance with metrical structure enables us to enter into the beauties of the rhythm, whilst our only clue to the exact meaning of the writer is not seldom given by the quantity of a vowel. Nor is the artifice of rhythm confined to poetical composition. Orators often shew themselves masters of this art; and in order to duly appreciate the flow of their eloquence, much more to reproduce it for ourselves, we must be skilled in the ordinary laws of metre. On this ground it is possible to commend the use of the manual of grammar which passes under the name of Alexander[2]; it is founded upon the great work of Priscian, but it is much more readily committed to memory on account of its metrical form. When the rudiments of prosody have been carefully learnt we shall find that proficiency is best gained by the daily reading of the poets. The works of Vergil must be learnt by heart, and recited as a regular task. In this way the flow of the hexameter, not less than the quantity of individual syllables, is impressed upon the ear, and insensibly moulds our taste. Other metres may afterwards be attempted, so that no form of ancient poetry be left neglected.

[1] The *De Musica* was in the library of Vittorino, supra p. 70.
[2] The *Doctrinale* of Alexander de Villa Dei.

§ 3. I have said that ability to write Latin verse is one of the essential marks of an educated person. I wish now to indicate a second, which is of at least equal importance, namely, familiarity with the language and literature of Greece. The time has come when we must speak with no uncertain voice upon this vital requirement of scholarship. I am well aware that those who are ignorant of the Greek tongue decry its necessity, for reasons which are sufficiently evident. But I can allow no doubt to remain as to my own conviction that without a knowledge of Greek Latin scholarship itself is, in any real sense, impossible. I might point to the vast number of words derived or borrowed from the Greek, and the questions which arise in connection with them; such as the quantity of the vowel sounds, the use of the diphthongs[1], obscure orthographies and etymologies. Vergil's allusion to the Avernian Lake:

> 'O'er that dread space no flying thing
> Unjeoparded could ply its wing,'[2]

is wholly missed by one who is ignorant of the relation between the name of the lake and the Greek word ὄρνις. Or again the lines of Ovid,

> 'Quae quia nascuntur dura vivacia caute
> Agrestes aconita vocant,'[3]

is unintelligible unless we can associate 'cautes' with the Greek (ἀκόνη). So too the name *Ciris* (κείρω), and the full force of *Aphrodite*[4] (ἄφρων) are but vaguely understood without a clear perception of their Greek etymologies. The Greek grammar, again, can alone explain the unusual case-endings which are met with in the declension of certain nouns, mostly proper names, which retain their foreign shape; such as 'Dido' and 'Mantus.' Nor are these exceptional forms confined to the

---

[1] Guarino Veronese wrote a treatise *De arte diphthongandi.*
[2] *Aen.* vi. 239 (Conington).
[3] *Metam.* vii. 418, 9.
[4] Cicero, *De Nat. Deor.* iii. 23. 59.

poetic use. But I turn to the authority of the great Latins themselves, to Cicero, Quintilian, Cato and Horace: they are unanimous in proclaiming the close dependence of the Roman speech and Roman literature upon the Greek, and in urging by example as well as by precept the constant study of the older language. To quote Horace[1] alone:

> 'Do you, my friends, from Greece your models draw,
> And day and night to con them be your law.'

And again,

> 'To Greece, that cared for nought but fame, the Muse
> Gave genius, and a tongue the gods might use.'

In such company I do not fear to urge the same contention.

Were we, indeed, to follow Quintilian, we should even begin with Greek in preference to Latin. But this is practically impossible, when we consider that Greek must be for us, almost of necessity, a learned and not a colloquial language; and that Latin itself needs much more elaborate and careful teaching than was requisite to a Roman of the imperial epoch. On the other hand, I have myself known not a few pupils of my father—he was, as you know, a scholar of equal distinction in either language—who, after gaining a thorough mastery of Latin, could then in a single year make such progress with Greek that they translated accurately entire works of ordinary difficulty from that language into good readable Latin *at sight*. Now proficiency of this degree can only be attained by careful and systematic teaching of the rudiments of the Grammar, as they are laid down in such a manual as the well-known Ἐρωτήματα of Manuel Chrysoloras, or in the abridgement which my father drew up of the original work of his beloved master. In using such a text-book the greatest attention must be paid to the verb, the regular form, with its scheme of moods and tenses; then the irregular verbs must be equally mastered. When the forms of noun and verb can be

---

[1] *De Arte Poetica*, ll. 268, 9; 323, 4. (Sir Theodore Martin's Version.)

immediately distinguished, and each inflexion of voice, mood and tense recognised,—and this can only be tested by constant *vivâ voce* exercises—then a beginning should be made with simple narrative prose. At this stage all authors whose subject matter requires close thought should be avoided, for the entire attention must be concentrated upon vocabulary and grammatical structure. Only when some degree of freedom in these latter respects has been secured should the master introduce books of increasing difficulty.

Our scholar should make his first acquaintance with the Poets through Homer, the sovereign master of them all. For from Homer our own poets, notably Vergil, drew their inspiration ; and in reading the *Iliad* or the *Odyssey* no small part of our pleasure is derived from the constant parallels we meet with. Indeed in them we see as in a mirror the form and manner of the *Aeneid* figured roughly before us, the incidents, not less than the simile or epithet which describe them, are, one might say, all there. In the same way, in his minor works Vergil has borrowed from Theocritus or Hesiod. After Homer has been attempted the way lies open to the other Heroic poets and to the Dramatists.

In reading of this wider range a large increase of vocabulary is gained, and in this the memory will be greatly assisted by the practice of making notes, which should be methodically arranged afterwards. The rules of Accentuation should now be learnt and their application observed after the same method. It is very important that regular exercises in elementary composition be required from the first, and this partly as an aid to construing. The scholar will now shortly be able to render a Latin author into Greek, a practice which compels us, as nothing else does, to realise the appropriateness of the writer's language, and its dignity of style, whilst at the same time it gives us increased freedom in handling it. For though delicate shades of meaning or beauties of expression may be overlooked by a casual reader they cannot escape a faithful translator.

But whilst a beginning is being thus made with Greek, continued progress must at the same time be secured in Latin. For instance the broader rules of grammar which sufficed in the earlier stages must give place to a more complete study of structure, such as we find in Priscian, and irregularities or exceptions, hitherto ignored, must be duly noted. At the same time the *Epistles* of Cicero will be taken in hand for purposes of declamation. Committed to memory they serve as one of the finest possible aids to purity, directness, and facility of style, and supply admirable matter in no less admirable form for adaptation to our own uses. Yet I would not be understood to claim the *Letters* of Cicero as alone offering a sufficient training in style. For distinction of style is the fruit of a far wider field of study. To quote Horace once more :

> ' Of writing well, be sure, the secret lies
> In wisdom: therefore study to be wise.'[1]

§ 4. But we are now passing from the first, or elementary, to the second, or more advanced, stage of grammar which I called ' Historice,' which is concerned with the study of continuous prose authors, more particularly the Historians. Here we begin with a short but comprehensive view of general history, which will include that of the Roman people, by such writers as Justin or Valerius Maximus. The latter author is also valuable as affording actual illustrations of virtuous precepts couched in attractive style. The scholar will now devote his attention to the Historians in regular order. By their aid he will learn to understand the manners, laws and institutions of different types of nation, and will examine the varying fortunes of individuals and states, the sources of their success and failure, their strength and their weakness. Not only is such Knowledge of interest in daily intercourse but it is of practical value in the ordering of affairs.

[1] *De Arte Poetica*, 309 (Conington).

Side by side with the study of history a careful reading of
the poets will be taken in hand. The true significance of
poetic fiction will now be appreciated. It consists, as Cicero
says, in the exhibition of the realities of our own life under the
form of imaginary persons and situations. Thus Jerome could
employ Terence in bringing home his exhortations to Temperance. Let us not forget that Vergil as a subject of deep
and regular study must always stand not first, but alone. Here
we have the express authority of Augustine, who urges the
supreme claim of the great poet to our life-long companionship.
Lucan may perhaps with good reason be postponed to a later
stage. Quintilian regarded him as 'the rhetorical poet': and
undoubtedly his poem has much affinity with certain aspects of
the forensic art. There is a certain strain of the keen debater
in particular portions of his work. So I should advise that
Vergil be followed by Statius, whose *Thebais*, fashioned upon
the *Aeneid*, will be found easy reading. The *Metamorphoses* of
Ovid form a useful introduction to the systematic knowledge
of Mythology—a subject of wide literary application—and as
such deserves close attention. The rest of the works of this
poet, if I except the *Fasti*—unique as a source of antiquarian
lore, and, alas! as incomplete as it is interesting—may very
wisely be omitted from the school course. The Tragedies of
Seneca attract us by the gravity of their situations and the
moral distinction of their characters by which they are
rendered specially useful for teaching purposes. Terence has
the sanction of Cicero as regards grace and appropriateness of
diction; he urged that parts of the Comedies should be committed to memory upon those grounds. If with Terence we
couple Juvenal, the greatest of Satirists, we shall find that these
two writers afford us a copious and elastic vocabulary for all the
needs of ordinary intercourse, and not that alone, but that
they provide us with a store of sound and dignified judgments.
It is objected, indeed, without sufficient reason, that Juvenal
is unsuitable for educational purposes in that he describes too

freely the vicious morals which come under his lash. But in the first place this applies to but very few passages, whilst the rest of the Satires must command the admiration of all earnest men : in the second, if we must shew our indignation in the matter we should direct it rather against the vices themselves than against their critic. Plautus is marked by a flow of eloquence and wit which secures him a high place in Latin literature. That the Muses, if they spoke in Latin, would choose 'the Plautine diction,' was a common saying ; and Macrobius placed the comic poet, in company with Cicero, at the head of the great masters of the Roman tongue. Horace throws unusual light upon the Art of poetry: he has a specially delicate sense of expression ; and in his choice of epithets is only surpassed by Vergil. His *Satires* again form the best introduction to that type of poetry : for Persius is much less clear. There are other poets of literary importance, but their study may be postponed to a later period. It will be of advantage that the reading of the poetical authors should be accompanied by occasional perusal of writers who have treated of Astrology and of Geography : such as Pomponius Mela, Solinus, and Strabo, which latter author has been lately translated from the Greek by my father. A clear conception, too, ought to be attained of the Ptolemaic Geography, to enable us to follow descriptions of countries unfamiliar to us.

The course of study which I have thus far sketched out will prove an admirable preparation for that further branch of scholarship which constitutes Rhetoric, including the thorough examination of the great monuments of eloquence, and skill in the oratorical art itself. The first work to claim our attention in this subject is the *Rhetoric* of Cicero[1], in which we find all the points of Oratory concisely but comprehensively set forth. The other rhetorical writings of Cicero will follow, and the principles therein laid down must be examined in the light of

---

[1] The *Rhetorica ad Herennium*, which Guarino Veronese had already determined to be unauthentic.

his own speeches. Indeed the student of eloquence must have his Cicero constantly in his hand; the simplicity, the lofty moral standard, the practical temper of his writings render them a peculiarly noble training for a public speaker. Nor should the admirable Quintilian be neglected in this same connection.

It will be desirable also to include the elements of Logic in our course of studies, and with that the *Ethics* of Aristotle, and the Dialogues of Plato ; for these are necessary aids to the proper understanding of Cicero. The Ciceronian Dialogue, in form and in matter, seems often to be modelled directly upon Plato. None of his works however are so attractive to myself personally as the *De Officiis* and the *Tusculans.* The former reviews all the main duties of life ; the latter exhibits a wealth of knowledge most valuable—both as to material and expression—to every modern writer. I would add that some knowledge of the principles of Roman Law will be helpful to the full understanding of Latin authors.

A master who should carry his scholars through the curriculum which I have now laid down may have confidence that he has given them a training which will enable them, not only to carry forward their own reading without assistance, but also to act efficiently as teachers in their turn.

§ 5. I now approach the second theme of my discourse : the method to be followed by those compelled to rely upon independent study. My first and most urgent precept is this. Let a young student regard himself habitually as likely to be called upon to teach the subject at which he is working at the moment. There is no better check to careless or superficial acquirement. For, as Quintilian long ago reminded us, one who knows that it will be his duty to teach the subject which he is studying will be diligent to examine it upon all sides, and in all its aspects, and will make himself secure upon every point that may fairly arise out of it. If opportunity offer, he will discuss the matter in hand with a fellow student, or in default of that he will devise an imaginary disputation in which he will expound or defend what he has acquired.

In reading an author it is not enough to be content with the exposition of a single Scholar. Every commentary of importance must be consulted to enable us to form our own judgment as to the precise meaning of the text and the force of each individual word. Our notes should be regularly written up, as carefully and as fully as though we destined them to publication. This practice quickens our intelligence and concentrates our attention : it tends to careful construing, to ready composition, to more exact recall of details. A volume of notes duly ordered serves the purpose of a common-place book. A student who is just entering upon a course of independent reading should direct his attention to those authors who have treated of a wide range of subjects, as Aulus Gellius, Macrobius, and Pliny, whose *Natural History* is indeed as wide as Nature herself. To these I may add St Augustine *De Civitate Dei*, so valuable for the light it throws upon the historic rites and ceremonies and the religious beliefs of the Ancient World. In such reading the practice of making extracts, where the interest of the subject matter suggests it, and of collecting parallel passages from different authors, is an important help to the student. Nor do I forget to urge the well-known device of the Pythagoreans, who in the evening revolved whatever of worth they had heard or had read during the day. Nothing more surely conduces to the clear memory of what we have acquired. I would propose, in addition to this, a monthly revision, upon a fixed day, of the entire course of our reading during the previous four weeks.

In Greek, the private student who has mastered the rudiments of the grammar, may confidently adopt a method which I know from experience to have proved effectual, in the absence of a teacher, in securing a high level of attainment in the language. He should select an author whose works have been accurately rendered into Latin. Keeping the original and the translation side by side let him make the most careful comparison of the two word by word : the vocabulary of Greek thus becomes readily familiar.   At the same time let him practise the habit of reading aloud to himself from a Greek author, a custom which has unfortunately been allowed to fall into neglect to the detriment of our scholarship.   I say 'reading aloud'; for each word must make its due impression upon the ear if attention is to be sharply aroused to it, and its true significance reach the mind.   Apart from its value mentally, reading aloud is physically beneficial, in the opinion of the experts in medicine.   Plutarch held that the action of the respiratory powers through the voice has direct effect upon the entire system, increasing the bodily heat, quickening and cleansing the blood.   So also Pliny and Ariston thought that the healthy activity of all the digestive functions is aided by the exercise of the voice.   Shouting and undue strain of any kind must, of course, be avoided, or injury to the throat results.

Another effect of this practice in reading will be to develope self-confidence in public-speaking, a quality of the utmost importance in an Orator but one by no means common.   For want of it Isocrates, 'the father of eloquence,' as Cicero calls him, could never deliver the speech as he had committed it to memory.   Now the points of good reading are not difficult to seize.   In the first place, however accurate the enunciation, however fluent the delivery, unless a fine perception of the author's meaning is conveyed in every tone of the Reader we pronounce the effort a failure.   In the next place, this implies a carefully trained intonation, with observance of recognised pauses, which correspond to the flow of ideas contained in the passage.   No pains must be spared by the student to achieve this nicely-adjusted relation of thought and expression.   For expression without thought, words without ideas, can never satisfy the lover of sound learning.

This leads me to the reflection that, whilst in Nature we

find some animals which are content to feed upon flowers, like bees ; others on leaves, like goats ; others again on roots, like swine ; the appetite of the Scholar demands the best of each and every kind of mental food. In purity and grace of style, in worthy deeds worthily presented, in noble thoughts nobly said,—in all these, and not in one alone, he finds the nourishment of his mind and spirit. In respect to poetry, however, a caution seems necessary. For like the Polypod, which, indeed, is pleasant enough to the taste, but provokes terrible visitations in the hour of sleep, so Poetry, whilst it feeds, as nothing else, our sense of delight, has yet in it a power to disturb and to excite the spirit. We need, then, to be careful in reading the fictions of the Poets to fix our thought rather on the underlying truths which are therein concealed than upon the imaginations in which they are expressed. In this way we are not disturbed by the impieties, cruelties, horrors, which we find there ; we judge these things simply by their congruity to the characters and situations described. We criticise the artist, not the moralist. Chrysoloras used to illustrate this canon of literature by analogy. We shrink from the touch, nay from the sight, of a snake or a scorpion : a clever drawing of either is a source of pleasure. Or we are afraid of the roar of the tempest, or we shudder at the grating of a saw, whilst a cunning imitation with the voice may provoke our laughter. What in real life repels us may in fiction win our admiration by its skilful presentation. But where the poet treats, with the same skill, of things in themselves noble, then we may accept his guidance without reserves.

In ordering our reading it is of great help to allot specific hours to each subject, and to observe the rule, once made, with strictness. In this way we may check our progress day by day. Hesiod long ago pointed the lesson, that the heap after all is only an accumulation of tiny grains. So to rescue even a few minutes each day for definite study of a particular author is always a gain. In the pursuit of learning as in other activities order and method are the secret of progress. A chorus sings in harmony of time and note, or it produces merely a noise; an army is a highly organised array of various arms, with its proper train of foragers, transport and camp followers, or else it is a bewildered and dangerous mob. Hence we see the crucial importance of system, which applies not less to study than to the captaincy of an army. For unless we map out clearly our course of reading and arrange our working hours in accordance with it, so many subjects claim our attention that concentration and thoroughness are impossible; our mind is divided between books of equal attractiveness, with the result that no solid work is done at all. When the day's reading is over, and we sit down to review and to secure what we have acquired, we find that our impressions are blurred and uncertain, that facts have escaped us and that definite conclusions, therefore, are not possible.

§ 6. Before I bring this short treatise to a close I would urge you to consider the function of Letters as an adornment of leisure. Cicero, as you remember, declares Learning to be the inspiration of youth, the delight of age, the ornament of happy fortunes, the solace of adversity. A recreation in the Study, abroad it is no hindrance. In our work, in our leisure, whether we keep vigil or whether we court sleep, Letters are ever at hand as our surest resource. Do we seek refreshment for our minds? Where can we find it more happily than in a pursuit which affords alike utility and delight? If others seek recreation in dice, in ball-play, in the theatre, do you seek it in acquiring knowledge. There you will see nothing which you may not admire; you will hear nothing which you would gladly forget. For good Books give no offence, call forth no rebuke; they will stir you, but with no empty hopes, no vain fears. Finally, through books, and books alone, will your converse be with the best and greatest, nay, even with the mighty dead themselves. A life spent amidst such interests deserves the title which the younger Pliny gives to it—' the true, the kingly, life': or, as Attilius was wont to say, no leisure could be more nobly occupied than that spent amongst books. Learned labour, he said, was pleasanter than any pleasures. The elder Pliny, indeed, took this ground when he gently reproached his nephew for using his leisure in taking walks; for no one was more careful in rescuing every minute for his beloved studies. His secretary was reading to him one day in the presence of a friend, who asked that a sentence carelessly read should be repeated; which was done. Pliny impatiently turned to his visitor, "Why interrupt? The sense was clear, and now we have lost ten lines or more by this stoppage." Cato of Utica would, in the Senate House itself, remain absorbed in books until the beginning of public business. Theophrastus was in the habit of reproaching nature for granting long years of life to the stag and the crow, who could not use them, whilst denying them to man who has before him the illimitable task of knowledge. Let us, then, heeding these great names, see to it that we allow not our short working years to pass idly away. To each species of creatures has been allotted a peculiar and instinctive gift. To horses galloping, to birds flying, comes naturally. To man only is given the desire to learn. Hence what the Greeks called 'παιδεία' we call 'studia humanitatis.' For learning and training in Virtue are peculiar to man; therefore our forefathers called them 'Humanitas,' the pursuits, the activities, proper to mankind. And no branch of knowledge embraces so wide a range of subjects as that learning which I have now attempted to describe.

I will end as I began. If this little work fulfils, perhaps more than fulfils, the promise which I held out, it is because it does but exhibit that order and method of study which my learned and revered father has followed for so many years in his own school. For as from the Trojan Horse of old the Greek heroes spread over the captured city, so from that famous Academy of my father has proceeded the greater number of those scholars who have carried learning, not merely throughout Italy, but far beyond her borders. You, as my pupil, are in a sense his intellectual heir. Continue to follow with all zeal the precepts herein laid down ; you will then fulfil the hopes I have always cherished of your future ; if it be possible, you will, I know, endeavour to surpass them.

At Verona.   xv Kal. Mar. MCCCCLVIIII.

A REVIEW OF THE EDUCATIONAL AIMS AND METHODS OF THE FIRST CENTURY OF HUMANISM.

THE purpose of the present chapter is to exhibit a general view of the Educational aims and methods of the Scholars of the first century of Humanism. In order to limit the enquiry to matter strictly pertinent I have confined attention to such sources as represent the definite educational practice of the time. The authorities referred to are, therefore, either actual schoolmasters, as Vittorino and Guarino, or Scholars of mark who compiled treatises upon one or another aspect of education. In this way I have practically excluded reference to the vast body of Commentaries, academic Addresses, or correspondence, produced in so great abundance by the Humanists of the fifteenth century. However interesting in the history of classical scholarship, they yield very little to the student of Education, in the strict sense, which is not to be found in more definite shape in the Treatises upon which I have mainly relied.

A singular harmony is presented by our authorities both as to the general aims pursued and the methods advocated to secure them. This renders it possible to offer in some detail a consistent and intelligible sketch of the higher type of educational practice of a period whose originating impulse is still, within that sphere, powerfully operative amongst us. Quotations are often given at some length, for the reason that my purpose has been to introduce the student to enquiry, at first hand, into an epoch of critical importance in the history of Education. And in this department of history, as in all others, a habit of direct acquaintance with original sources alone can obviate misunderstanding as to the true drift both of ideas and of facts. For the same reason I have generally abstained from criticism, and have allowed the authorities to exhibit their own case.

The principal Treatises upon Education of this period are the following :

1. Vergerius, *De Ingenuis Moribus*: (circ. 1393).

2. L. Bruni d'Arezzo [Leonardus Aretinus], *De Studiis et Literis* : (circ. 1405).

3. Francesco Barbaro, *De Liberorum Educatione*, a chapter (Lib. ii. 9) of his Tract *De Re Uxoria*.
   > This chapter was probably the result of the author's intercourse with Guarino Veronese, in whose house it was actually prepared for circulation[1]. (1428.)

4. Aeneas Sylvius Piccolomini (afterwards Pius II.), a Letter to Archduke Sigismund, to which we may give the title *Upon the Right Education of a Prince*: (circ. 1445).

5. The same, *Tractatus de Liberorum Educatione editus ad Ladislaum Ungariae et Bohemiae Regem* : (1450)[2].

6. Battista Guarino, *De Ordine Docendi et Studendi*: (1459).

7. Maffeo Vegio, *De Educatione Liberorum clarisque eorum Moribus*. In six Books : a systematic treatise modelled on that of Vergerius, but more copious in exhortation to good manners and to moral and religious duty. The work was the product of Vegio's later and more definitely religious stage of development: Augustine and Monica are more frequently referred to than Aristotle and Plutarch. (Circ. 1460.)

8. Gian Pannonio, *Silva Panegyrica ad Guarinum*: (circ. 1457). He was a pupil of Guarino, and specially

---

[1] See the Prefatory Letter: 'Erat is libellus pervetustus transcriptus quippe anno Domini MCCCCXXVIII die XXIX Novembris Veronae in domo Guarini Veronensis.' Ed. Paris, 1513.

[2] Large sections of this work, especially that dealing with Grammar, are borrowed with little or no modification from Quintilian Bk I. I have ventured to compress these in the version given above, p. 136.

intimate with his son Battista. This metrical description of Guarino's school and method is of interest, although, naturally, exaggerations abound. It was written during the life-time of Guarino. It contains about 2900 lines.

9. Jacopo Porcia, Count of Porsiglia (Purliliarum Comes), *De Generosa Liberorum Educatione*: (circ. 1470)[1].

The author is better known as a writer on the Art of War. This short Treatise has fallen into almost complete oblivion.

Certain Letters, mainly to Princes, are occasionally classed amongst Educational Tracts: *e.g.* 'Guarino to Leonello D'Este,' Rosmini, *Guar. Veron.* i. 113, and 'Filelfo to M. Triviano,' Id. *Vita di Filelfo*, ii. 463: and the works of Matteo Palmieri (circ. 1432), *Della Vita Civile*, and of L. B. Alberti, *Della Famiglia* (1431–1441), contain large and important sections upon the bringing up of children.

Of the above those referred to under 1, 2, 5 and 6, are given, in translation, in the present work.

There are notices of certain other Tracts which seem to be now lost:—

10. Gianozzo Manetti, *De Liberis Educandis.*

11. Secco Polentone, *De Ratione Studendi.* The writer was a pupil of Barzizza and a friend of Vittorino[2].

12. Nicolas Perotti, *De Puerorum Eruditione.*

13. P. C. Decembri, a work *De Studiis Puerorum.*

This list is, perhaps, incomplete, but I have purposely confined myself to the century which followed the death of Petrarch (1374). With Perotti we are introduced, as has been already said, to a more elaborate type of scholarship, which found

---

[1] Rösler shews that the date must be anterior to 1471 from the dedication of the book itself.

[2] A work in form of a Letter to Niccoli on the discovery of the bones of T. Livius is interesting as shewing his humanist enthusiasm : Patav. v Kal. Nov. 1414.

expression in the educational methods of the second period of Humanist education, viz. that marked by the Treatises of Erasmus, Sadoleto, Vives and Nausea, which, deeply interesting as it is, lies outside the scope of the present work.

§ 1. THE GENERAL PURPOSE OF THE HUMANIST EDUCATOR.

There is no doubt that the Humanists as a body were profoundly convinced of the *practical* character of Classical studies. It was said long ago of Vittorino[1] that his aim was the development of 'the complete citizen.' Vergerius[2], at the outset of our period, is anxious to set forth the ideal of Education as *the perfection of the man as Citizen,* which he found in Aristotle. The choice of studies and the temper in which they are to be pursued should be determined by this general aim. Learning[3] is not to be regarded as an excuse for withdrawal from active life and concern for the common good. Vittorino writes to Ambrogio, quoting Cicero with

---

[1] By Ticozzi : cf. his *Storia dei Letterati* etc., p. 19 : 'Soleva dire, non tutti i suoi discepoli aver bisogno per vivere onoratamente, di professare filosofia, legge, medicina,... ne tutti essere ugualmente da natura favoriti...; essere bensi tutti a vivere in società destinati ed a professare la virtu.'

[2] *De Ingenuis Moribus*, p. 479: 'Nam qui totus speculationi et literarum illecebris deditus est, is est forsitan sibi ipsi carus, ac parum certe utilis urbi aut princeps est aut privatus.'

Aen. Sylvius, *Opera*, p. 604 : 'Nec ego hos homines laudo qui sic se literis dedunt ut res caeteras parvi faciant, qualem fuisse Democritum Diogenemque constat.'

[3] For Vittorino's attitude we may refer to his motive for accepting the invitation to Mantua in 1423, and his actual life in that City. Sup. pp. 24, 79. Vergerius also writes in the same spirit : 'Ea mihi praestans philosophia visa est, quae in urbibus habitat et solitudinem fugit, quae cum sibi tum communibus studet commodis, et prodesse quam plurimis cupit.' *Epistol.*, ed Combi, p. xliv.

The Treatise of M. Vegio (vid. supra, p. 180) is written with the same end in view. 'Der berühmte und im Staate tüchtige Mann ist sein Ziel, nicht allein der Gelehrte,' says Voigt, *Wiederbelebung,* ii. 461.

approval: *virtutis laus omnis in actione consistit*[1]. That was his own ideal, and it was notorious that a full training for practical life was the leading purpose of the Mantuan school. This, indeed, is one of the characteristic marks of the lay spirit of Humanism, coinciding, as it did, with the objective temper of the Italian intelligence. Aeneas Sylvius impresses upon the young king Ladislaus a similar truth. He, too, quotes the sentence from Cicero in praise of action as distinct from self-absorption. He deprecates studies which may divert attention from the true ends of life ; he instances, especially, Dialectic and Geometry[2]. Such studies are legitimate in themselves, but their tendency is against practical interests. Letters, indeed, may be so studied that they produce a similar effect. But[3] the examples of Demosthenes, Aristotle, Caesar and Pliny, shew that, rightly pursued, literature proves the highest possible aid to genuine public spirit and to administrative capacity. Practical judgment in affairs is one main result of humanist teaching[4]. So far he is in accord with Vergerius[5], who lays down that 'sound judgment, wisdom of speech, and integrity of conduct' are the qualities cultivated by liberal learning. The Prince, especially, needs this training : by it he may safely count on being able to detect flattery, wilful imposition, insincerity of counsel[6]: his governing capacity

[1] Supra, p. 82.

[2] *Opera*, p. 989. 'Quamvis enim artes huiusmodi in veri investigatione versantur, earum tamen studio a rebus gerendis abduci contra officium est....Fugienda est omnis artis supervacua imitatio quae...ab utili negotio detrahit.' Supra, p. 155.

[3] Aen. Sylv. *Opera*, p. 604: 'Hi namque quod ex literis hauserant in administranda republica exercebant.'

[4] Ibid. p. 603: '...ut te in consilio loquente caeteri sileant, cum tu unus plus omnibus sapias.'

[5] Vergerius, supra, p. 108. See also his definition of Liberal Studies, supra, p. 102.

[6] Aen. Sylv. *Opera*, p. 607: 'At cum his servandum est quod supra dixi, ut temporis aliquod spatium concedas literis, quae reliquas virtutes

will be established on the firm basis of knowledge, and his wisdom will render him 'principum speculum,' and the adviser and moderator to whom neighbouring rulers will naturally turn. In the professional training[1] of the time, the study of antiquity when completed by its final course of ancient philosophy, was held to be the finest preparation for special studies, as Law, Medicine, or Theology. In Florence again no Humanist doubted that in Letters consisted the best preparation for the career of a Merchant or a Banker.

But apart from the broader effects of classical culture it was held that on nearly every side of practical life the best guidance attainable was to be derived from the study of ancient books. Aristotle's *Politics* is the soundest manual of statecraft : Vegetius and Caesar are the best guides to the Art of War ; Vergil, to agriculture. In ruling a household, Cicero, Plutarch *Upon Education*, and Francesco Barbaro, whose work *De Re Uxoria* was regarded as worthy of a place in the noble company, could be safely relied upon. In all departments of government[2], in war, justice, council, and domestic policy, Literature is the one sure source of practical wisdom.

Citizenship then being the highest end of education, we are prepared to find that the conviction of the Ancients, that the training of the young is a matter of State concern, is not lost sight of by the theorists. Vergerius[3] definitely affirms

tuas condiant et illustrent quibus si fueris, ut spero futurum, rite imbutus... non par aliis sed omnium principum eris speculum, teque vicini omnes suarum litium moderatorem et arbitrum facient.'

[1] Sassuolo da Prato (in 1443), of Vittorino, p. 71: '...sicque a se dimissos facit, affirmans illos cuicumque se arti et disciplinae dederint, vel Medicinae, vel Juri Civili, vel Theologiae, quidquid de illis et quantum voluerint facile confecturos.'

[2] Aen. Sylv. *Op*. p. 604: 'Nunc iudicium facies, nunc tenebis consilium, nunc arma tractabis, nunc rem familiarem respicies, et in his omnibus quid literae valeant experieris...et vel solus vel cum paucis orbe toto mirandus habeberis princeps.'

[3] *De Ingenuis Moribus*, supra, p. 99: 'Cum plurimum domesticae

this position, although it is in relation to character that he regards the action of the State as necessary. The Community is directly interested in the virtuous up-bringing of its future members, since good citizenship redounds to the profit of the State not less than to the advantage of the individual. Vergerius limits his principle to provisions safeguarding the young against moral dangers; nor is it clear how far he realised a method which should secure, in practice, the virtues of continence, moderation, and diligence by means of public regulation. We may remember, however, the close analogy of the Italy of this age and ancient Greece in respect not only of political but also of social and ethical problems. The attempt, therefore, to mould the social order on Hellenic lines was by no means wholly visionary.

But in the fifteenth century the conception of the 'perfect citizen' involved as a necessary condition that of the full development of the individual. To the humanist educator this carried the limitation of obedience to Christian faith and morality; in this way was secured a working compromise between the claims of Church, State and Personality, in the training of the 'complete man.' That the compromise was regarded as dangerous we know from the treatise of Giovanni Dominici[1]; and we are conscious of a certain uneasiness in many minds of the finer type as to the respective claims of religious obedience and unfettered devotion to scholarship. Vittorino[2] came serenely through a conflict of this kind, but his pupil and intimate friend Gregorio Corraro abandoned the humanities for the Cloister (1430), and the instances of Isotta

---

disciplinae permissum sit, nonnulla tamen solent legibus diffiniri, deberent autem, ut fere dixerim, omnia. Nam et Reipublicae interest iuventutem in civitatibus bene moratam esse, et si fuerint adolescentes ratione instituti, erit id quidem utile et civitatibus et ipsis bonum': p. 453.

[1] Supra, p. 120; a quotation from his invective is given, infra, p. 212.
[2] Supra, p. 20.

Nogarola[1] and Cecilia Gonzaga[2] shew the same tendency in learned women.

The broader aspects of the sense of Personality[3] amongst Italians of this time do not fall within the scope of this work. It is enough to trace its influence as an inspiring motive of the Humanist teacher. The *consciousness of personal distinction*, which perhaps best conveys the idea involved in the Italian use of the word *Virtus*, is, of course, by no means peculiar to this period. Dante, Boccaccio and Petrarch were all alike animated by it. It was intimately associated with the desire for the public acknowledgment of this distinction, and for its posthumous survival (*fama, gloria, laus posteritatis*). With the Humanist however, it becomes a definite educational end. Disadvantages of birth[4] may be overcome by a distinguished education, which again is an effectual safeguard against absorption in the less honourable side of life. For as to a vulgar temper gain and pleasure are the end of existence, to a lofty nature the consciousness of distinction and the repute which accompanies it are the dominant motives[5]. This higher nature is to be cherished by liberal studies, for from them proceed 'honor et gloria, quae sunt sapienti prima post virtutem proposita praemia.' Vergerius, further, in concluding his Treatise, reaches the climax of his exhortation by a direct appeal to the posthumous honour[6] which he will confer upon Ubertinus

[1] Upon Isotta see Sabbadini, *Guarino*, p. 128: 'L' ascetismo soffocò in lei l' umanismo.' See p. 250 below.

[2] Supra, p. 77.

[3] Upon Individuality and Fame as motives of Italian culture generally, see Burckhardt's admirable review, in his *Renaissance in Italy*, pp. 129 seqq.

[4] Vergerius, *De Ingenuis Moribus*, p. 443: 'quibus praediti rebus et obscura suae gentis nomina et humiles patrias attollere atque illustrare consueverunt.'

[5] Vergerius, *Op. cit.*, p. 459: 'Nam ut illiberalibus ingeniis lucrum et voluptas pro fine statuitur, ita ingenuis virtus et gloria.'

[6] Ibid. s. f.: 'Si probe itaque gesseris habebis quidem ab omnibus

by celebrating his literary distinction. Indeed it was held out[1] as one special attraction of Letters at the opening of the Century that their pursuit was as yet limited to a small number of select natures. Immediate renown was therefore the certain reward of proficiency. But the highest fame attaches only to those who are distinguished by a wide range of studies[2], which will have for their result both knowledge and a full, dignified life. They indeed may be further stimulated by the reflection of the fame they are bound to win for themselves[3].

Natural gifts are hardly sufficient to develop distinction; they must be reinforced by learning[4]. History teaches us that this was true of Princes in the past. A statesman of so remote a land as Britain[5]—Humphrey, Duke of Gloucester—is brought within the circle of Fame by his literary sympathies.

So far as concerned moral development, the humanist teacher was not willing to allow too much scope for the exercise of individual temperament. The accepted morality of the day, which was in large part identified with the practical Stoicism of the severer Roman writers, satisfied the better type of scholar. But it was not doubted that the moral nature

praesentem laudem; a me vero etiam litteris, si qua nobis eius modi facultas erit, posteritati commendabere.'

[1] L. Bruni, *De Stud. et Lit.*, p. 2: 'Et tua quidem laus illustrior erit, quam illarum fuerit...tu his temporibus florebis in quibus usque adeo prolapsa studia sunt, ut miraculi loco habeatur, videre virum nedum feminam, eruditam.'

[2] Bruni, *Op. cit.*, p. 17: 'Prorsus enim excellentia hominis illa admirabilis quae veram inclytamque famam nomini conciliat, non nisi ex multarum variarumque rerum fit cognitione.'

[3] Id. p. 34: '...currentem, ut aiunt, ad gloriam cohortari.'

[4] Aeneas Sylvius, *Opera*, p. 601: 'Nemo in clarum virum aut famosum principem potest evadere nisi cum naturae dotibus adiunctam habeat doctrinam.' P. 604: 'Omnes sane qui superioribus saeculis claruerunt principes studiosi fuerunt litterarum....Tu ergo (i.e. Sigismund) hos seque- ris, hosque audies, hosque leges, quos tibi praenominavi, si vis princeps toto in orbe...mirandus haberi.'

[5] Aeneas Sylvius, *Opera*, p. 602.

was in no slight degree amenable to the influence of liberal studies[1]. Patriotism, self-sacrifice, courage, restraint, and the active virtues, were regarded as amongst the most important fruits of a sound education : whence sprang also a more worthy view of life, its interests and its opportunities. In all this there was scope for *virtus* or *praestantia*, for the exhibition of the element of personality, not less than in the moral temper which defied, or simply ignored, the recognized standard of conduct. This nobler type of Christian individuality, so to call it, was one of the definite aims of humanist education. 'Omnis bene vivendi norma literarum studio continetur': this dictum of Aeneas Sylvius[2] represents, perhaps, the view of the theorist rather than of the Teacher of actual experience. Vergerius[3] devotes considerable space to the training of character by careful observation of individual temperaments and by adaptation thereto of the needful discipline. It is upon example and guidance that he relies rather than upon edification, whether drawn from Classical or Biblical sources. Guarino, however, attached weight to the moral lessons afforded by ancient literature. To him Terence was a teacher of morality of the highest value[4], and he used him largely in this sense. We are told that he invariably drove home the precepts which his authors suggested[5]. On the other hand it was clearly

---

[1] Bruni, *De Stud. et Lit.*, p. 34: 'Religionis studia et bene vivendi mihi praecipua sunt'; and this with the definite end of character in view. 'Caetera vero omnia,' he continues, 'ad ista referri debent vel adiuranda vel illustranda, *eaque de causa* Poetis et Oratoribus et scriptoribus inhaerendum. Providendum, autem in literis ut perceptio adsit ingenua et pervigil sollertia, nec unquam nisi optima probatissimaque legamus.'

[2] Aeneas Sylvius, *Opera*, p. 601.

[3] Supra, pp. 97 seqq.

[4] Sabbadini, *Guarino*, p. 145: 'Se poi voleva proporre un maestro di moralità, designava Terenzio.'

[5] 'Omnes enim lectiones, omnia documenta, omnia praecepta, ad bene beateque vivendum referebantur.' Ludovicus Carbo, a pupil of Guarino, quoted by Rosmini, *Guarino*, i. 115.

accepted that Learning was no guarantee against evil tendencies: that it might even serve as an instrument of depravity [1]. Vittorino, so we judge, although exceedingly vigilant in his choice of authors and undoubtedly careful to turn them to right account in moral teaching, seems to have studied to develope strength of will, sincerity and modesty, rather by the discipline of the playing fields, by wise religious observance, and by his own example. But it is characteristic of Humanism that morality is regarded as a subject for rational acquiescence: the broad duties of life are indeed pre-supposed, but there is no attempt made to pass beyond their mundane and objective significance, or to regard them as superior to all need of confirmation from non-Christian sources [2]. The attitude of Bruni [3] is a peculiarly noteworthy assertion of this position.

Distinction in social life was marked by power of conversation, and by personal carriage, by resourceful leisure and dignified old age. No Humanist teacher left these ends out of account in his view of education. They betoken a Society of ordered habit and of refinement, in which a definite standard of taste and manners is already recognised. To depreciate these elements of individuality as 'accomplishments,' pertaining

---

[1] Porcia, *De Generosa Liberorum Educatione*, p. 112: 'ex literarum studiis si boni natura sunt viri, meliores, si mali, deteriores fiant necesse est.' Vergerius, supra, p. 105 : 'persaepe sunt instrumenta perniciosioris iniuriae.'

[2] Aeneas Sylvius indicating the sources from which moral duty may be imbibed instances only Classical moralists, Cicero, Seneca, Boethius: and he is particularly anxious that approved writers only be selected for the purpose. *Opera*, p. 991; and supra, p. 158. So Bruni, *De Studiis* etc., p. 16: 'Nec sacris literis contentam esse volo, sed ad secularia traducam studia, videatque quid de his quae pertinent ad bene vivendum exculptissima Philosophorum ingenia tradidere.'

[3] Bruni, *De Studiis et Literis*, p. 30. He is defending the reading of ancient Poets by the example of Plato and Aristotle, when an imaginary opponent replies: 'Christianus sum, at illi forte suo more vixerunt.' 'Quasi vero honestas gravitasque morum non tunc eadem fuerit quae nunc est !' is his rejoinder.

merely to 'the leisure side of life,' would be to misconceive altogether the idea both of manhood and of citizenship as accepted in the Quattrocento. To be self-contained and yet to contribute some special or personal element to society was the double function of 'the complete man.'

The place occupied in Italian society of the Renaissance by polite intercourse, with its characteristics of discussion, romantic narrative, or polished conversation, needs to be recognised by the student of education in its true importance. This lay in its influence on the formation of public opinion in matters both of taste and morals. Social intercourse, even more than literature, tended to propagate common standards of intellectual and moral judgement. Humanism, at least, owed no small debt to this widely-ramifying but intangible force. It is not surprising, therefore, that the humanist educator should set forth definitely as one of his aims the higher art of conversation, through which, especially, intellectual individuality made its impress upon social opinion[1].

The Humanist insists that Learning should be available alike for action and for discussion. Bruni, writing on the place of studies in a woman's life, naturally places their social aspect in the forefront[2]. It is essential that knowledge should be allied with expression, each gaining distinction from the other. 'Indeed,' he declares[3], 'one may fairly ask what advantage it is to possess profound and varied learning unless one

[1] Aeneas Sylvius, *Opera*, p. 975: 'aequales tuos orationis ornatu gravitateque superare contendas.' Vergerius, supra, p. 102, refers to the power of conversation amongst children of higher intelligence.

[2] Bruni, *De Stud. et Lit.*, p. 32: 'sic enim resultat' (from wide reading and observation) 'plenum quiddam, ac sufficiens, ut copiosi, ut varii, ut ornati, ut in nulla re vacui rudesque videamur...nam et literae sine rerum scientia steriles sunt et inanes, et scientia rerum, quamvis ingens, si splendore careat literarum, abdita quidem obscuraque videtur.'

[3] Bruni, *Op. cit.*, p. 33: 'Et rogabo quid iuvat aliquem multa et pulchra scire si neque loqui de his cum dignitate possit.'

can convey it in language worthy of the subject. Only where this double capacity exists can we allow the highest title to distinction and to abiding fame.' In the training of a Prince this quality of a social leader is not to be lightly esteemed[1]. The essentials of good conversation are laid down with some care, and they include clear directions as to the cultivation of the voice[2]. Ease and lightness of touch, courtesy, willingness to listen are necessary qualities[3]. A too solemn manner repels, as does pertinacity in enforcing a point; whilst to allow your interlocutor the pleasure of convincing you is often a wise concession. Vehemence, loss of temper, arrogance, and exaggeration which amounts to falsehood, are destructive of all conversation.

Dignity of bearing was an essential factor in personal distinction. Vittorino, following Vergerius, desires to see grace of carriage express the corresponding qualities of the moral and intellectual nature[4]. The realisation of his own physical powers, not less than the consciousness of superiority of mind and spirit, was a necessary element in the development of the complete man. We shall see later how this function of education was treated in practice. It is enough to note here the place which it occupied amongst the general aims of the humanist.

Upon Relaxation and Old Age the Humanists have much to say. It is one of the ends of liberal studies to make a

[1] Aeneas Sylvius, *Opera*, p. 974: 'Dicendum existimamus, ut cum virilem togam induerit, quibus in modis puer non solum loqui sed ornate loqui prudenterque valeat.'

[2] Aeneas Sylvius, supra, p. 143; Vittorino's care in this respect is noted supra, p. 39.

[3] Aeneas Sylvius, *Opera*, p. 975: 'Adsit in colloquendo facilitas, in obvios compellendo suavitas, in respondendo benignitas. Nam graves in collocutionibus mores digna in se odia contrahunt. Absit pertinacia;... non solum vincere, sed forte vinci, speciosum est.'

[4] Aeneas Sylvius, *Opera*, p. 967: 'Gestus formae respondeant'; p. 968: 'Servandus est igitur in motu omnique statu decor': Vergerius, supra, p. 98.

man truly worthy of his freedom, to secure him against the tyranny of ignoble pleasures or of varying circumstance.   Man thus rejoices in that liberty[1] which alone deserves the name. Since in no other region of our life is this liberty so consciously realised as in our leisure, it is an urgent function of sound education to prepare us for its opportunity[2].   Hence Cicero is naturally appealed to in support of Literature ; Scipio or Cato on more general grounds : Domitian is the sad warning. Vergerius is especially eloquent upon the aim of education as the aid to the true use of leisure.   Learning is a resource against unworthy or unwelcome thoughts, it is the channel to the brightest and most elevating intellectual companionship.   But education, as the Humanist understood it, provided other alternatives of recreation[3]: music, singing, games, and outdoor accomplishments.   It aims at preparing the scholar to avail himself of all these in so far as each may contribute to a self-respecting, dignified existence.

§ 2.   Early Training—The Home.

The Humanist was keenly alive to the importance of the first years of infancy in the development of the child[4].   Parental care must be directed from the outset to each of the three sides of education.   It is most desirable that, wherever possible,

[1] Vergerius, *De Ingenuis Moribus*, supra, p. 102 : 'We call those studies *liberal* which are worthy of a free man ' etc.

[2] Id., supra, p. 106.   So Barbaro, *De Re Uxoria*, xxxi. *v.*: 'In his (early disciplines of mind and body) studium, animum et cogitationem adhibeant, quae grandioribus factis *decori, usui et iucunditati* sint.'   This conveys exactly the complete idea of humanist education, in its relation to action, distinction and leisure.

[3] Vergerius, *Op. cit.*, supra, p. 116.

[4] F. Barbaro, *De Re Uxoria*, xxix. *v.*: 'Restat educatio liberorum prorsus uxorii muneris maxime fructuosa et longe gravissima.'   Vergerius, *De Ingenuis Moribus*, p. 459: 'Oportet igitur a prima infantia his intendere et ad sapientiam omni studio conari': and supra, p. 102.

the mother should act as nurse to her child[1]; if resort must be had to strangers the greatest heed must be taken in their choice. Due regard should be had not to character only but to the manners, the speech, and accent of all who surround the child; rustic provincialisms are often acquired from the nurse and are with difficulty got rid of in later boyhood.

So soon as infancy is passed[2] the child begins to acquire knowledge, to form moral habits, and to develop physical characteristics. This training is still the chief responsibility of the Mother, to whom it falls to impart the first lessons of love towards God, Country, and Home, lessons which form the sound basis of future moral stability. So, too, the qualities of respect for elders, courtesy towards inferiors, frank ease with equals are inculcated at this stage[3]. Actual instruction is not on any excuse[4] to be omitted, though there may be reasonable question[5] as to the age at which it should be first pressed. This is, probably, a matter of individual capacity[6] and health.

[1] F. Barbaro, *Op. cit.*, xxxi. *r.*: 'Enitantur, igitur, nobiles feminae ut suos alant liberos.' But if impossible, 'nutrices...ingenuas, moratas, et exquisito sermone praeditas suscipiendas...ne tener infans corruptis et moribus et verbis imbuatur.' So also Porcia, *De Generosa Liberorum Educ.*, p. 108, dwells on the necessity of securing nurses who possess a good accent, and do not use provincialisms.

[2] F. Barbaro, *Op. cit.*, xxxi.: 'Postquam ex infantibus excesserint, ut animi et corporis dotibus excellant ingenium, curam, operam, impendant matres.'

[3] *L. c.*

[4] Porcia, *Op. cit.*, p. 107: 'Ad liberalem generosi pueri educationem licet multa quidem observanda sint nihil tamen magis quam ipsa institutionis initia a parentibus animadvertenda esse censeo.'

[5] Aeneas Sylvius, *Opera*, p. 966: 'Quidam fieri utrumque' (i.e. physical and intellectual training) 'simul censent ab infantia et primis, ut aiunt, ab unguiculis incipere debere institutionem pueri.'

[6] Vergerius, *Op. cit.*, p. 460: 'Est quidem ex natura in plerisque iuvenibus tanta ingenii celeritas....' Supra, p. 102. Erasmus, at a later period, wrote an important Treatise upon the necessity of beginning intellectual training at the earliest possible age: *De Pueris statim ac liberaliter instituendis*.

It is a mistake to suppose that early promise often leads to disappointment, and that forward children should, therefore, be deliberately kept back in the first stages of childhood[1]. It is at least as true that if time be lost in entering upon the pursuit of learning in early youth, that loss can never be adequately recovered in later years. We hear of reading and arithmetic taught by games[2], and we have a record of introductory grammars provided for the Gonzaga children before the age of six[3].

But the home training is to be devoted, primarily, to the formation of right personal habits, as, for instance, in eating and drinking, in which the most careful moderation should be inculcated from the first[4]. Amusements, and games[5]; intercourse with other children[6], who will never, by a well brought-up child, be reproached with the misfortunes or lower station of their parents; demeanour and bodily carriage; all these are points demanding close attention in the first five years of childhood. It will be needful to have regard to the dress[7] suitable to children, from the point of view of health and of self-respect: whilst such luxuries as beds of soft feathers[8], or too fine linen, or garments of silk, should be

[1] Vergerius, *l. c.*, 'Nec vero suscipiendum est, quod omnibus pene vulgo usurpatum est, ut existimemus eos qui iuvenes super aetatem recte sapiant, maiores factos desipere aliquando solere: quamquam et hoc in quibusdam non abhorreat a physica ratione.'

[2] Supra, pp. 38, 42 (of Vittorino).

[3] Supra, p. 69.

[4] Fr. Barbaro, *Op. cit.*, xxxi. *v.*: 'Cibi potusque temperantiam sic ediscant ut ad futuram aetatem omnis continentiae quasi fundamenta iaciantur.'

[5] Barbaro, *l. c.*: 'Voluptates illas effugere commonefaciant, quae ullo dedecore involutae sunt.'

[6] Barbaro, *l. c.*: 'Subinde praecipiant [parentes] ne inopiam maiorum ignominiam et ceteras calamitates ullis obiecerint, quibus ex rebus...arrogandi consuetudinem imbibant.'

[7] Porcia, *Op. cit.*, p. 112.

[8] Aeneas Sylvius, *Opera*, p. 967: 'Mollis educatio, quam vocamus

scrupulously avoided. Recourse to artificial heat[1], or the use of gloves[2], should be discouraged at the earliest possible age.

It is clear that a healthy, hardy habit of body, an affectionate and yet high-spirited moral temper, a reverent and modest bearing, and an intellectual passivity[3] rather than curiosity, are the main qualities which the home training of the first five years of childhood should aim at instilling. It is assumed that the example of parents[4], and of all who may come into contact with the young[5] will enforce precepts at this stage of education; and this influence may be early extended by pointing to the esteem in which fellow citizens of distinction are held, as an encouragement to youthful aspiration.

§ 3. THE LIBERAL STUDIES.

We consider next the general lines of the superstructure which the Humanists proposed to rear upon the basis of the home training here indicated, in their endeavour to satisfy the broad aims sketched in the opening section of this chapter.

Vergerius[6], at the outset of our period, had defined a

indulgentiam, nervos omnes et mentis et corporis frangit. Vitanda est plumarum mollities etc.'; supra, p. 137.

[1] Vegius, *De Educatione Liberorum*, p. 174. Supra, p. 35. Vittorino's practice referred to by Prendilacqua, p. 28 and supra, p. 35.

[2] Platina specially records this of Vittorino; Vairani, p. 24.

[3] Barbaro, *Op. cit.*, xxxii. *r.*: 'Pauca nisi iussos loqui doceantur.... Disciplinae enim impedimento erit si quod non satis exploratum sit impudentius explicare voluerint.' He explains that it is rather the duty of children to await the knowledge which the wisdom of their parents may lead them to impart. Vergerius, supra, p. 99, is in substantial agreement.

[4] Vergerius advises that children be sent early from home if the example and control of the parents is defective: supra, p. 101. Aeneas Sylvius, supra, p. 141.

[5] Vergerius, p. 98. Porcia, *De Gener. Lib. Educ.*, p. 113, thinks no stimulus equal to that of the example, ever pointed out, of distinguished living worth amongst citizens.

[6] Vergerius, supra, p. 102.

liberal education to be one which enables a man to attain to
and pursue a life of moral and intellectual distinction, and
which trains and develops his physical powers. Such an education will prepare men for the career of a statesman, of a
soldier, or of a simple citizen. But its object is not to train a
mere student[1]. This comprehensive aim is obviously suggested by the Graeco-Roman ideal, although it is at the same
time held to be in complete accord with the spirit of the
Christian life. In its practical working this education was
exhibited in the most developed form in the Mantuan school.
Vittorino claimed for his method, following Plutarch, the
title of 'encyclopaedic',[2] in that he definitely purposed the
threefold end of the moral, intellectual and physical training
of his pupils.

It was held that the most profound truths in all, or nearly
all, departments of life were to be sought for in the ancient
Literatures, in which were included the works of the greater
ecclesiastical Fathers, so far at least as their religious and
moral contents were concerned[3]. So whilst Letters form the
dominant study upon the intellectual side[4], philosophy[5] and
the Fathers the instruction in morals, gymnastic and military
exercises provide for physical culture. At the same time
Mathematics[6], the study of Nature, and Astronomy, have

[1] Vergerius, supra, p. 110.

[2] Platina, of Vittorino, p. 21: 'Laudabat illam quam Graeci ἐγκυκλοπαιδείαν vocant, quod ex multis et variis disciplinis fieri doctrinam et
eruditionem dicebat.' Vegio, *De Educatione Liberorum*, p. 263, urges the
adoption of that ancient education 'qui orbis doctrinarum appellatus est.'

[3] Bruni, *De Stud. et Litt.*, p. 15. He is referring to religious knowledge: 'quid est enim quod literata mulier ab Augustino discere non
possit?' See also, supra, p. 124.

[4] This of course runs through the writings of every Humanist.
Vergerius is typical of his class: supra, p. 105.

[5] Aeneas Sylvius, *Opera*, p. 991 in enumerating writers to be studied
for Morals confines himself to Roman classical writers. See Bruni,
supra, p. 127.

[6] Vergerius, supra, p. 108.

their due place; and music, singing and dancing, the latter with some reserves, are admitted. Drawing is treated as a technical rather than a liberal subject. Eloquence, recitation and reading are cultivated as aids to scholarship and for their own sakes. It is by no means assumed that every student can cover[1] the entire field of learning now thrown open to him. Ill-digested knowledge is condemned[2], for a restless curiosity that hurries from one subject to another is hurtful to all true progress. But amidst all this variety the essential feature of education consists in systematic discipline and practice. 'Natura sine disciplina caeca' was a doctrine universally accepted[3]. Where this is secured alternation of subjects[4], and corresponding change of masters, is desirable: indeed intellectual health demands variety. But it still remains true that to unite knowledge with style, to impart fact and truth in literary dress, was the humanist schoolmaster's ideal[5] on the side of erudition.

The curriculum proposed for a woman was, on its moral and intellectual sides, identical with that of a man, with, perhaps, a little less stress upon Rhetoric and more upon Religion[6]. There was no assumption that a lower standard of attainment is inevitable as a consequence of smaller capacity.

---

[1] M. Vegio, *De Educatione Liberorum*, p. 264: 'Non quo exacta omnium exigenda sit, id enim haud unquam fieri posset, sed quo ea transcurrentes per quandam quasi degustationem attingant.' Vergerius, supra, p. 109.

[2] Vergerius, supra, p. 110.

[3] Aeneas Sylvius, *Opera*, p. 966 and p. 601: natural gifts need to be trained by 'doctrina.'

[4] M. Vegio, *Op. cit.*, p. 264, urges variety of *subjects* as against the varied treatment of literary instruction alone. Out of these subjects one or two will, no doubt, be chosen for special study.

[5] Bruni, *De Studiis et Litteris*, p. 3: 'Eruditionem intelligo legitimam illam et ingenuam quae litterarum peritiam cum rerum scientia coniungit.' Vergerius, *De Ingenuis Moribus*, p. 469: 'Nam quae sine dignitate scribuntur ea nec sortiuntur fidem nec subsistere diu possunt.'

[6] Bruni, supra, pp. 126, 7.

It is, however, accepted that only women of leisure or position can expect to enter upon the pursuit of learning with that undivided mind which it demands.

Vittorino established the Renaissance tradition that in education ability is the test of a claim to share its privileges. The equality of scholars was his principle in accepting pupils: and his system of free education carried it to its fullest development. He, too, like all the great teachers of the period was a layman, and the secular character of the school in no way detracted from its high moral and religious temper. A comparison between the two famous schools of Northern Italy with the recent foundations of William of Wykeham in England enables us to realise the distinction between the humanist and the ecclesiastical ideal of education. Colet, in the following century, was the first Englishman to accept frankly the principle that education was primarily the concern of the layman and the citizen.

The age at which the child should enter upon a definite and systematic course of instruction is the subject of some divergence of opinion. Vittorino, we know, directed the training of the younger Gonzaga children before they reached the age of five[1]. Their mother was an exceptional woman, and continued to take the deepest practical interest in the training of the children. It seems likely that the Humanist urged the cooperation of the mother with a home tutor (praeceptor) after the fifth year[2]; although there is a tendency

[1] Supra, p. 29.

[2] Porcia, *De Generosa Liber. Educ.*, p. 110. Under a tutor the boy should remain at home, learning morals and manners; school he thinks is dangerous for young boys, owing to the mixture of classes, and consequent bad examples. However, 'exacto decennio publicas ad scholas accedant.' Vegio, *De Educ. Liber.*, p. 212: 'Proximum erit, ut cum firmari magis eorum anni coeperint, in publico, quo ceteri convenire pueri solent, auditorio doceantur, non domi sub privati praeceptoris cura habeantur.' He is anxious that boys should be plunged, as early as it could be safely done, into the society of their equals in age and ability.

to postpone regular lessons until two years later, or to leave the matter open to be settled by individual circumstances[1], School should begin at the tenth year in any case. There is a general agreement that the memory is at its best in the early years, and as the elements of learning fall mostly within the operations of that faculty, it is undesirable to delay the commencement of grammar beyond the fifth year.

Whether the child should remain at home[2] attending a day school, was much debated. On the one hand it was desirable on many grounds that a boy should live under the eye of his parents. But against this was to be set the risks which were incurred by retaining him amid the associations of women-folk, whose foolish indulgence and ignorance of moral discipline retarded the right development of manliness and self-reliance[3]. It was, therefore, often advisable to send boys away from home, even though they remained in their native city[4]. In the choice of a school at a distance, it was of importance to take into account the moral and intellectual distinction of the city in which it was placed[5]. Not to speak of the proper pride which boys ought to take in their school and their adopted city, the stimulating atmosphere of a famous place of learning reacts directly upon the youthful mind and keeps a generous youth from sinking to a lower level of aspiration. Parents should consider it a duty to hear the recitations[6] learnt for school; they should cultivate the use

---

[1] Vegio, *Op. cit.*, p. 211.   Aeneas Sylvius, *Opera*, p. 972.

[2] So Vegio and Porcia; Vergerius (supra, p. 101) affirms that this depends entirely on the character of the parents themselves.

[3] Vegio and Vergerius state this very strongly.

[4] Vergerius, supra, p. 101.

[5] M. Vegio.   A boy should not be sent to school in a city, 'ubi nulla dignitas morum, nulla habitatorum generositas et elegantia habeatur;...sunt enim, ut hominum ita et civitatum, a natura insita singularia quaedam ac propria ingenia.' ' Ad celebres doctisque refertas praeceptoribus urbes mittantur.' *De Educ. Liber.*, p. 214.

[6] M. Vegio, *Op. cit.*, p. 216.

of sound Latin in the family circle, and should carefully regulate and supervise home preparation[1].

The subjects of instruction available for children at this first stage of their education would seem to have been these : reading, taught by moveable letters, arithmetic, taught by games, writing and drawing; the Psalms, Creed, Lord's Prayer, and Hymn to the Virgin, learnt by heart; Latin, acquired in conversation, with the first rudiments of accidence as contained in a metrical form, with a vocabulary or phrase book in Italian and Latin. The vernacular language was probably ignored as a subject of instruction, but the habit of exact enunciation and of refined conversation in Italian was regarded as of much importance. Children's stories existed in abundance. Vegio[2] tells us, from his own experience, that it was customary to make children acquainted at a very early age with the subjects of ancient history and mythology, with the view of rendering them familiar with the contents of the literature which afterwards formed the staple of their education. Partly in the form of lessons, partly of conversations and for amusement, an introduction to Livy, Vergil, Homer and Plutarch was thus provided for young children. Vegio records that the stories of the *Aeneid*, told by a skilful master by way of relaxation to the class, were never forgotten. Training in virtue and manners was afforded by careful religious observance, by teaching moral stories from the Bible or Plutarch, and by the stress laid upon reverent and modest demeanour at home. No criticism is less justifiable than that which charges against humanist education that it ignored childhood.

The choice of the Tutor (praeceptor, paedagogus) is a matter demanding much forethought. On the one hand he must be selected mainly for his personal character[3]; for his relations with his charge and with the whole home circle are

---

[1] Porcia, *De Generosa Liber. Educ.*, p. 112.

[2] *De Liber. Educ.*, p. 262.

[3] Porcia, *Op. cit..* p. 110.

necessarily close, and should be thoroughly easy and confidential. But he should be at the same time a man of genuine
ability[1]. Too much care can scarcely be bestowed upon the
first rudiments of learning. Philip engaged Aristotle to teach
Alexander to read. It would be better almost that a boy
be left ignorant than be so ill-taught that the schoolmaster
has to undo the mischief of bad preparation. Thus the tutor
should be on all grounds a man who commands respect:
though parents are sadly careless upon this point[2]. The true
light in which to regard him is that he stands 'in loco pa-
rentis[3],' and this will carry with it the habit of treating him
with courtesy and of upholding his authority. The father
will do well to imitate the example of P. Aemilius who took
a close personal interest in the work of the schoolroom, for
this will encourage the tutor and stimulate his charge[4]. Indeed,
it belongs to the parents no less than to the master to inculcate
habits of study and love of knowledge.

Vittorino and Guarino were, as regards the Gonzaga and
the D'Este princes, at once tutors and schoolmasters (magistri). The tie which united Vittorino to his pupils was, as
we have seen, that of mutual affection, marked by respect and
veneration on one side and deep personal interest on the
other. This was the realisation of the humanist ideal. For

---

[1] B. Guarino, *De Ordine docendi*, supra, p. 162. Vergerius, supra,
p. 110.

[2] Vegio, *Op. cit.*, p. 220, denounces the indifference of many parents of
wealth to the education of their sons. 'They will not greet their boys'
Tutor, nor even acknowledge his existence. They pay him as little as they
can and that, too, with the air of one who is losing a tooth or an eye.'
Aeneas Sylvius, supra, p. 137.

[3] B. Guarino, *Op. cit.*, p. 4: 'In praeceptore colligendo paternam sibi
constituant sanctitatem....' He adds that 'our ancestors held the Tutor to
stand in a quasi-parental relation to his pupils that so he might realise
more deeply the responsibility that was entrusted to him.'

[4] Vegio, *Op. cit.*, p. 219: 'Debebit autem paterfamilias, cum idoneum
erudiendo filio magistrum nactus fuerit, magnopere studere ut eum habeat
quam familiarissimum.'

the master should have under his charge only so many pupils as he can know and guide individually[1]. His responsibility is that of the father of their moral and intellectual nature[2]; and by this presumption he will be determined in his devotion to his work in the discipline[3] which he enforces, and in the example[4] which he himself sets forth.

The humanist teacher, true to his aim of developing individuality, attaches the greatest importance to the observation and encouragement of the personal taste and capacity of his scholars. Both Vergerius[5] and Vegio devote much attention to the recognition of varying disposition. But the study of the intellectual powers of each individual child was a matter of more urgency still. It is, in the first place, a duty of every parent[6] to afford the right mental occupation to their young children. When the master steps in to undertake their charge he takes over this responsibility. Unless he be an acute observer of mental bent and ability he will prove a failure. Vittorino held it his first function to thoroughly understand his

---

[1] Vegio, *De Ed. Lib.*, p. 218, and B. Guarino, supra, p. 163, urge smallness of numbers, especially in the earlier stages. With older boys larger classes stimulate the master.

[2] Aeneas Sylvius, *Opera*, p. 967 : 'non minus amabis praeceptores quam ipsa studia, et parentes esse non quidem corporis sed mentis tuae iudicabis.' Vegio, *De Educ. Liber.*, p. 223: 'non aliter ac filios omni cura et amore prosequentur.'

[3] 'Placidi et mitis ingenii…, nam praeceptorum inhumanitas atque, ut ita dixerim, ariditas maxime impedit profectum qui ad literas in ea aetate sit.' Vegio, *l. c.*

[4] This was the strong point in Vittorino's discipline. 'Il maestro doveva sopratutto essere ai suoi discepoli uno specchio vivente di onestà e costumatezza,' says Sabbadini, *Guarino*, p. 100, speaking of the method by which these two great masters enforced their unique authority.

[5] For Vergerius, vide supra, p. 97 seqq.; Vegio, *Op. cit.*, Lib. i. § 18.

[6] Vergerius, *Op. cit.*, p. 446 : 'Principio igitur erit unicuique suum ingenium per se spectandum…parentes ceterique quibus curae erimus animadvertere debebunt et in quas res natura proni aptique fuerimus eo potissimum studia nostra conferri et in eis totos versari conveniet.'

material and then to adapt both subjects and methods to its needs[1]. Prendilacqua has an important passage, illustrating Vittorino's practice, which confirms all that we gather from other sources on this head. ' In truth, so Vittorino used to say, we are not to expect that every boy will display the same tastes or the same degree of mental capacity; and whatever our own predilection may be we recognise that we must follow Nature's lead. Now she has endowed no one with aptitude for all kinds of knowledge, very few indeed have talent in three or four directions, but everyone has received some gift, if only we can discover it. Then he went on to compare the human intellect to the soil, with its varying degree of fertility, here good, here poor, but even the worst capable of some return to suitable cultivation. Hence he sought out that subject and that method of instruction which he believed to be best adapted to each individual intelligence. Upon the dullest he would bestow infinite pains, that by devising simple tasks or some special form of training he might meet the needs even of the least promising scholars[2].' Vergerius shews much insight into the differences of mental capacity[3]. Where the intelligence has a fine and keen edge difficulties of subject-matter serve only to stimulate exertion. Danger then lies rather in reliance upon cleverness to the neglect of memory, by which alone knowledge is secured for future use. But in the case of those whose intellect is dull—to be compared to lead rather than to steel—the master must provide the constant stimulus of oral

---

[1] Prof. Brambilla, in his edition of Prendilacqua, p. 97, says, ' E così fatta osservazione (attenta, perspicua, continua) fu, per così esprimermi, il capolavoro del massimo Vittorino e la vera forza del suo metodo educativo.'

[2] Prendilacqua, p. 42.

[3] Vergerius, supra, p. 109. His preference for the practical and concrete interests of one type of mind as contrasted with the speculative and abstract studies which appeal to another is essentially Italian.

teaching and questioning[1]. Let the master study carefully the taste of such boys, in order that they may devote themselves to those studies which they are likely to pursue with most pleasure and profit. We may not count upon capacity for Letters in every child: and Literature though the best, is not the only educational instrument. It is obvious that business, agriculture, or the profession of arms are all careers for which due preparation may be made in other ways[2]. The end to be kept in view must be to interest and occupy the learner's mind and to devise a curriculum accordingly.

There is, however, practically little definite suggestion as to the course of instruction to be followed by those whose tastes do not fit them for classical learning. We shall see how difficult it is to form any clear conception of an instrument of instruction which was not either Letters or the training of arms. It is unlikely that the elder Guarino, his son Battista, or Lionardo Bruni contemplated an education in which Letters should occupy an inferior place. At least, it may be said with confidence that taste for, and proficiency in, classics was held by every Humanist to indicate with certainty the possession of the higher type of intelligence.

The observation of individual character and ability naturally determines the methods of Discipline[3]. By discipline the Master both stimulates and restrains. The friendly personal

---

[1] Vergerius, *De Ingenuis Moribus*, p. 482.

[2] Vegio, *Op. cit.*, p. 290 : 'Non omnium ingenia literis affecta deditaque esse possunt.' Even those who are best trained by methods of literature should not confine themselves to that subject alone. Vergerius, *Op. cit.*, p. 477, remarks : 'ita sunt coniunctae doctrinae omnes ut nulla quaevis, ignoratis prorsus aliis, egregie percipi valeat.' Bruni lays great stress on the necessity of uniting ' scientia rerum ' with ' peritia literarum.' Supra, p. 132. ' Res,' however, by no means implies external and concrete realities. It covers simply contents as distinct from literary form.

[3] Vegio, *Op. cit.*, p. 195 : ' Summa vero ante omnia opus erit prudentia atque mentis iudicio in cognoscenda filiorum natura, discernendaque varia ingeniorum indole, ut in emendandis eorum moribus...adhibeantur cuique vitio atque animi morbo contraria etiam affectionis remedia.'

relation of teacher and pupil is the prime factor in either regard[1]. The scholar responds to the quasi-parental affection of the Master. He is encouraged by praise[2], which must, however, be sparingly used, partly lest jealousy be aroused. Healthy emulation, between individual boys or sections of a class[3], is needful in early stages of school life; flattery, sometimes resorted to, is but weak indulgence; boys are not pet dogs[4]. A desire for personal distinction may, in later years, be safely relied upon; and as the boy nears manhood the force of reason will supersede all forms of external stimulus[5]. The restraint of corporal punishment will rarely be needed; with younger boys it is to be strongly condemned. In all cases it is an indignity, and carries with it 'servile quiddam[6]': it engenders indifference to, or positive dislike of, learning, and not seldom arouses a passionate hatred to the master. If, like a wise physician, the teacher carefully observes the nature of the moral disease[7], he will learn to rely upon patient rather than forcible remedies. Thus the master must possess a calm but firm temperament; he may indulge the expression of indignation but he must keep it well under control; he must

[1] Sabbadini, *Guarino*, p. 100 : 'La base fondamentale del Metodo didattico di Guarino era l' intimo legame del Maestro con gli scolari.'

[2] Vegio, p. 227 ; and p. 234 : ' Ita ergo modice laudandi sunt ut laudis amore aequales suos virtute ac literis superare, non indignari illis, aut irasci, aut odio infensos esse, contendant.'

[3] Especially urged by Vegio, from his own experience. He gives an interesting personal reminiscence of a method employed by his own Master, a humanist teacher of eminence. The class was divided into small groups, who were exercised in disputation, under the direction of the ablest boy, in the presence of the Master. 'Non possum satis dicere quantum me, ne inferior aliis saltem iudicarer, ad sustinendam omnem vigiliarum studiorum-que molem incendebat.' *De Educatione Liber.*, p. 228.

[4] Vegio, p. 203.

[5] Vergerius, supra, p. 97, and B. Guarino, supra, p. 163.

[6] B. Guarino, *l. c.*

[7] For instance, irascible natures need to be controlled by a low diet. Vergerius, supra, p. 99.

lay aside harshness, sarcasm and vindictiveness in all his
dealings with boys[1].

There is no doubt that the discipline of Vittorino, on the
side both of stimulus and of restraint, was a successful application of these principles. The secret of this success has already
been indicated. It is to be noted further that small classes
and much individual teaching[2] are essential factors, and where
the further condition of genuine devotion to the work itself is
present, as was the case with Guarino, and apparently with
certain of Vittorino's pupils, we can well understand that the
need for severity seldom arose. Further, it would seem to be
of importance to consider the circumstances of the teaching art
itself at the time. The oral type of instruction, rendered
necessary by the absence of text-books, the personal, and
therefore elastic, methods of treating the entire apparatus of
learning, which belonged to a tentative stage of education, and
a certain patriotic enthusiasm for the literature which formed
its staple subject-matter, all contributed to secure a higher level
of interest, and, therefore, an easier discipline, in the early, as
contrasted with the later, period of Humanism[3]. We know

---

[1] Vegio, *Op. cit.*, p. 234 : ' Talem, in summa, se exhibebit discipulis, ut
sit austerus sine tristitia, comis sine scurrilitate ;...irascatur sed modice,
obiurget sed non contumeliose, corrigat sed non acerbe,' etc.

[2] Rosmini, *Guarino*, i. 86. Guarino devoted the entire evening to
private tuition of his pupils, who came to him with any subject which they
happened to be reading. The pupils who lived in his own house were
systematically taught in this way : ' a questi ripeteva la sera insino a notte
molto innoltrata le cose insegnate (i.e. in his public lectures), e secondo la
loro inclinazione e i bisogni in varie altre scienze istruiva.' The section
of Rosmini's work dealing with Guarino's actual practice at Ferrara,
i. 78 seqq., is still well worthy of study : it has not been superseded
by Sabbadini's recent and in most respects far more accurate and
instructive biography.

[3] This important characteristic of the first period of humanist education
is not recognised by Paulssen or Schmidt in their histories of education,
nor by any of the critics of the education of the Renaissance.

that punishments were savage in the common schools of Petrarch's day[1], and again that they were hardly less so a century later when Erasmus was a boy[2]. But, beyond a doubt, the early humanists not only contemplated, but actually exhibited, an educational practice in which the capacity of the teacher and the inherent attractiveness of his subjects made the ideal discipline both possible and effective.

The art of Reading was diligently cultivated. The earliest steps were gained by means of moveable letters employed in the form of play[3]. The first object aimed at was the attainment of clear and effective enunciation[4], which received attention from the outset of school life. The faults to be avoided are repeatedly dwelt upon. Tone must be full, not thin, shrill, or tremulous, like that of a woman, whilst all overbearing loudness must be avoided[5]. To secure this, each organ of the voice[6] must do its part: the breathing[7],

[1] Supra, p. 64.

[2] Erasmus, *De Pueris statim etc.*, *Op.* i. 504; a most significant autobiographical passage. He adds : 'nec ulli crudelius excarnificant pueros quam qui nihil habent quid illos doceant,' p. 505.

[3] Supra, p. 38. Platina, p. 21: 'literarum formas variis coloribus pictas ad lusum pueris proponebat' (of Vittorino).

[4] Guarino writing to Leonello d'Este : 'Primum quidem non introrsum aut sub lingua immurmurare, sed clariore pronunciare voce jubebat' [Chrysoloras]. Rosmini, *Guarino*, i. 113. Vegio, *Op. cit.*, p. 249: 'Exercenda erit eorum vox, debitisque ac castigatis rationibus informanda.' Aen. Sylvius, *Opera*, p. 975, 'Formanda est inprimis vox.'

[5] Aen. Sylvius, *l.c.*: 'ne [vox] feminea exilitate frangatur, neve similiter tremat, aut nimium boet.' B. Guarino, *De Ordine*, p. 26: 'vox clamosa et violenta raucitatem inducit.' Vegio, *l.c.* 'vox distincta sit, robusta, sonora.'

[6] B. Guarino, *Op. cit.*, p. 6: 'obscura est intra dentes murmuratio et verborum conculcatio.'

[7] Aen. Sylvius, *l.c.*: 'expressa sint verba, suisque literis totis enuncientur; non excidant extremae syllabae, non audiatur vox in faucibus, atque expedita sit lingua et os, absolutior, expressiorque sermo.' Platina, p. 21 : 'vetabat eos aut in faucibus aut in extremis labiis, quod exsibilationem prae se ferrent et audientes laederent, enunciare.'

the throat, the teeth, the lips. Each word must be completely uttered; the final syllable must not be slurred, nor may the words run indistinctly into each other. Exercises were devised to secure practice in words involving various difficulties of utterance[1]. It was important, also, that enunciation should not be accompanied by marks of undue effort, such as grimaces or uncouth gestures[2].

In pronunciation and intonation the most important element is careful, deliberate pace[3], which enables the reader to grasp the meaning of the passage and consequently to express it with judgment and taste. As the sense may demand, the reader will increase the speed[4], lower or raise the tone, and indicate the rhythm with which a great prose-writer instinctively adorns his composition[5]. The observance of the pause, in order to mark parenthesis, clause or period, of accent, and of quantity, is essential to all good reading. The mere mechanical delivery of a succession of words and sentences is not reading at all[6].

Good reading serves various ends. Grace, self-possession and readiness in conversation and public speaking[7] are amongst

---

[1] Aen. Sylvius, *l.c.*; supra, p. 143. So Quintilian, i. 1. s. f.

[2] Vegio, *Op. cit.*, p. 249. He urges practice of controlling movements of the mouth and all gestures during reading: the uncouthness of the rustic and the elaborate facial play of the actor are both objectionable. Vittorino was most particular in this matter: Platina, p. 24.

[3] L. Bruni, *De Studiis et Literis*, p. 8: 'Illud ex hac lectione consequetur, ut verba suo tempore proferat, neve properet, cum immorandum est, neve cum properandum sit immoretur.'

[4] Vegio, *Op. cit.*, p. 249: 'quando vel attolli, vel moderari, vel deprimi debeat [vox]; ubi suspendendus est spiritus, ubi claudendus sensus.'

[5] L. Bruni, *Op. cit.*, p. 8: 'ea ergo cum alte leget manifestius deprehendet repleri aures veluti harmonia quadam.'

[6] B. Guarino, *De Ordine*, supra, p. 174.

[7] Aen. Sylvius, *Opera*, p. 974: 'ut cum virilem togam induerit non solum loqui sed ornate loqui prudenterque valeat.' B. Guarino considers that 'audaciam' in public speaking would be much assisted by practice in reading: *l. c.*

them. The habit of reading Greek or Latin aloud is a valuable aid to entering into general drift and meaning of the passage. So Chrysoloras advised, and Guarino urgently enforces the practice[1]. Matter thus read is far more securely impressed upon the mind. The exercise, too, reacts beneficially upon the reader's own style, and, especially in view of composition, it is desirable to read aloud model passages before attempting to write either in prose or in verse[2]. Apart from the intellectual and social advantages involved, definite physical benefits accrue. Vittorino urged reading aloud as a better remedy for cold than artificial warmth. B. Guarino agrees with Plutarch and Pliny that nothing is more favourable to the digestive processes than vigorous reading and recitation[3].

The custom of speaking Latin at home, so much encouraged by humanist teachers, served as the natural introduction to the more systematic study of Grammar. This was begun very early, soon after the close of the fifth year. During our period the *Doctrinale* of Alexander de Villa Dei—the Latin accidence in hexameters—seems to have served as the first text book, which would be in parts learnt by heart. This was gradually supplemented by the *Elementarium* of Papias, the *Regulae* of Guarino, or Donatus, and superseded in the case of more advanced scholars by Priscian. Where means permitted, each pupil would possess a copy of these works, but in the great majority of cases he would be required to take down from dictation such passages from the text book in use as the master should select.

It is probable that by degrees each successful teacher provided his own manual for the use of his pupils: and that

[1] Rosmini, *Guarino, l.c.*, 'cum aures ipsae, quasi aliud extrinsecus sonat, mentem moveant, te ad cognoscendum acrius exsuscitent.' See also Sabbadini, *Vita di Guarino*, p. 103, where this letter is referred to.

[2] L. Bruni, supra, p. 125. Vittorino's practice in regard to composition, supra, p. 56.

[3] Supra, p. 35; B. Guarino, supra, p. 174; Guarino Veronese (Rosmini, *l.c.*) values Reading on this ground.

this was cast in the form of question and answer, like that of Ognibene da Lonigo[1], or that of Chrysoloras, which was the accepted accidence of Greek. This was accompanied by a small phrase book, such as Filelfo compiled, and such as we see in the large Grammar of Perotti[2], where Latin and Italian sentences are given side by side. Further, selected passages— either extracts from Classical writers, or model letters of Barzizza or Guarino, or short narratives composed to exhibit syntactical rules[3]—were then introduced, and recitation, from Ovid or Vergil, required.

But 'Grammatica' in its broadest sense was sometimes held to include the whole range of Latin literature and composition, which, otherwise, under the terms 'Literae' and 'Rhetorica,' were regarded as the edifice of which grammar was but the foundation. Indeed Latin and Greek grammar was still in the inductive stage; it could only be studied by the actual reading of the great writers[4]; orthography, accidence, syntax, prosody and style were alike far from being crystallised in authoritative rule and usage[5]. On the deductive side, as a practical art, grammar was still only in the making. But we trace at the same time, the growth of the conception of Grammar as a body of rules to be deductively applied in reading and in composition. So Vergerius[6] treats it thus as the introduction to Letters; its function is to determine orthography, inflexion, the order of words and clauses. Grammar is the essential instrument of teaching, and its study lies at the

---

[1] Supra, p. 88.   [2] Supra, p. 40 (note).   [3] Supra, p. 45.

[4] Aeneas Sylvius, supra, p. 148, and L. Bruni, supra, p. 124.

[5] I refer, of course, to the substitution of classical for mediaeval standards of Grammar and usage, a slow and laborious process tentatively begun by Petrarch, continued by Barzizza and Vittorino, but hardly attained during the lifetime of Guarino (ob. 1460).

[6] Vergerius, *Epistolae*, ed. Combi, p. 5: 'Grammatica, primordialis scientia pedagoga, dirigit et administrat singulas facultates....Haec fundamentum solidum cuiuslibet alterius disciplinae.' Aeneas Sylvius, *Opera*, p. 976: 'Grammatica doctrinae cuiusvis ostium dignoscitur.'

root of all intellectual progress. So, too, Vittorino[1], treating it as an introductory subject, 'diligentissime omnia in erudiendo primum adolescente prosequenda arbitratur.' B. Guarino[2], who terms this function of grammar *Methodice*, or the exposition of the formulae of language, speaks of it as the 'foundation of the house': it 'treats of everything which concerns the right construction of the sentence'[3]. So Perotti[4] defines it 'ars recte loquendi recteque scribendi, scriptorum et poetarum lectionibus observata.' It is again[5] 'ratio (method) congrui sermonis'; here, with Aeneas Sylvius[6], we pass into a wider view of its function, for it embraces 'recte loquendi scientia' (conversation and oratory), 'poetica et aliorum auctorum enarratio' (composition in prose and verse), 'scribendique ratio' (the epistolary style).

It is important to notice the weight attached to orthography and etymology[7], to the use of diphthongs, to transliteration of Greek names[8], and to the distinction of archaisms[9]. By careful instruction in early years, by much repetition[10], by practice in oral and written exercises[11], but above all by constant observation in reading[12], this essential body of knowledge could be so firmly acquired as to become almost a mechanical aptitude.

[1] Sassuolo da Prato, p. 56.

[2] *De Ordine docendi*, p. 7: 'Ut enim in aedificiis...ita et in studiorum ratione nisi principia optime calleant quo magis progrediuntur eo magis imbecillitatem suam sentiunt.' He borrows the technical terms directly from Quintilian i. 9.

[3] Ibid. p. 10.   [4] *Grammatices Rudimenta*, f. 3.

[5] Vergerius, *De Ingenuis Moribus*, p. 473.   [6] *Opera*, p. 976.

[7] Vergerius, *Epistolae*, p. 5. Aeneas Sylvius, *Opera*, p. 979. Vegio, *Op. cit.*, p. 244.   [8] B. Guarino, *Op. cit.*, supra, p. 164.

[9] Aen. Sylvius, supra, p. 147. Vegio, *l.c.* The affectation of archaism is condemned by Quintilian, i. 7.

[10] E.g. B. Guarino, *Op. cit.*, p. 7: 'Saepe repetens (magister), iterum iterumque memoriam in iis puerorum exerceat.'

[11] B. Guarino, *l.c.*, if boys are so trained 'expeditam consequentur et in scribendo et in loquendo promptitudinem, quam illud quoque vehementer augebit si Latine loqui continue assuefiant.'

[12] Aen. Sylvius, supra, p. 148. Bruni, supra, p. 124.

There was no difficulty in deciding upon the choice of Latin writers for the young scholar. After an introductory book of simple narrative, Phaedrus or Valerius Maximus[1], the *Aeneid*, and the *Letters*[2] or the Catiline speeches[3] of Cicero were at once entered upon. 'To begin with the best'[4] was the uniform precept of the Humanists. The Epic strain[5] was specially attractive to boys, whilst the style of Cicero[6] was lucid and his subject matter generally easy of comprehension. Ovid was sometimes read before Vergil, and Lucan and Sallust[7] placed in close connexion.

In viewing the general estimate of Latin literature for school purposes we turn first to the poets. The question was fiercely debated by the opponents of the new education as to the suitability of the classical poets for the training of the young[8]. The Dominican Father Giovanni[9], of Sta Maria

[1] M. Vegio, *Op. cit.*, p. 255: the moral fable is the best introduction to literature for the youthful mind. B. Guarino, supra, p. 169.

[2] Porcia, *De Generosa Liber. Educ.*, p. 112. At the period of beginning school, 'Ciceronis Epistolas audiant, his studeant, has sibi familiares faciant, bibant,...has et loquendo et scribendo semper imitari nitantur.'

[3] The Catiline speeches are urged by Vegio, *l.c.*

[4] Vergerius, supra, p. 110. Aeneas Sylvius, supra, p. 152.

[5] Aeneas Sylvius, *Opera*, p. 981: [Magister] 'et subtilitate Heroici carminis animus puerilis assurget et ex magnitudine rerum spiritum ducet et optimis imbuetur.' Vegio, *Op. cit.*, p. 255, 'ab unguiculis pueros assuefacere praestat,' i.e. to heroic poetry.

[6] Aeneas Sylvius, *Opera*, p. 984: 'Cicero iucundus incipientibus et apertus est satis.'

[7] Giovanni Dominici, *Regola del Governo*, p. 134, speaks of Ovid as the poet usually read first. Vittorino read Lucan along with Vergil. Porcia, *Op. cit.*, p. 112 urges that Sallust, 'historicorum princeps,' should be one of the earliest authors studied.

[8] L. Bruni, supra, p. 130, Aeneas Sylvius, supra, p. 149. Guarino's famous controversy at Ferrara with G. da Prato turned on this subject: Sabbadini, *Vita di Guarino*, p. 147.

[9] Supra, p. 120. *Regola del Governo*, *l.c.*: 'Ora si crescono i moderni figluoli e così invecchia l' apostatrice natura nel grembo degl' infedeli, nel mezzo degli atti disonesti sollicitanti la ancora impotente natura al peccato, ed insegnando tutti i vituperosi mali si possono pensare, nello studio

Novella, specially denounced their study on the score of the mythological and licentious stories from which they drew their themes. No doubt he but expressed a vein of sentiment common at the time (circ. 1400). Most Humanists took an opportunity of rebutting such strictures. They pointed out that the great Fathers, Basil, Jerome, and Augustine, following the example of Paul himself[1], quoted the poets or advised their study. May not Augustine and Lactantius[2] be said indeed to have reverenced Vergil? No one is seriously disturbed by the old mythology as a body of beliefs; whilst there is much even in them which reveals the praise of virtue, of faithfulness and self-sacrifice[3]. Poetry, moreover, is not to be taken literally; many truths are conveyed by figure. Again, when the poet portrays moral weakness or vice, we recognise the skill of the artist who developes his characters consistently[4]; it is not his purpose to exhibit evil for its own sake. It was allowed that the reading of the ancient poets needed careful discrimination[5]. A woman would avoid Juvenal[6], although

d' Ovidio maggiore, delle pistole *de Arte Amandi* e piu meretriciosi suoi libri e carnali scritture. Così si passa per Vergilio, tragedia, e altri.... E che peggio è, quella teneruccia mente si riempie del modo del sacrificio fatti agli falsi iddii...prima diventando pagani che Cristiani e prima chiamando dio Iuppiter o Saturno, Venus o Cibeles, che il sommo Padre, Figliuolo, e Spirito Santo; donde procede la vera fede essere dispregiata, Dio non riverito, scognosciuto il vero, fondato il peccato....Tutto procede dalla velenosa malizia dell' antico serpente.'

[1] Aeneas Sylvius, supra, p. 150: B. Guarino, supra, p. 170.

[2] L. Bruni, *l.c.*

[3] Bruni quotes especially Penelope and Alcestis, supra, p. 131.

[4] B. Guarino, supra, p. 175. So the elder Guarino, defending Terence, affirmed in reply to G. da Prato, that if the dramatist represents his characters as vicious or evil-tongued this is due to the necessities of the play as a work of art, and is not a symptom of moral perversity in the writer. Sabbadini, *Guarino*, p. 147.

[5] Vegio, *Op. cit.*, p. 250: 'Non negamus multorum qui poemata scripserunt interdicendam esse pueris lectionem'; this applies to the elegists, and some lyric poems of Horace and Catullus. Aeneas Sylvius, *Opera*, p. 983.

[6] L. Bruni, supra, p. 132.

there is nothing in his satires ' non laudabile, non Christiano homini maxime congruum' ; a boy should not be directed to the Elegiac poets, or to the Comic dramatists, or to the Satirists, who should be read at a later stage[1]. But who can desire to be ignorant of Vergil?

The standpoint of the Humanist teacher is intelligible. Most of the practical virtues are common to Christianity and to the higher type of Paganism[2]. So far as the poets celebrate these, and enforce them by their art, they may serve as models alike of life and of literary form[3]. The superstitions of mythology are at least harmless: if we can interpret them as allegories, they may even be helpful, whilst the poetic gift which clothes them in attractive dress is always admirable. Episodes there are, as indeed in Scripture, by no means edifying[4]; but their number is insignificant in comparison with nobler themes. Truths of natural philosophy[5], lessons of practical life, are scattered throughout the greater poems of antiquity. But, further, there is a direct correspondence between the instincts of our intellectual and emotional nature and the poetic harmonies[6]. Poetry is thus indicated as the fitting instrument of the finer training of the spirit. Its variety of form, and of subject ; the ease with which it may be learnt, and retained as an adornment of life ; its power of inspiring the mind from our earliest youth, all alike compel us to give noble poetry a high place in education. In a word, without a sound knowledge of the poets no one can attain to 'praestantia literarum.'[7]

---

[1] Vegio, *l.c.*; so Vittorino: 'Satirici qui graviores fuerint tantum admittentur' (Vegio): 'Persium et Horatium non omittebat...posthabito in lectione publica Iuvenale, quod aperte nimium et obscene loqueretur': (Platina, p. 22, of Vittorino).

[2] L. Bruni, supra, p. 131.

[3] Aeneas Sylvius, *Opera*, p. 983: 'Cum excellentium virorum dicta aut facta commemorant, tunc tota mente moveri et inflammari lector debet.' Like bees we may extract honey even from poisonous flowers.

[4] L. Bruni, supra, p. 131.   [5] Ibid. p. 129.
[6] Ibid. p. 130.   [7] Ibid. p. 131.

The poets to be preferred, after Vergil, whose 'ars,' 'eloquentia' and 'gloria'[1] are unsurpassable, are Lucan, the 'rhetorical' poet, and Statius[2]: Ovid's *Fasti* and *Metamorphoses* are more suitable than his other poems: Seneca's Tragedies[3] are prized for the gravity both of their style and sentiments. Horace[4] is 'parum minor Vergilio'; Claudian[5] is the purest of the later poets. Terence and Plautus are excellent for the conversational style[6]: though Vittorino and Guarino differed as to the advisability of reading the comic dramatists with school-boys. There is no mention of Lucretius[7]. Martial[8] is rigorously forbidden.

Emphatic claims are made for a prominent place amongst liberal studies on behalf of History[9]. A well known passage of Cicero[10] was quoted in support of this judgment of the Humanist. But for educational purposes the term covers only

[1] Aeneas Sylvius, *Opera*, p. 984; Platina, p. 21 (quoting Vittorino).

[2] B. Guarino, supra, p. 170. Aeneas Sylvius, *Opera*, p. 603: 'Statius sententiis gravibus usque refertus.'

[3] B. Guarino, *l.c.*   [4] Aeneas Sylvius, *l.c.*

[5] Aeneas Sylvius, *l.c.*

[6] Vittorino admired them 'quod hi plurimum eloquentiae conferrent. Eorum tamen lasciviam nocere ingeniis non bene substitutis affirmabat.' Platina, p. 22.

[7] The Italian scholars were entirely ignorant of Lucretius until the discovery of a complete copy by Poggio, a transcript of which reached Guarino late in 1416 or early in 1417. F. Barbaro, on July 6 of this latter year, writes to congratulate Poggio on the discovery of this amongst other lost classics. But nothing more was heard of the original MS. until after the death of Niccoli, who had jealously kept it to himself. We do not know what use was made of Guarino's copy. But neither in point of style nor of matter would Lucretius appeal favourably to the Humanists of this period. Vid. Sabbadini, *Guarino*, p. 37, for the dates.

[8] Aeneas Sylvius, *l.c.*: 'perniciosus' is his epithet for Martial.

[9] Vergerius, for instance, places it first in the category of liberal studies; supra, p. 106. Guarino says 'plurimum sane et ad studia et ad vitam conducit' in writing to a pupil. *Museo Italiano di Ant. Class.* II. ii. 415.

[10] *De Oratore*, ii. 9, 36: 'Historia testis temporum, lux veritatis, vita memoriae, magistra vitae, nuntia vetustatis.'

the literary presentation of the history of Rome and, in a less degree, of Greece.   When Bruni[1] speaks of the importance of studying 'the origins of our own history' he is thinking of Aeneas or Romulus, of Scipio or Augustus.   The records of the period subsequent to the decline of the old Empire are hardly worthy of consideration.   Vernacular histories or monastic annals are to be studiously eschewed.   A history[2], for instance, of the Bohemian or Hungarian nation may possibly yield some grains of worth, but to search for them is, even for a prince whose destiny it is to rule over these peoples, an empty labour.   Such productions, the work of uncultured minds, are destitute of all merit, whether of accuracy, of style, or of didactic usefulness.   The great histories, which alone deserve attention, are at the same time literary monuments. To study these is the right educational use of history.

History, thus studied, fulfils various functions.   It is of much value, first of all, to those who may be called to handle affairs[3].   For by it we acquire insight into the institutions and customs of other countries[4]; we learn the secret of the development of our own.   Again, we perceive the virtues which in the past have proved beneficial, the vices which have proved fatal, to the state: we are able to trace the policy which has built up or undermined its power.   From history we learn the varying fortunes of kings and of free peoples, and thus determine our own state-craft to-day.   For no one, whether he be soldier or statesman, can from his own individual experience

---

[1] Supra, p. 128.

[2] Aeneas Sylvius, *Opera*, p. 984: 'Nullo autem pacto vel Bohemorum historias vel Ungarorum atque his similes...tradi puero permiserim.   Sunt enim ab indoctis scriptae, multas ineptias continent, multa mendacia, nullas sententias, nullos ornatus.'

[3] Bruni, supra, *l.c.*; Vergerius, supra, p. 106.   Aeneas Sylvius, *Opera*, p. 604: in his advice to Sigismund he dwells at length upon the value of history in training the judgment: and supra, p. 141.

[4] Bruni, supra, p. 128: B. Guarino, supra, p. 169.

gain that breadth of wisdom which the study of books provides[1]. But there is another aspect of history, which renders it still more attractive as an instrument of education. If the philosopher lays down principles by which conduct should be guided, the historian alone can illustrate it by concrete examples[2]. We wish to know not only what ought to be done, but what has been done in the past, and the manner of doing it. History, written by men of notable gifts of style, affords us lessons, not only impressive in themselves, but couched in a form which renders them readily available whether for instruction or for public utterances. We may affirm with confidence that this didactic use of history determined the method by which it was taught in the Humanist schools[3]. Moreover, it was urged[4] that history, an attractive study to every learned man, is peculiarly easy as an educational subject. It is mainly a matter of memory. 'There is nothing in its study subtle or complex,' says Bruni; 'it consists in the narration of the simplest matters of fact, which, once grasped, are retained without difficulty.'

We see that history is not regarded by the Humanists upon its constructive side, as the creation, from diverse sources, of a continuous picture of a nation's development. Nor is it held to be a subject of critical enquiry[5]. Mediaeval or contemporary histories are scarcely contemplated, if we except

---

[1] Aeneas Sylvius, *Opera*, p. 603 : 'Nunquam tam multa experiundo videbis quam multa legendo perdisces.'

[2] Vergerius, supra, *l.c.*; Bruni, supra, *l.c.* Petrarch, *De viris illustribus*, ed. Razzolini, i. 6. 'Hic enim, nisi fallor, fructuosus historicorum finis est, illa persequi quae vel sectanda legentibus vel fugienda sunt.'

[3] That this was true even of Erasmus is shown by Benoist, *Quid de Puerorum &c.*, p. 138.

[4] Bruni, supra, *l.c.*

[5] We should, however, bear in mind the tentative critical method of Valla, who was in some respects the most powerful intellect of this period.

the conspicuous instance of Biondo[1], or the purely literary effort of Poggio[2]. The sources of history, indeed, are fixed, they are entirely literary, and their authority is determined by attractions of style, and by their aptness for moral edification. Vittorino, confronted by scepticism as to the accuracy of Livy, indignantly rejects the suggestion that a sound Latinist, an elegant narrator, and a Paduan, could possibly be historically untrustworthy[3].

Valerius Maximus[4] was much employed in schools, since he provides a store of examples for the moralist. Justin, Q. Curtius, Florus[5], and the Latin version of Arrian by Vergerius are recommended for beginners. Plutarch, in Latin, or at a later stage, in the original Greek, was the favourite historian : for the biographical method lent itself specially to the inculcation of moral precepts[6]. A translation of the life of Camillus or Pelopidas was an acceptable offering to a patron, and to read or declaim such a version a profitable exercise of the school. By Bruni[7] Caesar was regarded as the chief historian. But Vegio and Porcia, following the common opinion, preferred Sallust[8]; Vittorino Livy, whom indeed he first introduced into schools. Suetonius[9] was not

---

[1] *Historiarum ab inclinatione Romanorum Decades.* Basil., 1559.

[2] *Historia Florentina*, in eight Books. It was translated by his son Jacopo and often printed in that form.

[3] Platina, p. 22.

[4] B. Guarino, supra, p. 169. For Vittorino's judgment, Platina, p. 22: 'Valerii Maximi lectionem frequentabat propter varietatem historiarum et copiam exemplorum.'

[5] Aeneas Sylvius, supra, p. 152. For Florus, Sabbadini in *Museo Ital., l.c.*

[6] Guarino writes of Plutarch to Leonello d'Este (Rosmini, *Guarino*, i. 118) that the *Lives* are the best training for the practical duties of a Prince. He proposes to present him with a special selection of passages throwing light upon this grave subject.

[7] Supra, p. 128.

[8] Porcia, *Op. cit.*, p. 112: 'Maiori cura Sallustium historicorum principem in manibus habeant, foveant, amplectantur.'

[9] Aeneas Sylvius, supra, p. 152.

permitted to boys; Tacitus[1], hardly known as yet to scholars, and, as a stylist, always doubtfully viewed, is never mentioned. Further, carefully selected narratives from the Old Testament, and the Apocryphal books (especially the Second Book of the Maccabees) are included[2], Aeneas Sylvius indeed devoting much space to the lessons to be drawn by a young prince from the records of the Kings of Israel and Judah.

The practice of oratory is based upon the close study of the masterpieces of classical eloquence and the rhetorical treatises which have survived from antiquity. The high value attached to this art, not by scholars alone, but in public affairs, in diplomacy, in social and ceremonial functions, led to that elaborate study of ancient rhetoric which characterises the Humanist schools. The speeches of Cicero or the rhetorical compositions inserted in the histories of Sallust and Livy are the main oratorical material. Their value in education consists, in the eyes of the Humanists, first, in the profound moral lessons, civic and personal, therein enforced. Bruni[3], for example, looks upon eloquence as giving the emotional impulse to the individual will in carrying out in practice the principles suggested by philosophy and exemplified in history. Nowhere are virtues so persuasively set forth or vices so forcibly condemned. Next we learn from the orators the practical arts of Dialectic, by which conviction is brought home to differing minds[4]. The power of argument is for

[1] Sabbadini, *Codici Latini*, p. 450. During the whole of the first half of the 15th century Tacitus was practically unknown to the Humanists ; and although Guarino, about 1444, is eager to obtain a transcript of the archetype at Florence, it is perfectly safe to say that this historian was entirely without influence upon the Latinity or the historical knowledge of the time.

[2] Vegio, *Op. cit.*, p. 252.

[3] Supra, p. 128.

[4] Vergerius, *De Ingenuis Moribus*, p. 472 : ' per eloquentiam possumus graviter ornateque dicere, qua una re maxime conciliantur multitudinis animi.'

purposes of affairs[1], of legal discussion, and of conversation, of prime importance. Where can this be more fruitfully studied than in the forensic orations of Cicero? To enable a boy to realise the force of ancient oratory, he should be taken to hear some eloquent citizen, or great pleader in the Courts[2]. There he will perceive how gesture and delivery combine with logical skill to illustrate a case, and so learn to supply by imagination an element which is of necessity absent from recorded speeches. Lastly, the whole subject of style is exhibited, in example or in precept, or in both, by such writers as Cicero and Quintilian[3]. Vocabulary, metaphor, exposition, persuasiveness, all the arts of expression, are cultivated best by an intimate knowledge of the orations of Cicero.

The reading of Cicero is accompanied by constant practice in the declamation[4] of his Speeches. His oratorical treatises must all be studied, especially the *De Oratore*, which in the hands of Barzizza and Vittorino formed one of the chief Latin text books. The precepts therein laid down should be illustrated by suitable extracts from the speeches themselves. Quintilian, also, will be in perpetual use as a commentary upon Roman eloquence[5]. But besides the classical examples, Lactantius[6], the Cicero of the Church, Ambrose, Augustine and Jerome provide material thoroughly sound in substance, and acceptable in style. Even modern writers, themselves students of ancient eloquence, Bruni, Guarino, or Ambrogio Traversari, are held to be valuable models of oratorical prose, and their orations deserve, therefore, attention in the schools.

[1] Vergerius: eloquence he terms, ‘civilis scientiae quaedam pars’: it has three forms, iudiciale, deliberativum, demonstrativum.

[2] Porcia, *De Generosa Lib. educ.*, p. 114; he is referring to boys of twelve or thirteen years of age.

[3] Supra, p. 125, for Bruni's opinion, which is indeed that of every Humanist from Petrarch downwards.

[4] B. Guarino, supra, p. 172.

[5] Guarino, *l.c.*

[6] Aeneas Sylvius, supra, p. 151.

It is a marked characteristic of Humanism to limit Philosophy, as a serious study, to Ethics, to the entire exclusion of
Metaphysic[1]. But by Ethics was meant little more than the
common-places of Roman Stoic morality as expounded by
Cicero and Seneca. It was avowedly practical in intent, but
personal rather than social in its application. Reverence,
self-control, modesty, truthfulness, and courage, the virtues of
the individual, were dealt with in some detail and with copious
illustration from classical sources. More complex questions,
such as the relation of patriotic duty to personal ambition or
opportunity, or the opposition between Christian self-repression
and the self-assertion—intellectual and moral—of the Roman
'virtus,' or the nature of the ultimate sanction of morals, and
the influence of Religion upon it, all these are ignored. Here,
as in certain other departments of practical enquiry, the fixed
usage of the best age of antiquity is accepted as a sound
working standard. It follows, therefore, that the method of
teaching morals was mainly literary and didactic[2]. Thus the
study of Cicero, of Aristotle, and of Seneca, with illustrations
from Livy, and above all from Plutarch, provided an important educational instrument[3].

In the training for public life (to which so many of the
pupils of Vittorino and Guarino would look forward), or for

[1] Some qualification of this statement is due in the case of Vergerius;
but the entire temper of the man was opposed to any but practical and
objective intellectual interests so far as concerns education. See his aim
expressed in his own words : 'insisto multo studiosius ' (than upon Logic)
'philosophiae, non solum ei quae naturam rerum ostendit, sed ei quoque
in qua omnis recta ratio vivendi consistit,' *Epistole*, LXXIV, p. 100.

[2] Aeneas Sylvius, *Opera*, p. 972 : ' philosophia absque literis haud
facile percipi potest.' So also Bruni, supra, p. 127.

[3] Platina, p. 22, for Vittorino's opinion : ' Cum omnem honesti iustique
disciplinam omnemque item Academicorum, Stoicorum, Peripateticorum
doctrinam ad tollenda animi vitia et formandum optimum doctissimumque
virum duceret pernecessariam esse. Ciceronem, egregium Platonis, Aris-
totelis, Zenonis aemulum, legendum continuo dicebat, quia illinc omne quod
ad publicam ac privatam vitam facit sumeretur.'

private station, moral philosophy ranks second to history alone. It covers all life, and all conditions of men. Hence its essential place in education, for boys and for girls alike. In practice, no doubt, religion, example and discipline were relied upon[1], but sound training in the principles of conduct is derived from the reading of ancient books[2]. These, indeed, are illustrated and suggested by poet, historian and orator, but the moralists must be studied for the systematic understanding of this grave subject.

In the choice of moralists it is of urgent importance that works recognised as sound in style and in matter alone be adopted. Plato, Aristotle, Cicero, especially the *De officiis* and the *Tusculans,* Seneca and Boethius cover the ground. Vittorino went further afield and included Augustine and other ecclesiastical writers, as did Bruni. But the necessity for careful attention to style brought about in practice the supremacy of the classical moralists in actual teaching[3]. Bruni thus claims the fullest liberty in the choice of authors, deprecating only, as does Aeneas Sylvius, recourse to mediaeval or modern Churchmen. It was the custom of Vittorino and

---

[1] By Vittorino and Guarino, and doubtless by all practical teachers; but even by them the sanction of Cicero or Plutarch was highly valued in enforcing duty.

[2] Vegio, *De Educ. Liberorum,* p. 288: 'Mores a nullis procul dubio melius quam a philosophiae (quae vitae nostrae magistra est) studiis consequentur.' So Aeneas Sylvius, supra, p. 141. Formal discussions, in which the ancient authors would be mainly relied upon as material, are urged by Bruni, supra, p. 127.

[3] It is a remarkable fact that the *Meditations* of M. Aurelius are never alluded to by any Humanist scholar. Petrarch's reference to their author, in his Treatise *De Officio et Virtutibus Imperatorum,* is obviously a mere platitude; but none of the Greek scholars of the fifteenth century seem aware of the survival of this important monument of ancient Ethics. In the preceding century, however, certain copies seem to have been made, and detached passages were introduced by Planudes into a collection of extracts upon Morals. The Ed. Princeps did not appear until 1559, which is in itself significant.

Guarino to impress with much care the moral lessons afforded by the daily classical reading, or again to distinguish, where necessary, between the moral confusions of an ancient author and the literary or dialectic skill with which they were expressed.

There is, however, amongst Humanist writers upon education occasional reference to a wider conception of philosophy as the 'mater omnium artium,' or as equivalent to 'amor sapientiae'; and this wisdom is defined as 'the knowledge of all things, whether divine or human, their laws and their causes[1].' Vittorino, as we know from Platina[2], included Natural Philosophy in his course, and the curious intermixture of science, ethics and mathematics reminds us of the conjunction of moral and natural philosophy in the Chair of Philosophy at Padua. But in treating philosophy in this wider sense of the term, apart from mathematics which were valued for their own sake, the main end in view of the Humanist teacher was gradually confined to the provision of just so much information as would enable a boy to understand the allusions to Astronomy, Geography or Natural history contained in the ancient poets and historians[3]. As classical education became more precisely defined, these subjects ceased to obtain an independent place, and 'Philosophy' lost all other content than that of Ethics. The works of the elder Pliny, of Solinus and Pomponius Mela, valued for the variety of their subject-matter by earlier Humanists[4], then dropped out of the school curriculum.

---

[1] Aeneas Sylvius, *Opera*, p. 991 ; Vergerius, supra, p. 108.

[2] Platina, p. 21 : ' Asserens perfectum virum de natura, de moribus, de motu astrorum, de linearibus formis, de harmonia et concentu, de numerandis dimetiendisque rebus disserere oportere.'

[3] This is the position taken by B. Guarino, supra, p. 171. A knowledge of the geography of Strabo is recommended for the same reason. Poggio, however, shews a genuine feeling for geography and travel in the account of the journeys of Niccolò Conti which he included in his work, *De Varietate Fortunae*. But Vergerius and Vittorino treated natural philosophy more seriously, perhaps as a result of the influence of Padua.

[4] B. Guarino commends Aulus Gellius, Macrobius and Pliny, upon this

At the outset of the period with which this survey is concerned, we find Vergerius lamenting, like Petrarch before him, that Greek literature was still sealed against western scholars[1]. But within a very few years he is found sitting with Guarino and Bruni in the lecture room of Chrysoloras at Florence rejoicing in the dawn of a new age. To Guarino at Venice and Vittorino at Mantua was due the introduction of Greek into the school course. No one attached more importance to the subject than Vittorino, and to him mainly was due the elaboration of the order and method of study, reading, and composition in the language. Neither Vergerius nor Bruni refer to Greek in the treatises before us; Aeneas Sylvius mentions it only to regret the lack of opportunity for its study in Hungary or Germany[2]. The elder Guarino at Ferrara laid less stress upon Greek than did Vittorino at Mantua. Public opinion, indeed, regarded Greek as standing on a wholly different footing, educationally, from Latin. For Latin was, in a true sense, the historic tongue of Italy, its use was an urgent necessity in many careers in life, and a knowledge of Roman literature indispensable to social distinction. Greek, on the other hand, appealed to a narrower interest. Its study was regarded as a valuable aid to the full understanding of Latin, both as language and as literature; and it was held in reverence as the key to Homer, Plato and Demosthenes. But not until the middle of the fifteenth century, when the multiplication of texts and the settlement of accidence and syntax rendered its acquisition a simpler matter, did the influence of Vittorino and Guarino make itself generally felt, so that it was possible to lay down that no one ignorant of Greek could claim the title of educated[3].

ground. The *Historia Naturalis* 'non minus varia est quam ipsa natura.' 'Possedere un Gellio era per un umanistà una necessità, essendo esso uno dei più ricchi prontuari antichi,' says Sabbadini.

[1] Supra, p. 106.

[2] Supra, p. 149.

[3] B. Guarino, supra, p. 166.

The Gonzaga children under Vittorino began the subject early. Cecilia knew the declensions and conjugations at the age of seven : and this was not exceptional. Greek and Latin were taught side by side so soon as the necessary grounding in Latin grammar had been secured[1]. A higher knowledge of this subject, as presented by Priscian, was not considered possible until a beginning had been made with Greek. Much attention was paid at this stage to the light thrown by Greek etymologies upon Latin orthography. The *Erotemata* of Chrysoloras was the one available manual. It was specially edited and abridged, with a parallel Latin version, by Guarino. A reading book of easy prose was provided, and the Gospels[2], with or without the Latin version written side by side, served as the first continuous work read. Reading aloud in Greek was from the first practised as an aid to the more ready grasp of the sense of the author ; whilst translation into Latin, with composition in Greek, formed the usual exercises.

Homer, both as the father of Epic poetry[3], and therefore attractive to boys, and as helpful to the better appreciation of Vergil, was the poet first studied. The Attic tradition was not as yet formulated by the Humanists; for Apollonius Rhodius, Herodotus, and Xenophon were the books next studied. We may recall the estimation in which Vittorino[4] held the chief writers of Greece, determined by their value for instruction. Isocrates was specially prized by Battista Guarino. The Dramatists seem to have been read before Thucydides or Demosthenes[5]. But our information as to the order or choice of the authors adopted in school is very limited. We know, however, that Plutarch occupied an important place, and that the Greek Fathers, Basil and Chrysostom, were frequently read.

---

[1] Platina, p. 20 : 'quod utraque alterius cognitione facilior videretur.'

[2] Cecilia Gonzaga was reading the Gospels in Greek before she was eight. Luzio, in *Arch. Venet.*, 1888, p. 329, seqq. Poliziano began Greek with Piero de' Medici before his pupil was seven (1478), using Gaza's grammar.

[3] B. Guarino, supra, p. 168.   [4] Supra, p. 49.

[5] Under Vittorino, however, boys began early to read Demosthenes.

Guarino was able to turn out pupils who after twelve months' instruction could translate competently from the authors just mentioned[1]. He encouraged rapid reading by aid of a Latin translation. He, however, deprecated the advice of Quintilian to begin with Greek in preference to Latin. It is possible that Vittorino did, with some few clever pupils, try this experiment[2].

The Scriptures and the Fathers are constantly recommended for school purposes. Vegio is anxious that selections only from the Old Testament, especially in the case of the book of Genesis or Ezekiel, should be placed in the hands of the young. The Psalms, to be learnt by heart, will be followed by the Proverbs and Ecclesiasticus, and the Maccabees; the second Book of the latter 'approaches in dignity of style the finest examples of Roman literature[3].' Elsewhere we meet with advice to use Genesis, the Books of the Kings, Esther, and Esdras; and from the New Testament, the Acts of the Apostles[4]. The choice is limited for most part to the simpler historical narrative, read both as moral teaching and as history[5].

Amongst the Fathers Lactantius stands first for grace of

[1] Supra, p. 167.

[2] Prendilacqua, speaking of Alessandro Gonzaga, says, p. 45: 'Fu nella puerizia eccellentemente nutrito di greche lettere, nell' adolescenza di latine, e nell' età più matura di studi sacri.' Alessandro was the scholar-poet of the family, much beloved by Vittorino.

Our information upon the school teaching of Greek and the authors read is limited to the practice of Vittorino and the Tract of B. Guarino.

[3] Vegio, *De Educat. Liber.*, p. 252: the Book of Genesis, Ezekiel, and Song of Songs should not be taught until the 20th year.

[4] Aeneas Sylvius, *Opera*, p. 603. 'Scripturam sacram semper domi habebis, et nunc Vetus nunc Novum intueberis Testamentum.'

[5] Aeneas Sylvius, *Opera*, p. 605, lays great stress upon the lessons to be derived from the Old Testament histories. He assumes that a knowledge of the Creed, Lord's Prayer, and other simple formularies will be acquired early, supra, p. 141.

style, in which he is often compared to Cicero[1]. Augustine holds the second place, and in subject-matter he has perhaps the higher claim. Vegio[2], indeed, takes the account which Augustine gives of his own early training as the text of his Treatise. The Humanists, at least during this earlier period of the New Learning, were eager to appeal to the authority of this Father in support of their educational ideals[3]. The other ecclesiastical writers included in the school courses of the humanist teacher were Jerome, Ambrose, Cyprian, Chrysostom, Gregory Nazianzen, and Leo[4]. Later writers, especially the Scholastic theologians, were under a severe ban. We suspect that inferior Latinity was, in their case, an objection at least as weighty as the nature of their writings[5]. We notice the confident appeal to the judgment of learned society, whether clerical or lay, in Italy, in support of this position.

As regards methods of exposition of a classical author, some light may be derived from the occasional references to the

[1] Supra, p. 124.

[2] Vegio, *Op. cit.*, p. 140.

[3] E.g. upon the use of the ancient Poets, supra, pp. 165 and 170 (Guarino) ; p. 149 (Aeneas Sylvius).

[4] Aeneas Sylvius, *Opera*, p. 603. Guarino ' sacras literas non negligebat, sed maxime Cipriani, Lactantii, Hieronymi et acutissimi Augustini studiosus erat...quapropter non seculares modo, verum etiam religiosi et monachi et Christo amici homines Guarinianum auditorium frequentabant.' Lud. Carbo, a pupil of Guarino, quoted by Rosmini, *Guarino*, i. 115.

[5] Aeneas Sylvius, *Opera*, p. 604: (to Sigismund) ' Haec quae nunc scribo, si quis doctus extra Italiam legeret, me maxime argueret quod inter auctores legendos non numeraverim Hugonem de Sancto Victore, aut Alexandrum de Ales, vel Magnum Albertum, vel Petrum Blesensem, vel Nicolaum de Lira, et Alanum, et hanc novorum turbam. Sed tu cave ne istos audias. Nam etsi docti sunt, docere tamen alios nequeunt. Ego tibi id suadeo quod per me rectum puto, nec somnio. Sed vivos totius Italiae peritissimos in hanc sententiam habeo concurrentes...Illis in auctoribus te exerce qui sunt probatiores. Suscipere namque semper optima debemus ad imitandum.' With this compare Bruni's protest against the reading of contemporary religious writings, supra, p. 127.

subject met with in the records of the two great school-masters[1].
The conditions under which class-work was necessarily carried
on have been alluded to.   The scarcity and inaccuracy of
texts, the absence of dictionaries and of commentaries, the
undeveloped state of syntax, especially in the case of Greek,
made preparation by the class difficult, and compelled the
master to rely largely upon the method of lecture and dictation.
There was, however, scope for variety in the form of the lesson
even under these limitations.   A section of the text of the
author having been dictated Guarino called for it to be read
aloud[2].   If the passage did not yield, on a first reading, from
the rhythm and structure of the sentence, an intelligible
meaning, the process was repeated.   When a bald construe
had been attained, the art of the master came into play in
arriving at an exact and elegant version.   In the case of a
Greek classic this version would be in Latin.   Here there was
an opening for skilful questioning.   We know that Guarino
denounced the method of learning syntax by acquiring rules by
heart[3].   Grammar was taught by him through the medium of
speaking and reading Latin[4]; and only when examples in
illustration of syntactical principles could be framed by the
pupil, was he expected to commit a formula to memory.

The construing secured, and oral practice in accidence and
syntax with it, the lesson tended to take the form of a lecture.
Parallel passages were quoted and recorded : e.g. in reading
Homer, Vergil would be constantly referred to[5].   Mythological,
geographical and other allusions were explained, and a body of
knowledge accumulated in note-books for future use.   More
especially 'sententiae', reflections upon characters whether

[1] For Vittorino's practice see p. 46 above.

[2] Rosmini, *Guarino*, i. p. 113, Guarino's letter to Leonello.

[3] Id. *Op. cit.*, i. 85.

[4] Gian Pannonio, *Silva Panegyrica*, ll. 520 seqq., gives a poetical
description of Guarino's grammatical expositions.

[5] B. Guarino, supra, pp. 168, 173.   Platina, p. 21.

historical or other, would occupy a large part of the lesson. It is obvious that there was here no little temptation to mere display of heterogeneous learning; but the masters of whose practice we know most were conspicuous for the simplicity of their method and their perseverance in appealing to the intelligence of their least advanced pupils[1]. Special portions of the author thus treated, which contained, perhaps, a smart anecdote, clever repartee, striking simile or metaphor, were committed to memory, and once a month such passages were revised and classified. The notes taken were copied, and their substance incorporated into carefully arranged volumes[2].

In reading an Oration of Cicero the master would devote special attention to questions of style: and the work would be treated not only as literature but as a model for composition. The same method was pursued in handling Vergil and Ovid, in which case paraphrase in prose and in verse was required from the class. In teaching older pupils the whole field of rhetoric was open to the master, but during the period before us the higher elaboration of the art was not practised in schools and was, indeed, discouraged.

Great stress was laid by scholars of the first rank upon the use of the best available texts[3]. In private reading of Greek, the use of a sound literary translation side by side with the original, as advocated by Guarino, was regarded as a remarkable

---

[1] Platina notes this as the special characteristic of Vittorino : ' varius erat, distinctus...ex ingeniis auditorum ac lectionum qualitate,' p. 19. ' Adeo humaniter, adeo benigne, adeo patienter interrogantibus respondebat Guarinus, ut facile animadverteretur eum vehementissime cupere, ut quicquid ipse sciebat in auditores transfunderet.' L. Carbo, quoted by Rosmini, *Guarino*, i. p. 115. But the evidence of the simplicity and thoroughness of the teaching of these two great masters does not depend on isolated opinion. The selection of books whose subject-matter is intelligible and interesting is noted as a necessary point of good teaching by B. Guarino, supra, p. 168.

[2] B. Guarino, supra, p. 173.

[3] B. Guarino, supra, p. 164 ; Vergerius, supra, p. 106.

discovery in method, and the rapidity with which his pupils learned to construe at sight was certainly noteworthy : we must remember however that Guarino, like Filelfo, could speak Greek.   But the strongest point in the teaching of the early Humanists consisted in their persistent individual work[1].   They were careful of the first steps in grammar and composition, and took great pains to adapt themselves to the needs of each individual pupil.   The working hours both of master and scholars were inordinately long[2].

The importance of Composition in the eyes of the Humanists is manifest in all that they said and wrote.   Style is the indispensable condition of permanence[3], almost indeed of credibility, in a literary work ; in Society it is accepted as the obvious mark of an educated man.   The functions of eloquence—by which is meant style, whether in conversation, in composition or in oratory,—are of supreme dignity.   For whilst it is the end of philosophy to exhibit canons of excellence in thought and character, and the use of history to illustrate them, it belongs to eloquence alone, by fitting stimulus, to enforce their application.   It has often been said that the Humanists (at least those of the later age) provide with difficulty a place for the spiritual forces of a personal religious faith in their ideal of life ; and so far as this is true, the explanation lies in the fact that scholars persuaded themselves

---

[1] Sabbadini, *Vita di Guarino*, p. 139.   Guarino 'facceva doppia scuola ; alla pubblica dedicava il giorno, alla privata la sera.   La lezione pubblica era doppia, nella mattina spiegava un poeta e un prosatore Latino, nel pomeriggio leggeva ordinariamente Greco.   La sera e la notte erano dedicate ai convittori ; essi lavoravano sotto i suoi occhi e l' avevano sempre lì presente e pronto a rispondere a tutte le difficoltà che incontrassero.'

[2] Five hours' sleep was considered ample for a scholar really in earnest.

[3] Vergerius, *De Ingen. Moribus*, p. 469 : 'Si quid pluribus exemplaribus vulgatum est, non facile potest interire, si modo et dignitas accedat orationi.   Nam quae sine dignitate scribuntur, ea *nec sortiuntur fidem, nec subsistere diu* possunt.'

that Style could fulfil the function of a religious impulse, that argument and illustration drawn from an authoritative past, and driven home by exhortation couched in classical literary form, could serve as a spiritual force to the individual life[1].

Next, we must remember the high practical value of a good prose style. Its possession was a prime qualification for a public or professional career apart from its element of personal distinction. We are thus prepared to find that, once the canons of purity defined, the reading of ancient authors is largely guided by the wish to acquire a habit of sound writing. In the period with which we are now concerned, the schoolmaster had not learned to regard 'epideictic' or artificial rhetorical display as the highest aim of composition. With Vittorino, as we have already seen, the striving after oratorical effect found no favour. To write perspicuous prose, free from ostentation and ornament, was the purpose of his teaching[2]. So we find it laid down that boys are to be taught to strive after 'oratio plana, perspicua, dilucida, nulliusque interpretis indigens auxilio'[3]; words should be chosen from no affectation of archaism[4], but be such as are generally accepted. Though Cicero is the natural model for the philosophical and oratorical style, it is not necessary to erect him into a tyrant: we may employ words 'domestica et usitata,' if we keep before us the general

[1] Bruni, supra, p. 128.

[2] So Guarino required, first, clearness, secondly, 'proprietas verborum,' or the right choice and use of words, and only when these were secured would he pay regard to the third point of good composition, style. See Rosmini, *Guarino,* i. 84.

[3] Dialectic so far as it formed part of a humanist curriculum was chiefly treated as an aid to composition, and as a department of Rhetoric. Vittorino and Vergerius broke entirely away from the scholastic methods and regarded Logic merely as a means to clear and precise expression. Supra, p. 60.

[4] The unsettled orthography of Latin was a matter of grave concern to scholars, and pedantic efforts at archaistic spelling were common. The true bases of orthography, literary and philological, were obviously beyond the reach of the Humanists.

principles of his sentence-structure.   There is a third function
of composition which is indeed less important than the others
but which was gradually felt to be educationally valuable.
This is the place of Latin and Greek composition in compelling rigorous study of the literature upon which it is
modelled[1].   Both subject-matter and expression are reduced
to their simplest elements before a version or an original
theme can be produced.   Paraphrase of poetry into prose[2],
the translation of Greek into Latin, and the reverse exercise,
and direct imitation of a proposed model passage, were all
inculcated as means to rigid analysis of classical style.   On
the other hand no one can hope to write well who does not
carefully observe the literary methods of the best authors[3].
Hence the importance of the right choice in classical reading.
Only in this way can we imbibe, unconsciously as it were, the
indefinable charm of style, which consists in ' sonus, elegantia,
concinnitas et venustas[4].'

This training should begin early[5].   Verse composition, in
which Ovid and Vergil are the natural models, will prove a
useful aid to facility in prose[6].   Speech in Latin provides an
easy introduction to continuous composition, and care must be
taken in insisting on sound literary examples to grammatical
rules, whether provided by the master or sought out by the
class[7].   An exercise frequently employed was the declamation
of the Letters of Cicero[8], and their imitation, whilst the practice
of reading aloud and committing to memory large portions of

[1] B. Guarino, supra, p. 168.

[2] Vegio, *Op. cit.*, pp. 235, 6.

[3] Aeneas Sylvius, supra, p. 148.

[4] Bruni, *De Studiis et Literis*, p. 5.

[5] B. Guarino, supra, p. 168, speaks of the importance of Greek composition, so soon as a boy begins the language.

[6] Vegio, *Op. cit.*, p. 235.   Prosody was taught early; but lyrical metres
received little attention.

[7] Supra, p. 164.

[8] B. Guarino, supra, p. 169.

the best prose writers in Greek and Latin bore directly upon the acquisition of vocabulary and cultivation of style. Bruni especially would have the student note and prize the rhythmical element present in the best prose with a view to its imitation [1]. Vittorino [2] and Guarino gave much individual attention to the exercises in composition. In later stages when the more complex arts of Rhetoric were introduced, with the elaborate study of metaphor, simile, figure, and elegance, arts which had scarcely reached their full importance in our period [3], original production both in prose and verse [4] were required. Vittorino [5] devised special practice in forensic oratory, in public addresses, and, though more sparingly, in complimentary speeches. His aim, we are told, was to cultivate readiness and self-confidence in view of the future career of his pupils [6]. But here as always, in judging the scholarship of the Humanists, we must remember that the school of which Vittorino is the most characteristic representative cultivated the study of antiquity, and reproduced it, with the definite purpose of reconciling it with the culture and the activities of the time. Hence, in composition the

[1] Bruni, supra, p. 125.

[2] Platina, p. 24 : 'Emendabat ipse diligentissime quae a discipulis scribebantur, quaedam adiciens, plurima detrahens.' Upon Vittorino's method in teaching composition, see supra, p. 56.

[3] Vittorino himself wrote 'omni pompa ac fastu verborum amoto'; 'nullo fuco aut ambitu orationis utens.'

[4] The Hexameter was the metre mainly used in composition exercises: but the other metres were used by older pupils. Guarino, supra, p. 165. There is little or no reference to methods of teaching verse composition in Greek.

[5] Sassuolo da Prato, p. 64: 'Cuius (i.e. rhetoricae) cum contrita illa praecepta perceperint, exercitationibus declamatoriis assidue illos exerceri iubet, fictis scilicet causis propositis forensibus, popularibus, senatoriis': 'ut ad dicendum paratiores ac promptiores in forum in curiam in contionem prodirent.'

[6] L. Carbo, a pupil of Guarino, acknowledged, even as a young man, the authorship and circulation of more than 10,000 hexameters and over 200 orations in the grand style. As a consequence, he had, says Rosmini, 'soverchia buona opinion di se stesso.'

stamp of personality was not rejected in obedience to the
necessity of exact imitation of Cicero and Livy: so that
criticism which may fairly be levelled against the stylistic
methods of the following century is beside the point when
applied to the more sincere and direct Latinity of Vergerius
and his immediate successors[1]. It may, however, be admitted
that no doubt was felt that by diligent study and imitation of
Cicero and Vergil[2], combined with due observance of the
precepts of Rhetoric, and the Art of Poetry, a persevering
student might count upon becoming not only a scholar but
a poet or orator as well. In practice, however, verse composition was regarded as an accomplishment[3], whilst a good
prose style was a definitely practical aptitude.

§ 4. MATHEMATICS, SCIENCE, MUSIC.

The position of Mathematical studies in Italy during the
fourteenth and fifteenth centuries needs further research.
There is no doubt that after the close of the period with
which this review is concerned, Italians held the foremost
place in the pursuit of this as of the other sciences. No
doubt, the absorbing interest of Letters in the fifteenth century
tended to hinder the appreciation of Mathematics as a subject

[1] The following quotation from an address by Dr. Sabbadini to the
University of Catania, 1893, confirms the position taken up in the text.
'Scuole umanistiche l' Italia ne ebbe due: una grande e una piccola,
quella degli eroi del Quattrocento e quella degli epigoni del Cinque-
cento. I latinisti del Quattrocento riproducevano tutte le forme
letterarie della cultura romana per il bisogno di riprodurre, ma vi
imprimevano la propria personalità potente e viva, riuscendo nell'
imitazione originali, dovechè i cinquecentisti non facevano che bamboleg-
giare ciceroneggiando.' *Prolusione al Corso di Letteratura Latina*, 1893–4,
p. 18.

[2] B. Guarino, supra, p. 171; for Vittorino's close study of the *De
Oratore*, see supra, p. 48.

[3] Vergerius, supra, p. 107. We must remember that the *art* of poetry
came within the general scope of Rhetoric.

of school instruction. The study remained always one of professional importance to the architect and the navigator, just as Drawing[1] to the artist and the builder, but only by exceptional teachers was either admitted to a leading place amongst liberal studies.

About the year 1400 Padua was more closely identified with Mathematics than any other University. But Pelacani[2], whose industry is shewn by the immense body of MS. work, even now mostly unexamined, which survives, had no public Chair in the subject. Vergerius and Vittorino[3], both deriving their educational ideals from Padua, attached great weight to the inclusion of Geometry and Astronomy, and what we should now call elementary Mechanics, in a complete course of training. Bruni[4] and Aeneas Sylvius[5], however, allow only a subordinate place to these subjects, whilst Guarino and his son ignore them altogether.

Geometry was evidently the department of pure Mathematics commonly taught, presumably through Euclid[6], for Algebra is barely alluded to. Euclid was definitely regarded as a better substitute for the scholastic Logic, which was decried by every

---

[1] Drawing is not admitted to the circle of the Liberal Studies (supra, p. 107). It is a technical aptitude of the Painter. It may however be regarded as a preparatory training in writing, and so deserves attention. Vegio is clearly inclined to modify the usual humanist judgment, on reflecting that Aemilius expressly wished his sons to learn to draw and paint. *De Educ. Lib.* p. 281. To Writing importance was attached, both by Guarino and by Aeneas Sylvius. The autograph of Guarino himself (Brit. Mus. Add. MSS. 12,008) is a beautiful example of clear and elegant script.

[2] Gloria, *Mon. della Univ. di Padova*, ii. 415—6.

[3] Vergerius, supra, p. 108. For Vittorino, supra, p. 43, and Sassuolo da Prato, p. 64.

[4] Supra, p. 126.

[5] Supra, p. 156. Mathematics fall within those subjects of natural or external interest which are inferior in rank to 'the weightier things which concern character and action.

[6] Supra, p. 43 (note).

Humanist. The training in rigid deductive reasoning supplied by Geometry is held of great value to the young mind[1]; the subject may therefore be introduced early. It is a corrective of hasty inference, and encourages a habit of requiring demonstration. It developes also quickness of observation. Vittorino, grouping together arithmetic, geometry and astronomy, prized them as the only exact knowledge we possess, and as the finest possible stimulus to precise thought. Slow or wandering intellects could best gain power of quickness and concentration from arithmetic which, moreover, in a strong native intelligence developes as nothing else can the higher practical gifts[2]. Geometry, too, has its utilities, for Archimedes prolonged the defence of Syracuse by his science[3]. Although a certain type of mind finds much attraction in it[4], too much devotion to the abstract side of the subject is a form of trifling[5]; so that a passable knowledge of general principles is all that is necessary to the educated man.

As regards Astronomy we must bear in mind the larger place which this subject filled in the general knowledge of earlier centuries. *La Divina Commedia* indicates a wide popular acquaintance with the map of the heavens and the laws of the constellations. Calendars, clocks, the compass, and maps have displaced much of this traditional lore. Humanist masters, however, retained the subject in their courses, the more readily that certain late Roman writers were available as authorities. An acquaintance with Astronomy was necessary, also, to the explanation of frequent allusions in classical

---

[1] Sassuolo says that without this training there is risk lest a boy 'in ceteris [studiis] perpetuo vagari et errare cogatur': p. 65. Aeneas Sylvius, supra, p. 156.

[2] Sassuolo (who was assistant in Mathematics to Vittorino) argues that the Florentines derived their business capacity from their training in arithmetic, p. 65.

[3] Supra, p. 156.

[4] Vergerius, supra, p. 109.

[5] Aeneas Sylvius, quoting Cicero, supra, p. 155.

literature[1]. Vergerius[2] recommends a knowledge of the constellations, planets, the sun and moon, so far as relates to the
laws of their revolutions or conjunctions, as a delightful
(iucundum) study. No particular educational motive is as-
signed, but apart from its practical utility, the main value
of this knowledge lies apparently in its cultivation of a certain
spirit of awe which lifts the mind above mundane cares. Vittorino followed Vergerius, although we hear nothing of his
method of treating the subject; Aeneas Sylvius approves of a
moderate acquaintance with it, and quotes from classical
history incidents in which ignorance of the laws of eclipses
proved a crucial factor in war.

The position of the Humanists respecting Astrology is
easier to define, and it is of great significance. Vergerius has
not a word to say upon it; Vittorino discarded it; Bruni is
contemptuous of it; Aeneas Sylvius, a man of the world, does
not believe in it, but he is aware that in actual life it is still
held in superstitious respect. Hence a prince must know
something of it, and make what use of it he can[3]. The first
great onslaught against the whole body of astrological lore was
due to Petrarch[4]: no Humanist believed in it; and not a few,
like Pico, openly denounced it. The contribution to scientific
truth made by Humanism in ridiculing this powerful strong-
hold of superstition needs recognition.

The period of the Renaissance in Italy was marked by
much curiosity about strange animals and plants, and beauty
of colour in marbles or precious stones was highly prized. To
collect such rarities was a mark of distinction in a city or a
personage. This interest in natural objects was associated
with the delight in the tales of distant travel which was felt

---

[1] Aeneas Sylvius, supra, p. 156.

[2] Supra, p. 108.

[3] Aeneas Sylvius, supra, p. 156. He commends Alfonso for being
contemptuous of astrologers: *Opera*, p. 493.

[4] *Epist. Sen.* iii. 1: (Ed. Fracassetti, *Lettere Senili*, i. p. 143).

even by ardent Humanists[1], and to some extent with the study of medicine. It is not surprising, therefore, to find the study of Natural History commended[2] for purposes of education as 'intellectui humano consona atque conformis,' or that Vittorino regarded a knowledge of it as indispensable to the 'vir perfectus.' It is, however, difficult to realise the extent to which this teaching of Nature was pursued. If we enlarge our view so as to include the practice advised by Erasmus, we should have to admit that instruction 'de meteoris, de plantis, de animalibus,' was regarded as fit only for young children not yet able to grasp more serious matters. His exposition of the use to be made of pictures in such cases is interesting, and indicates that the school method of the Humanists in the subject of science had made little or no progress during the preceding century. 'The picture[3] of an elephant attacked by a dragon is presented. The master states the Greek name, which is identical with the Latin; he gives the nominative and the genitive, 'elephantus, -i'; then the name of the trunk both in Greek and Latin. He then describes the tusks, giving the product, ivory; and the process of breathing. Next the Indian dragon is referred to in detail; the name in both languages, with its feminine, is noted. The teacher proceeds to an account of the combat between the two beasts, and gives any other particulars which may be suggested by the questions of the class. A hunting scene, again, will provide opportunity for teaching the names of trees, plants, birds, animals in a most attractive way.'

Now there is every reason to believe that this is a typical illustration of the Humanist method of handling Natural Science. Two things are thus obvious: that the knowledge

[1] Supra, p. 223, note.
[2] By Vergerius, *De Ingen. Moribus*, p. 476. Vittorino's opinion is given by Platina, p. 21.
[3] Erasmus, *Opera*, i. 510.

imparted was uncritical[1] and trivial, and that it was regarded mainly as an aid to vocabulary, or as helpful in understanding classical allusions. We may feel confident that Bruni and Guarino regarded natural history in this light; whilst Aeneas Sylvius thinks it wise to warn a boy of ten against absorption in 'naturalibus studiis et contemplationibus.' As the tyranny of style crept over classical education, towards the close of our period, the interest in external nature encouraged by Vergerius and Vittorino sank into indifference.

Upon the propriety of including Music and Singing amongst the subjects of instruction humanist feeling was somewhat divided. It was recognised, on the one hand[2], that the Greeks honoured skill in music and song, reckoning the bard amongst the messengers of the gods, and refusing the dignity of 'the complete man' to one who could neither play nor sing. On the other hand, Italian self-respect hardly admitted of emotional display in public, and Christian sentiment was averse to self-surrender to the sensuous charm of sound. The Romans, it was also remembered, were not unanimous upon the wisdom of permitting music to the young.

As life is mainly concerned with action, should education, it was asked, take account of a subject which developes neither wisdom, judgment nor conduct[3]? Yet the Spartans, under rigid limitations, indeed, encouraged song; David, Gracchus, Cicero, all of them men of affairs, practised the art. So, too, Pythagoras and Socrates sanctioned it: it was regarded as a means of inciting to noble deeds, and of soothing the disorders of the mind.

But yet in actual life music was felt by the Humanist to be

---

[1] Bruni, supra, p. 129, clearly implies that the literary authority of ancient writers extends to their views on Nature.

[2] Vegio, *Op. cit.*, p. 280: 'Apud antiquos merito musici inter vatum et sapientum numerum...' and one ignorant of the art was held 'minime ingenue doctus.'

[3] Aeneas Sylvius, supra, p. 155.

a dangerous indulgence, unless safeguarded with peculiar care[1].
'The greatest watchfulness is needed,' says Vegio, 'in teaching
Music, for we see so many promising youths lose all vigour of
mind and character in their absorption in unworthy harmonies';
'the popular music of our time,' says Sassuolo[2], who taught
the art at Mantua under Vittorino, is 'inquinata, impudens,
corrupta atque corruptrix,' although in its intention music was
given to man to be the guardian and inspirer of all that is
best and noblest in human thought and emotion. Singing-
masters[3] had ordinarily a bad name; they were men of inferior
stamp, unfit to be trusted with impressionable natures. A
facile skill in the *Canzone* or with the lute led to dubious
company, or generated a self-conceit which was ruinous to
all serious habits of study.

Yet with scarcely an exception the educators of the period
admitted music, with reserves. They seem to lay special stress
upon its value as a recreation[4], and a diversion from the cares
of life. Extreme skill is not desirable[5]; that is the part of
the professional musician. Yet the subject should be taught
well within the required limits[6]. Stringed instruments were
preferred: to play with the finger is more dignified than to

[1] Vegio, *l.c.*, 'maxima adhibenda est cura': 'nam et nequitia et ignavia
ex musica praesertim hoc tempore exoriri solent,' says Porcia, *De Generosa
Liber. Educ.*, p. 113.

[2] Sassuolo, p. 69.

[3] Aeneas Sylvius, *Opera*, p. 989: 'si praeceptores non vitiosi reperi-
rentur.'

[4] Vegio, *l.c.*, 'ad degendam recte in otio vitam'; Vergerius, supra,
p. 117.

[5] Aeneas Sylvius, *l.c.*: 'non...huius disciplinae mediocris fugienda
cognitio.' Vegio, *Op. cit.*, p. 302, considers it unworthy that a girl, 'literis
Graecis et Latinis doctam, psallere et saltare elegantius quam necesse sit.'
He would prefer that she should not sing or dance at all.

[6] Platina, of Vittorino, p. 19: 'Magistros conduxit qui cantibus et lyra
eos erudirent quos maxime idoneos cernebat; hac quoque in re, ut in
ceteris, Atticos doctores imitatus, quod his etiam excitari animos concentu
et harmonia ad laudem et pulchritudinem virtutis diceret.'

distort the face by blowing. Hence the violin in various forms, and the larger and more elaborate 'clavicembalo' were the accepted instruments[1]. In singing the solo was preferred to the chorus; and in song and instrumental music alike only severer melodies were allowed, such as philosophers would commend as carrying definitely elevating suggestion[2]. Dancing to music was apparently approved by Vittorino, though in this he differs from Vergerius and also from Porcia, who, writing at the very close of our period, finds it unworthy of a gentleman. This judgment, however, was not in accord with the social opinion of the age. For, as tending to cultivate grace and courtliness of bearing, dignified and graceful dancing was an accomplishment of no slight importance.

§ 5. MORAL AND RELIGIOUS TRAINING.

A few remarks may be added upon moral and religious training, mainly by way of supplement to what has been said above respecting discipline and the study of moral philosophy[3]. The virtues upon which most stress was laid by the Humanist teachers under review were reverence, self-restraint, modesty and truthfulness. Special qualities were inculcated, in the case, for instance, of a Prince, who is exhorted to clemency and to humility, or of a court official who is warned against intrigue[4].

We find that both Vittorino and Guarino insisted upon daily attendance at Worship; Vittorino further urged upon his elder scholars regular Confession and reception of the

---

[1] Burckhardt, *Renaissance in Italy*, p. 392.

[2] The Socratic distinction of harmonies, and of their influence on character is, it need not be said, present to the minds of all Humanists.

[3] Supra, p. 204, and p. 221.

[4] By Guarino: Sabbadini, *Vita di Guarino*, p. 103. Guarino translated for Leonello a work of Isocrates on the duty of the Sovereign as a guide to princely duty. The letter of Guarino to his son Jerome upon his conduct at the court of Naples is printed by Rosmini, *Guarino*, i. 119.

Eucharist. All writers on Education without exception dwell urgently on the duty of religious observance and of respect for the doctrines and ordinances of the Church. Regulation, however, was with the great school-masters the least important element in their religious training.

It cannot be too strongly affirmed that a close acquaintance with the actual work of Vittorino and Guarino, and with the aims of Vergerius[1] and Vegio, reveals a thorough sincerity of religious conviction which permeates all their educational practice. Vittorino's great achievement was to effect a reconciliation between the Christian life and Humanist ideals : in this he was followed by other masters, though rarely with the same unfaltering consistency[2]. It is a fair description of the motive underlying Vittorino's method that he regarded Humanist education as the training for Christian citizenship. He himself took a leading part in the religious teaching of the school ; and by addresses, by private conversations, and above all by his own example, he brought the full force of his personal character to bear upon his pupils in the critical years of their life. He expressly encouraged a sense of responsibility towards the poor and suffering, and never forgot his civic obligation, and its religious sanction. Upon the princes of the House he specially impressed the duties of their station, using Scripture and ancient moralists to enforce conviction. His share in the resolution of Cecilia to take the Veil has been already alluded to. Reverence towards parents and elders, towards learning and goodness, regard for the higher courtesies of daily life were regularly inculcated from the Bible and from antiquity : and any lapse into impiety or profane language was severely punished.

Vittorino, no doubt, was an exceptional man, and his

---

[1] On Vergerius, supra, p. 15; on Vittorino, p. 27.

[2] Aeneas Sylvius, supra, p. 141, supports Humanist studies on a somewhat different ground, namely, that pagan literature has itself an underlying religious spirit.

loveable character and personal sacrifices in maintaining poor scholars at his own charge gave him a peculiar influence. But after all his method represents the ideal which we find set forth in all the treatises of the time : though we can well believe that few masters attained to so high a level in actual practice. Francesco Barbaro, the young Venetian patrician, strikes the same keynote, when he urges that the inculcation of reverence towards God and home, is the foundation of all education ; and to secure this the example of parents and of teachers is of prime necessity.

Next to reverence, capacity for self-restraint appeals most strongly to the teacher of this age. In all that concerns the body temperance is held up as the true norm of conduct, in the interests of the physical nature itself. There is no suggestion of ascetic contempt for the physical frame. On the contrary, its health, its suppleness, and its dignity are perpetually before the mind of the true Humanist educator, who whilst impressing the antique ideal of the discipline of the flesh has no sympathy with the mediæval churchman's concept of the worthlessness of the body.

It was indeed easy enough to treat of the right principles of living by didactic methods, and by literary illustration ; and in the case of Aeneas Sylvius we are conscious—not unreasonably—rather of platitudes of Roman morality than of deep personal sincerity. But in the actual practice of the best schools, close intercourse with masters of the type of Vittorino and Guarino, coupled with the constant discipline of games, sports, and martial exercises, formed the surest safeguard of a healthy moral standard.

It may seem more difficult to reconcile the Humanist ideal of conscious personal distinction with the stress laid upon the virtue of modesty and self-effacement in educational treatises[1]. But we must remember that nowhere was the penalty of

---

[1] E.g. by Barbaro, *De Re Uxoria*, p. xxxii.

premature or unwarranted self-assertion so swift and so overwhelming as in the Italy of the Quattrocento.   Hence in the
training of the young it is the duty of parent and teacher to inculcate as a mark of highest excellence that children be silent in
the presence of elders, that they refrain from asking questions
in company[1], that they be unobtrusive in dress and bearing.
The obligation of truthfulness forbids, also, boasting or exaggeration, and all forms of ostentation in speech and writing;
the use of metaphors and flights of fancy are unbecoming.
Pertinacity, malice, or impropriety in conversation are condemned as indicating a froward temper[2].   To be convinced
of ignorance and yet determined to excel, to be conscious of
power but reserved in exhibiting it, were the signs of a
disposition which promised well for a personal distinction
which would have no need to conceal itself in after years.

§ 6. Physical Training.

It must not be forgotten that the education of the earlier
Humanists was, in one aspect of it, a development of the
courtly and military training of youth characteristic of the
preceding century.   The ideal of humanist education was not
the product of the free City, or of the University, but of the
Court.   Venice, Florence, Padua all had schools which in the
early decades of the fifteenth century were imbued with the
humanist spirit.   But such schools were, as we know, tentative,
and did but partially realise the aims of the men who initiated
them.   Only at a Court like that of Mantua or Ferrara could
humanism exhibit its complete educational ideals.   One reason

----

[1] This did not in any way imply that eager curiosity in school was
regarded as other than a mark of intelligence, and by the wiser masters
encouraged.   Vittorino prized the quality above memory, then usually
accepted as the token of excellence.

[2] Aeneas Sylvius, supra, p. 144.

for this lay in the fact that there only did they find free scope
and encouragement upon the side of physical training.

From the treatise of Vergerius we see that the distinction
between the training of Letters and of Arms is definitely
recognised. Either is commendable; the combination of the
two forms for a man of position the ideal education. But,
even at the Court schools, there is a much larger class—that
of town-dwellers and youths of private station—for whom a
military career offers no attraction. For them, Vittorino,
applying the full antique conception of training for the first
time[1], devised systematic methods of physical instruction.
At the outset habits of hardy nurture laid the foundation of
health and inured the boy to regular exertion. Care was taken
to increase the strain upon physical endurance by slow degrees[2],
a responsibility which involves careful observation of individual
children. Lessons were broken by regular and liberal intervals
for spontaneous play[3], which it was urged should not be of
less than two hours' duration in all. A tendency to moroseness,
unsociable habits and reluctance to join in games was checked
with firmness. Amongst outdoor games for young children
ball-play[4] in its various forms was most prized, next to that
running and jumping, as compelling active movement. Dancing,
however, is often condemned in spite of its many advantages:
partly, it would seem, because it familiarised a boy with softer
and less stimulating influences. After the age of ten, sports
and exercises requiring regular training in skill are introduced,

---

[1] Burckhardt, *Renaissance in Italy*, p. 389, and Sabbadini, *Guarino*,
p. 102 ; both agree that to Vittorino was due the special place given to
physical culture generally, and to carefully devised gymnastics in particular.

[2] Vergerius, supra, p. 114.   M. Vegio, *De Educ. Liber.*, p. 281.

[3] Porcia, *De Generosa Lib. Educ.*, p. 111.

[4] Vegio, *Op. cit.*, p. 286: 'Pilae ludus et honestus et liberalis videtur.'
Ball games included foot-ball, throwing and catching: the 'trigonalis pila'
is still obscure. Porcia, *l.c.*, objects to allowing well-born youths to play
with 'rustici aut plebeii.' Guarino appeals to the precedent of Alexander
and Scaevola, who keenly enjoyed games with the ball.

such as archery, fencing, the use of the sling and the first steps in military training[1]. Emulation should be encouraged by prizes for exceptional quickness and endurance. Skill in arms is cultivated as a necessary training for civic duty, that each citizen may be capable of taking his part in the defence of public liberty and independence[2].

In order to develope habits of manly yet graceful bearing, to which as the outward mark of distinction[3] much importance attached, special training was devised. No Humanist disregarded the advantages to a boy of dignified carriage in society, exhibited in walking, sitting or standing with ease and grace. Vittorino was probably the first to teach, with this end in view, gymnastics as an art, deserving of perseverance for its own sake, apart from military training or mere recreation[4]; and after his time it became incorporated into Italian education of the higher type. Guarino imitated his practice at Ferrara, though perhaps with less insistence. Riding and swimming were encouraged as indispensable to the soldier and useful attainments in everyone. Guarino's argument for swimming is characteristic. 'As an art, swimming gives elasticity to the muscles; it adds another aptitude to the physical powers, since by it a man ceases to be merely a denizen of dry land. It is more important to remember how many illustrious persons have been good swimmers. Let it be enough to mention Horatius Cocles, Alexander and Caesar: and the story of the imprudence of the Macedonian will warn Leonello to be cautious in bathing.' Hunting, as developing endurance and courage, is advised where opportunity offers.

For older students quieter recreations may be desirable: as walks[5], especially on bright days, amid fine scenery or by

---

[1] Porcia, *Op. cit.*, p. 113.

[2] Vegio, *Op. cit.*, p. 282: 'summe necessaria studia.'

[3] Aeneas Sylvius, supra, p. 137 sq.

[4] Sabbadini, *l.c.*

[5] Vegio, *Op. cit.*, p. 287. So Guarino and Porcia.

the sea, riding, with a pleasant companion, fishing, hawking and snaring birds. The latter, however, are pastimes for adults, rather than exercise for the young and vigorous.

The ends which the Humanist master had in view probably varied somewhat with individuals. To preserve health[1] and to secure that the mental activities should be as free and vigorous as possible was, no doubt, always foremost amongst them. Next, the actual acquirement of bodily aptitudes was, in the earlier stage of Humanist education, an integral factor of individual excellence. Not, however, that these were to be sought 'in morem athletarum'; a professional skill would imply an unworthy stress upon what is, after all, the least important side of human faculty. But the value of games as a healthy moral stimulus[2], and as a security against indulgence, meanness, and selfish unconcern for the interests and happiness of others was probably the argument which with the practical school-master weighed most strongly in the fifteenth century as it does to-day.

§ 7. HUMANISM AND THE EDUCATION OF WOMEN.

It is often said that in the education of Girls the Humanist contemplated a standard of attainment and a range of subjects identical with those proposed for boys. This, however, so far as it applies to our period, needs some qualification.

The distinction seems to be, not so much in a difference of educational subject-matter, as in the altered stress which is laid upon certain elements in it. The Humanist has not attempted any revolution in the position of women. Home, social life, the rearing of children, the practice of charity and religious obligation are still their first duties. There is, undoubtedly, a

---

[1] Vegio, *De Liber. Educ.*, p. 281, 'roboris et bonae valetudinis gratia.' The 'gravior tristiorque frons,' is not desirable in a boy, and is best banished by out-door sports, p. 283.

[2] Vegio, *l.c.*

new element present, that, namely, of intellectual distinction; and the ideal wife of Bruni or Vegio was a more interesting figure than the house-mother of Alberti's well-known book[1]. And, as with a boy so with a girl, this 'praestantia' can only be attained by a training in Letters[2].

The practice of religion, and the example of a well-ordered life will be a woman's first care[3]. Both Bruni and Vegio lay the greatest stress on this aspect of her training. But in her studies, also, she will keep the same ends constantly before her. For Bruni, enthusiastic scholar though he is, regards literature from a special point of view when treating of the reading suitable for a woman. In studying Latin literature she will turn first to the Fathers, notably to Augustine and Lactantius[4]. And here the characteristic feeling of the Humanist reveals itself. For both these writers are commended as stylists as well as theologians. There are possibly edifying doctors[5], who may be helpful to a woman's inner life, amongst contemporary churchmen, but on no account should their productions be read lest her literary taste be corrupted. Further, there is no warrant for limiting the study of moral precepts to the ecclesiastical authors; such writers as Cicero and Seneca are capable of affording profound lessons in the virtues: and discussions on the principles of morals may suitably follow. The standpoint, however, is never lost sight of. The true motive for the study of ancient literature is the cultivation of the higher faculties of our nature[6], although it will, at the same time, grace social position and give dignity to leisure. Certain elements of classical training will be omitted, such as the subtleties of rhetoric: and the choice of authors read will need judgment. History is a peculiarly suitable

[1] *Il Governo della Famiglia*, which represents the older type of Tuscan life.

[2] Bruni, supra, p. 123 and passim.

[3] Vegio, *Op. cit.*, p. 302.

[4] Supra, p. 124, 127.

[5] Supra, p. 127.

[6] Bruni, *s.f.*, supra, p. 133.

subject for a woman ; who, however, will not shew too much interest in such meaner studies as Arithmetic or Geometry : and she will be superior to Astrology[1].

The education of a girl is, in reality, a matter which needs the careful supervision of the mother, for practical morals and religious temper are of chief importance. Letters must be held subordinate to manners and character. Still, as she may not be encouraged to excellence in singing, playing or dancing, she will find intellectual interests in the study of Greek and Latin. Such is the advice of M. Vegio[2], who approaches education avowedly from the point of view of a Humanist churchman, and whose highest admiration is reserved for Augustine and Monica his mother. Vittorino does not appear to have received the daughters of other Houses than the Gonzaga ; but Cecilia's scholarship was certainly not inferior to that of her brothers ; her early progress in Greek, which astounded Ambrogio, has been already mentioned[3].

Guarino, whilst teaching at Verona, had in Isotta and Ginevra Nogarola two of his most enthusiastic pupils[4]. Isotta attained much celebrity for her learning ; and like Battista di Montefeltro she was a woman of sincere Humanist sympathies. She wrote excellent Latin both in prose and verse ; in her correspondence with Guarino she quotes Greek authors, and classical and modern Latinists, and handles anecdotes and illustrations in strict Humanist fashion. But the case of Isotta shews us that Society did not approve of a tendency to emancipation from the accepted rules which governed the conduct of a lady. It was considered an impropriety that she should write to Guarino, so that she came under the ban of the social opinion of Verona. Thus, although a lady might be, should be indeed, deeply versed in the literature of the Fathers, the moralists, and the chief poets of antiquity ; should

---

[1] Supra, pp. 126, 128.

[2] Vegio, *Op. cit.*, p. 302.

[3] Supra, p. 50.

[4] Sabbadini, *Guarino*, p. 125.

write elegant Latin and, if possible, Greek; should read History; and should have a wide field of knowledge available for discussion and conversation[1] in Society, yet she must not presume to pass beyond the conventions which regulated the moral and social duty of a woman of position. It is possible that a sense of irksomeness was, as a consequence, engendered in some more vigorous minds, just as we know that others amongst scholarly ladies became conscious of an opposition between their religious instincts and the attractions of pagan literature. Both of these causes, combined with the need of sanctuary in troubled times, may serve to explain why, in not a few cases, the Humanist impulse gave way before an ascetic motive, and learned women, like Isotta, Cecilia, Paola her mother, and Battista di Montefeltro, took the veil.

It is evident, lastly, that Humanist culture was sought and attained by a limited proportion only of the wives and daughters of leading families. It was more common amongst them in Florence and Venice than in the smaller cities. But those whose fame has come down to us, and they must be but representatives of a large number, strike us as thoroughly womanly in temperament, not seldom of strong practical gifts, and respected in their own day not less for their domestic virtues than for their refinement and cultivation.

[1] Bruni, supra, p. 132; and infra, p. 190.

TITLES OF WORKS QUOTED AND
REFERRED TO.

The following List has been compiled to facilitate the identification of and reference to the works actually quoted in the text and notes of the present volume. It in no way represents the whole body of available authorities nor of those which have been consulted for the purposes of this work.

ADDA (Marquis Gerolamo d'). *Indagini storiche, artistiche e bibliografiche, sulla Libreria Visconteo-Sforzesca del Castello di Pavia,* parte i. 8°. Milano 1875.

ALEXANDER DE VILLA DEI. *Das Doctrinale des Alexander de Villa Dei:* kritisch-exegetische Ausg., bearbeitet von Dietrich Reichling (*Monumenta Germaniae Paedagogica,* Bd. xii). 8°. Berlin 1893.

ANTOGNONI (Oreste). *Appunti e memorie.* 8°. Imola 1889.
  [Literary essays, including one on "Vittorino da Feltre e un suo biografo" (F. Prendilacqua).]

BANDINI (Angelo Maria). *Catalogus Codicum Latinorum Bibliothecae Mediceae Laurentianae.* 3 voll. fol. Florentiae 1774.

BANDINI (Angelo Maria). *Catalogus codicum manuscriptorum Bibliothecae Mediceae Laurentianae, varia continens opera Graecorum patrum.* 3 voll. fol. Florentiae 1764–70.

BARBARO (Francesco). *De re uxoria libelli duo* [with two letters commendatory of the work by Poggio Bracciolini and P. Vergerius. Edited by A. Tiraquellus]. 4°. In aedibus Ascensianis: [Parisiis] 1513.

BENOIST (A.). *Quid de puerorum institutione senserit Erasmus.* 8°. Parisiis 1876.

BERNARDI (Jacopo). *Vittorino da Feltre e suo metodo educativo.* 12°. Pinerolo 1856.

BISTICCI (Vespasiano da). *Vite di uomini illustri del secolo* XV...rivedute sui manoscritti da Ludovico Frati. 3 voll. 8°. Bologna 1892.

BORSA (Mario). *Pier Candido Decembri e Umanismo in Lombardia* (in *Archivio Storico Lombardo*, Mar. 1893). 8°. Milano 1893.

BOTFIELD (Beriah). *Praefationes et Epistolae Editionibus Principibus auctorum veterum praepositae.* 4°. Cantabr. 1861.

BRUNI (Lionardo) Aretino. *De studiis et literis.* 8°. Parisiis 1642.

BURCKHARDT (Jacob). *The Civilisation of the period of the Renaissance in Italy,* trans. by S. G. C. Middlemore. 8°. London 1892.

CASTIGLIONE (Francesco di). [A biographical fragment upon Vittorino da Feltre quoted in the *Vita Ambrosii* prefixed to *Ambrosii Traversarii Epistolae,* ed. L. Mehus, q.v.]

CASTIGLIONE (Count Baldassare). *Il Cortegiano; or the Courtier:* written by B. Castiglione, and a new version of the same into English.... To which is prefix'd the *Life of the author* by A. P. Castiglione. 4°. London 1727. [Italian and English text.]

CLERVAL (L'Abbé A.). *Les Écoles de Chartres au moyen-âge du Vᵉ au XVIᵉ siècle.* (*Mémoires de la Société Archéologique d'Eure-et-Loire.* tome XI). 8°. Chartres 1895.

COLLE (F. M.). *Storia scientifico-letteraria dello Studio di Padova.* 3 voll. 4°. Padova 1824.

COMBI (Carlo A.). See under ' Vergerius, P. P.'

CORTESIUS (Paulus). *De Hominibus Doctis.* [in P. Villani *Liber de Civitatis Florentiae famosis civibus*]. 4°. Flor. 1847.

DAVARI (Stefano). *Notizie Storiche intorno allo Studio Publico ed ai Maestri del Secolo XV e XVI che tennero scuola in Mantova.* 8°. Mantova 1876.

DENNISTOUN (Jas.). *Memoirs of the Dukes of Urbino.* 3 voll. 8°. Lond. 1851.

DOMINICI (Giovanni). *Regola del Governo di Cura Familiare.* Testo... illustrato con note dal Prof. Donato Salvi. 8°. Firenze 1860.

ERASMUS (Desiderius). *Opera omnia, emendatiora et auctiora*: cura J. Clerici. 10 voll. fol. Lugd. Bat. 1703-6.

FABRICIUS (Joannes Albertus). *Bibliotheca Latina Mediae et Infimae Aetatis.* Ed. J. D. Mansi. 6 voll. 4°. Patav. 1754.

FILELFO (Francesco). *Exercitatiunculae Latinae et Italicae.* (Hain-Copinger 12,957.) 4°. Mediol. 1483.

FIORETTO (Giovanni). *Gli Umanisti, o lo studio del Latino e del Greco nel secolo XV in Italia.* 8°. Verona 1881.

GASPARY (Adolf). *Storia della Letteratura Italiana* [a translation into Italian of ' *Geschichte der italienischen Literatur.*' Berlin 1855]. 2 voll. 8°. Torino 1889.

GAZA (Theodore). *Grammaticae Institutionis liber primus,* sic translatus per Erasmum Roterodamum. 4°. Basil. 1516.

GEBHART (Émile). *Les origines de la Renaissance en Italie.* 8°. Paris 1879.

GHERARDI (Alessandro). *Statuti della Università e Studio Fiorentino dall' anno* MCCCLXXXVII *seguiti da un' appendice di documenti dal* MCCCXX *al* MCCCCLXXII *pubblicati da A. Gherardi.* fol. Firenze 1881.

GIOVIO (Paolo). *Elogia veris clarorum virorum imaginibus apposita.* fol. Venetiis 1546.

GLORIA (Andrea). *Monumenti della Università di Padua.* 3 voll. 4°. Venezia 1884–88.

GUARINO, Battista. *De Ordine Docendi et Studendi.* 4°. s. l. et a. [? Modena, 1496], (Hain 8129).

GUARINO VERONESE. *Erotemata Guarini* [an abridged Latin version of τὰ ἐρωτήματα of M. Chrysoloras]. Venetiis 1512.

GUARINO VERONESE. *Regulae Guarini.* 4°. s. l. et a. [? Bologna 1475].

GUASTI (Cesare). *Intorno alla Vita e all' insegnamento di Vittorino da Feltre,* lettere di Sassolo Pratese volgarizzate. [With emended Latin text.] 8°. Firenze 1869.

HODY (Humphrey). *De Græcis illustribus linguae literarum humaniorum instauratoribus.* 8°. Londini 1742.

IANUS PANNONIUS. *Silva Panegyrica ad Guarinum Veronensem praeceptorem suum [in Iani Pannonii Opera].* 8°. Traiecti ad Rhenum 1784.

Index Bibliothecae Mediceae [1536]. 8°. s. l. et a. [Florentiae, 1883].

KLETTE (Theodor). *Beiträge zur Geschichte und Litteratur der italienischen Gelehrtenrenaissance.* 3 voll. 8°. Greifswald 1888–90.

    (i)   Johannes Conversanus und Johannes Malpaghini von Ravenna.

    (ii) Leonardi Aretini ad Petrum Paulum Istrum Dialogus.

    (iii) Die griechischen Briefe des Franciskus Philelphus.

LEGRAND (Émile). *Cent-dix lettres grecques de François Filelfo* (d'après le Codex Trivulzianus 873). 8°. Paris 1892.

LEGRAND (Émile). *Bibliographie Hellénique, ou description raisonnée des ouvrages publiés en grec par les Grecs aux* XV*ᵉ et* XVI*ᵉ siècles.* 2 voll. 8°. Paris 1885.

LUZIO (Alessandro). *Cinque Lettere di Vittorino da Feltre* [in *Archivio Veneto,* t. xxxvi.]. Venezia 1888.

MANCINI. *Vita di Lorenzo Valla.* 8°. Firenze 1891.

MANETTI (Giannozzo). *Chronicon Pistoriense a condita urbe, usque ad annum* MCCCCXLVI [in Muratori (L. A.) *Rerum Italicarum Scriptores,* tom. xix. p. 985 sqq.]. fol. Mediolani 1731.

MARTÈNE (Edmond) & DURAND (Ursin). *Veterum scriptorum et monumentorum, historicorum, dogmaticorum, moralium, amplissima collectio.* 9 voll. fol. Parisiis 1724–33.

MAZZUCHELLI (Giovanni Maria). *Gli Scrittori d' Italia.* 2 voll. fol. Brescia 1753-6.

MEHUS (Lorenzo). *A. Traversarii...Latinae Epistolae...Adcedit Eiusdem Ambrosii Vita.* fol. Florentiae 1759.

MITTARELLI (Johannes Benedictus). *Bibliotheca Codicum Manuscriptorum Monasterii S. Michaelis Venetiarum.* fol. Venetiis 1779.

MULLINGER (James Bass). *The University of Cambridge from the earliest times to the royal injunctions of* 1535. 8°. Cambridge 1873.

NOLHAC (Pierre de). *La bibliothèque de Fulvio Orsini: contributions à l'histoire des collections d'Italie et à l'étude de la Renaissance.* 8°. Paris 1887.

NOLHAC (Pierre de). *Pétrarque et l'humanisme.* 8°. Paris 1892.

NOVATI (F.). *Il Epistolario di C. Salutati,* a cura di F. Novati. 2 voll. 8°. Firenze 1891.

OGNIBENE DA LONIGO [Omnibonus Leonicenus]. *Grammaticae libellus ...[sive] de octo partibus or[ati]onis liber.* 4°. Per Jacobū Gallicū : [Venetiis] 1473. (Dedicated to Fredericus de Gonzaga.)

PAGLIA (Enrico). *La casa Giocosa di Vittorino da Feltre in Mantova* (in *Archivio Storico Lombardo,* 1884). 8°. Milano 1884.

PEROTTUS (Nicolaus). *Rudimenta Grammatices.* fol. Romae 1473.

PETRARCA (Francesco). *De viris Illustribus Vitae,* ed. Luigi Razzolini : [with Italian version of Donato da Pratovecchio]. 2 voll. Bologna, 1874, 1879.

PETRARCA (Francesco). *Epistolae de rebus familiaribus et variae,...*studio et cura I. Fracassetti. 3 voll. 8°. Florentiae 1859–63.

PETRARCA (Francesco). *Lettere senili...*volgarizzate e dichiarate con note da G. Fracassetti. 2 voll. 12°. Firenze 1869–70.

PICCOLOMINI (Enea Silvio), Pope Pius II. *De liberorum educatione,* ad Ladislaum Ungariae et Bohemiae regem [in Æn. Sylvii *Opera,* p. 965]. fol. Basileae 1551.

PLATINA (Bartholomaeus). *Commentariolus Platinae de vita Victorini Feltrensis,* ex codice Vaticano [in Vairani, q.v.].

PORCIA (Jacopo di), Comes Purliliarum. *De generosa liberorum educatione,* ed. J. Alenus Cremonensis. 12°. Basil. 1541.

PORCIA (Jacopo di), [Comes Purliliarum]. *Opus Epistolarum familiarum.* fol. [? Venetiis 1540].

PRENDILACQUA (Francesco). *Intorno alla vita di Vittorino da Feltre.* Dialogo...tradotto e annotato dal professore Gius. Brambilla. 8°. Como 1871.

RACKI (Franjo). Ivan Ravenjanin (in *Rad Jugoslavenske Akademije,* lxxiv.). 8°. Agram 1885.

RASHDALL (Hastings). *The Universities of Europe in the Middle Ages.* 2 voll. 8°. Oxford 1895.

REUMONT (Alfred von). *Lorenzo de' Medici, the Magnificent*...translated from the German by R. Harrison. 2 voll. 8°. London 1876.

ROSMINI (Carlo de'). *Idea dell' ottimo precettore nella vita e disciplina di Vittorino da Feltre e de' suoi discepoli.* 8°. Bassano 1801.

ROSMINI (Carlo de'). *Vita e disciplina di Guarino Veronese, e de' suoi discepoli.* 3 voll. 4°. Brescia 1805-6.

ROSSI (Giuseppe). *Niccolò di Cusa.* 8°. Pisa 1894.

SABBADINI (Remigio). *Briciole Umanistiche* (in *Giornale Storico della Letteratura Italiana*, xviii.). 8°. Torino 1891.

SABBADINI (Remigio). *Briefe des Guarino von Verona* (*Vierteljahrsschrift für Kultur und Litteratur der Renaissance* I. p. 103). 8°. Leipzig 1886.

SABBADINI (Remigio). *Codici Latini posseduti, scoperti, illustrati da Guarino Veronese* (in *Museo Italiano di Antichità Classica*, II. ii.). Firenze 1887.

SABBADINI (Remigio). *Della Biblioteca di Giovanni Corvini* (in *Museo Italico d' Antichità Classica*, I. iii.). Firenze 1888.

SABBADINI (Remigio). *Epistolario di Guarino Veronese.* 8°. Salerno 1885.

SABBADINI (Remigio). *Guarino Veronese e le opere retoriche di Cicerone.* 8°. Livorno 1885.

SABBADINI (Remigio). *Lettere inedite di Ognibene da Lonigo*, con una breve biografia. Lonigo 1880.

SABBADINI (Remigio). *L'ultimo ventennio della vita di Manuele Crisolora*, 1396-1415 (in *Giornale Ligustico*, ann. xvii., 1890).

SABBADINI (Remigio). *Notizie sulla vita e gli scritti di alcuni dotti Umanisti del Secolo XV.* 1. Crisolora. 2. I due Maestri Giovanni da Ravenna. 3. Francesco Filelfo. 4. Antonio Beccadelli. 5. Giovanni Lamola. 6. Poggio. (in *Giornale Storico della Letteratura Italiana*, vol. v.) 8°. Torino 1885.

SABBADINI (Remigio). *Storia del Ciceronianismo nell' età della Rinascenza.* 8°. Torino 1885.

SABBADINI (Remigio). *Studi di Gasparino Barzizza su Quintiliano e Cicerone.* 8°. Livorno 1886.

SABBADINI (Remigio). *Vita di Guarino Veronese* (in *Giornale Ligustico*, ann. xviii.). 8°. Genova 1891.

 The same work, reprinted as an independent volume, Genova 1891.

SANTI (Giovanni). *Federigo di Montefeltro, Duca di Urbino, Cronaca.* Zum ersten Male herausgegeben von Dr Heinrich Holtzinger. 8°. Stuttgart 1893.

SASSUOLO DA PRATO [Saxolus Pratensis]. See under 'Guasti (Cesare).

SCHMIDT (Karl).   *Die Geschichte der Pädagogik.*   3 voll. 8°. Berlin 1894.

SCHMIDT (Otto Eduard).   *Die Visconti und ihre Bibliothek zu Pavia.*
(in *Zeitschrift für Geschichte und Politik,* 1888).   Bd. II.   8°. Stuttgart
1888.

SHEPHERD (William).   *The life of Poggio Bracciolini.*   4°. Liverpool
1802.

SYMONDS (John Addington).   *The Renaissance in Italy:* i. The Age of the
Despots ; ii. The Revival of Learning.   8°. London 1875-7.

THUROT (Charles).   *De l'organisation de l'enseignement dans l'Université
de Paris au moyen-âge.* [*Thèse présentée à la Faculté des Lettres de
Paris.*]   8°. Paris, Besançon 1850.

TICOZZI (Stefano).   *Storia dei Letterati e degli Artisti del Dipartimento
della Piave.*   tom. I. (all published).   4°. Belluno 1813.

TRAVERSARIUS (Ambrosius) Camaldulensis.   *Hodoeporicon,* ex bibliotheca
Medicaea a Nicolao Bartholino Bargensi publicae luci assertum.
4°. Flor. et Lucae [1680].

TRAVERSARIUS (Ambrosius).   See also under ' Mehus (L.).'

VAIRANI (Tommaso Agostino).   *Cremonensium Monumenta Romae ex-
tantia.*   fol. Romae 1778.
    Contains *Comment. De Vita Victorini Felt.* by Platina.

VEGIO (Maffeo).   *De educatione liberorum.*   Ed. J. Alenus Cremonensis.
8°. Basileae 1541.

VERGERIUS (Petrus Paulus).   *Dei nobili costumi di Pierpaolo Vergerio,*
trad. da Everardo Micheli.   16°. *Siena* 1878.

VERGERIUS (Petrus Paulus).   *De Ingenuis Moribus.*   Ed. J. Alenus
Cremonensis [with treatises by L. V. Roscius and others].   12°.
Basil. 1541.

VERGERIUS (Petrus Paulus).   *Epistole di Pietro Paolo Vergerio.* [Collected
and edited by Carlo A. Combi.]   4°. Venezia 1887.

VIVES (Joannes Ludovicus).   *De tradendis disciplinis.*   Colon. Agr. 1536.

VOIGT (Georg).   *Die Briefsammlungen Petrarca's und der venetianische
Staatskanzler Benintendi* (in *Abhandlungen der k. bayerisch. Academie
der Wiss.* III. Cl. XVI. Bd. III. Abth.).   4°. München 1882.

VOIGT (Georg).   *Die Wiederbelebung des classischen Alterthums: oder das
erste Jahrhundert des Humanismus.*   3te Aufl., besorgt von Max
Lehnerdt.   2 voll. 8°. Berlin 1893.

VOIGT (Georg).   *Enea Silvio de' Piccolomini als Papst Pius der Zweite
und sein Zeitalter.*   8°. Berlin 1856.

ZARDO (A.).   *Il Petrarca e i Carraresi.*   8°. Milan 1887.

INDEX.

W.

Eugene F. Rice, Jr., Professor of History at Cornell University, was born in Lexington, Kentucky, in 1924. After receiving his B.A., M.A., and Ph.D. from Harvard University, he taught history there from 1953 until 1955, when he joined the Cornell faculty. Professor Rice has written several articles and reviews for scholarly journals of history and was editor of Theodor E. Mommsen's *Medieval and Renaissance Studies* (1959). His books include *The Renaissance Idea of Wisdom* (1958) and *The Prefatory Epistles of Jacques Lefèvre d'Etaples and Related Documents* (in preparation).